The Turning Point That Changed Everything

Choosing to accept the unpredictable

By
Dr. Wallace R. Pratt

Copyright © 2009 by Dr. Wallace R. Pratt

The Turning Point That Changed Everything
Choosing to accept the unpredictable
by Dr. Wallace R. Pratt

Printed in the United States of America

ISBN 9781615795215

All rights reserved solely by the author. The author guarantees all contents are original and do not infringe upon the legal rights of any other person or work. No part of this book may be reproduced in any form without the permission of the author. The views expressed in this book are not necessarily those of the publisher.

Unless otherwise indicated, Bible quotations are taken from The The Hebrew-Greek Key Word Study Bible, King James Version. Copyright © 1991, Revised Edition.

www.xulonpress.com

To: Lovie,

Thank you for your interest in ministerial education.

Dr. Wallace R. Pratt
10/9/13

Table of Contents

Acknowledgements vii

Foreword by Dr. Hector Ortiz xi

Introduction xv

Chapters
    1 A Personal Crisis of Faith 21
    2 Unbelievable Events vs. Uncertain Future 39
    3 Between a Peripeteia and a Peripety 59
    4 Resistance and the Control Factor 77
    5 Unmanageable Change 98
    6 If Bishops Become Kings, So What? 117
    7 The Improbable Degree of Reversal 139
    8 The Tyranny of the Urgent and God's Liberation 160
    9 The Arrival of Anagnorisis 182
    10 The Plan of God in the Church Age 202

Conclusion 223

Endnotes 227

Acknowledgements

It is with sincere modesty that this book has been written. No one in my position could ever assume to be an expert or seer when it comes to understanding why a person or corporate body experiences a major turning point. But I have simply tried to study many transitions; and others will hold differing views to my conclusions, yet I gratefully can say I began with no presupposition that forced me to view events with any prejudice. Therefore, I give God all the glory for helping me finally put down on paper what I have observed, heard, discussed, prayed over, and experienced in the last thirty-eight years of academia and leadership. The turning point began in my life in 1984 and in my church organization in 1990. While the beliefs and basic presuppositions of many key leaders were always privately debated, there was no massive underlying party pushing "the envelope" for change.

This book is more than an autobiography or a reminiscing of turbulent times. Rather, it is a book birthed out of my experience/spirit. Perhaps you could say it is a study about the drama of life. My intention is to give a sincere and straightforward examination of why things often occur and why they often fail to live up to expectations. It is also a plea for courage and faith when things do not occur as we once thought they would. In reality, it is a cry for patience to go further than some would want, as well as a caution to other leaders not to allow change to run amuck like a wild river destroying everything in its path.

I am grateful to my beloved wife Judy that has for several years encouraged me to finally sit down and share with a broader audience my observations, experiences, and faith about the future. She has been my best and truest counselor. In fact, she read and edited my first draft before anyone else was trusted to analyze the preliminary draft. I also thank my family, especially my daughters Cherry and Melissa, who always make me feel like a sage and a hero when such terms would make others possibly giggle.

Contrary to some who believe they are blessed with unusual talent or giftedness, my cup holds no such abundance. I realized years ago that everything I am or anything I ever did would come from a merciful and wonderful Father. I am a common man with an uncommon Savior. So, above all other acknowledgements, I thank Jesus Christ for giving me a spirit of adventure. While my earthly father (Lee) gave me a good work ethic and my mother (Elizabeth) an example of prayer, I was blessed with good literary mentors who helped me love to read books. Names like C. S. Lewis, Francis Schaeffer, Dietrich Bonhoeffer, A. B. Bruce, Charles Swindoll, Chuck Colson, and Philip Yancey were my constant inspiration through the last forty years. Then, there were friends such as Raymond Pruitt, Billy Murray, J. Wendell Lowe, and John Doroshuk who provided me with living examples of how men like organizations can have a significant turning point.

Specifically, I give thanks to the hundreds of parishioners and scores of pastors who listened and shared with me their own frustrations, enthusiasm, and perspectives. They gave me courage to dare to be called a "rebel," a title that many have given me over the years. Some did so with critical hearts, but most of my peers gave me the nickname with affection. There will be others to thank as this book is evaluated and rewrites become a part of the usual task of anything worth reading, but none more than Virginia Chatham who edited and assisted tremendously in the final preparation of the book for publication. I am deeply indebted to her for our friendship and professional eye that kept this project focused toward a worthy conclusion.

Special appreciation is extended to my three colleagues who offered to read and evaluate the contents of the original manuscript to examine my contents, motives, and thoughts. Bishop R. E. Howard (present General Overseer of the Church of God of Prophecy), as well as Dr. Héctor Ortiz and Dr. Tony Charalambou have been friends I've trusted and relied on for many years. They are also men of rich heritage in leadership and continue to be catalysts for progress in the institution we serve. To them, I give thanks for their integrity, courage, and forward mindedness. It has been my honor to serve our Great Master with them.

Finally, I acknowledge the inspiration of an Almighty God who never ceases to amaze me with His divine intervention. In the opening chapters, I will speak about miraculous and total transformations of people and organizations, which would not be possible if there was no Heavenly Conviction moving in the hearts of the most humble of men. It is mind-boggling to me what God can do with such ordinary people who rise up to lead in pivotal points of history both nations and organizations. I have been graced by Jesus Christ to witness such events, and I am the better for it. In fact, we are all better for great turnarounds, and I pray they will occur with more frequency and with a broader influence than heretofore realized.

Note: If and when scriptural quotations are applicable, all such quotations are from the King James Version of the Bible unless a reference is given identifying the other translation being used. Bear with each reader's preference because I will utilize various translations as appropriate or deemed more understandable. All the opening quotes appearing at the beginning of the introduction and each particular chapter are not cited since these statements are now commonly used and have become public domain.

Foreword

By Dr. Héctor Ortiz

I have known Dr. Wallace R. Pratt for more than twenty-five years. I know him as a child of God, a servant leader, a family man, a churchman, and a friend. Our friendship was re-enforced in the crucible of serving together on the Biblical Doctrine and Polity Committee of our church denomination. We have not always agreed, but we have forged a bond of friendship, which is more important than disagreements and agreements. It is a privilege to write the foreword to his book, *The Turning Point That Changed Everything.*

The Turning Point is a narrative about the journey of Dr. Pratt's life, experience, and his heart. The reader is invited to see how the writer will unmask some very catalytic experiences in his Christian journey. He is to be commended for being willing to bear his soul for all to see. Also, the reader will discover that the book is inspirational, sermonic, and didactical.

All writers have the task of selecting what to include in a book and what to exclude. Also, each writer has to make a selection of audiences and methodology. The audience that Bishop Pratt has chosen is general, as it will speak to leaders, pastors, leaders of leaders, and to "powers that be" in Ecclesial bodies. The book is framed in the usage of Performing Arts of ancient times to the more contemporary cinematography of Hollywood. The writer does not invite one to agree with him on all he has to say but has hopes that a tender ear will listen to the narrative of His heart.

Bishop Pratt points to two great "turning points" in his spiritual narrative—one for his personal life in 1984 and the other concerning the Ecclesial body that he belongs to, which is the Church of God of Prophecy. The writer has chosen to use the terms *peripeteia*, which is "a sudden turn of events or an unexpected reversal" and *anagnorisis*," which is "the learning of something previously unknown." A *peripeteia* coupled with *anagnorsis* can be negative or positive, captivating or liberating, but it is always transforming. It is well understood that transformation causes change and that there is no such thing as change that does not change.

The writer galvanizes the concept of a radical "turning point" by applying the biblical concept of "You intended to harm me, but God intended it for good to accomplish what is now being done, the saving of many lives" (Genesis 50:20 NIV). This type of divine reversal is known in theological circles as *"voluntas mali approbens."* Also, that radical turning is strengthened by an encounter with *Missio Dei*—"For it is God who works in you to will and to act according to his good purpose" (Philippians 2:13 NIV).

Dr. Pratt will walk you through a series of personal heroic narratives concerning his family's heroes. He will share his frank presentation of his joys and pains as he ministered in the Ecclesial body that he loves, but, as with many leaders, he has experienced the fulfillment of "'What are these wounds on your body?' he will answer, 'The wounds I was given at the house of my friends.'" (Zechariah 13:6 NIV).

Although Bishop Pratt does not claim to be an expert on change process, he does emphasize the importance of understanding some of the dynamics of change. Dr. Pratt states in the book, "My Goal is simply to bring to light the transformation that occurred within my church body," which began in 1984 and was brought to a visionary catalyst under the leadership of Bishop Billy D. Murray, General Overseer of the Church of God of Prophecy.

It is in reliving the trauma of "the Turning Point," to reverse the structure of legalism, institutionalism, and autocracy that the pains of great effort, sacrifices, and losses would be most realized. I appreciated the honest confession that "the Turning Point" could have used better management. In the writer's words "Being swept up in the wave of change, my mistakes were many . . . the methods and speed was terminal to those unable to cope with the abruptness of it all . . . for I too would be guilty and would confess it openly. If any of them are reading this, I love you and ask you to forgive us for lacking understanding how to implement and manage the change." I affirm this confession and add my name to the confessional of the miscarriage of judgment concerning "the Turning Point" of the Ecclesial transition.

Dr. Pratt uses many historical illustrations concerning the dynamics of resistance and control factor that makes change so difficult. The noble speech of *I have A Dream* of Dr. Martin Luther King has taken decades to move closer to its realization due to resistance and control. Old dreams do not fade, gracefully; they fight to the death.

The writer is concerned with the lack of biblical holiness among many would-be famous voices heard through the medium of the "gospel media." The "purpose philosophy gospel" and the "prosperity gospel," with its weak emphasis on true grace, are ever moving toward "cheap grace." These and many more are a concern in dealing with the plan of God for the church (Ephesians 1:11). The readers may not agree with all of Dr. Pratt's views concerning God's plan for His church, but we all must acknowledge that Christ loves His church; and as Savior of His Ecclesial body, He will ensure that "the gates of Hades will not overcome it" (Matthew 16:18 NIV). The details of how the divine plan will unfold may not be fully known, but the finale is already signed, sealed, and it will be delivered!

Thank you, Wallace, "amigo." You did well, and may you and yours be blessed as you travel on your spiritual journey toward some more narratives of other "turning points."

A Field Hand,
Dr. Héctor Ortiz

Introduction

If you want things to stay as they are, things will have to change.
—Giuseppe di Lampedusa

There is a popular myth today that long-established institutions can never change. Organizations, whether religious or secular, are generally set in concrete after thirty or forty years. A forgotten television commentator once observed that religious institutions are like Congress—you can change the faces in the seats and the names on the office doors, but in reality nothing is ever really different. For more than four decades, I grew up and participated in an institution that practiced the proverbial "no real change" concept like it was perfection and God-ordained. Then in front of the backdrop of one day, a turning point was made that would suddenly begin changing everything as I had once known it. The old power brokers cursed it, more ignored it, a few selfishly used it, but there were many who welcomed it like a cool breeze on a hot summer evening. Unexpected and so refreshing!

The Turning Point That Changed Everything

Recently, while working on this very book, an issue of my monthly subscription to the *Smithsonian* arrived in the mail. Being a historical buff and a geographical "nut," receiving this magazine each month is like another fresh breath of air because I've usually read and reread the last issue by then. In December 2007, I received an issue with the lead story entitled, "1908: The Year That Changed Everything." It had to be either a lucky circumstance or a designed gift to enhance my work. The article written by Jim Rasenberger explored the year 1908 when astonishing events, inventions, predictions, breakthroughs, and incredible achievements propelled America into the modern age. Looking back over the last 100 years, one has to marvel at how almost everything in the United States of America was impacted by those 366 days (leap year). From foreign affairs to family life, nothing would remain the same. A metamorphosis occurred because automobiles, airplanes, communications, politics, sports, immigration, architecture, and environmental changes were impacting a nation. It was a turning point so dramatic that it inspired Thomas Edison to say, "Anything, everything, is possible."[1]

This is the kind of turnaround that most people never envision, but a few men like Thomas Edison, Henry Ford, President Theodore Roosevelt, and Wilbur and Orville Wright could anticipate and usher in the transformation that was coming. Leaders of churches, educational institutions, corporations, parachurch organizations, and even governmental bodies are not exempt from these powerful influences or the need to make such 180 degree turn in their structure, practices, vision, and even within their rank-and-file workers. Historically, "the leader of leaders" does not welcome such changes. The resistance is so strong at the top leadership positions and even among the grassroots' constituency that many organizations get stuck in the roundabout, leaving them in worse condition than they were before the watershed event. We have all witnessed those churches, religious organizations, companies, and various entities as they were bogged down by complacency, fear, or infighting that left them anemically unable to reach complete and positive results.

Oftentimes, turning a group around will depend greatly on the relational qualities of those who lead such incredible breakthroughs. In 1908, those idealistic industrialists, inventors, innovators, and explorers like Admiral Robert Peary were also men of unusual and deep relationships.[2] Many of those who worked with such enthusiasts were driven by the "relationship power" of those people we call giants today. Reawakening or reinventing any organization, especially churches and educational institutions, requires "relationship power" that many leaders never have developed in their lives.[3]

All the above being true, this book is not altogether about leadership and change; it is an exploration into the extraordinary reversal of circumstances or direction that comes as an outworking of God's plan within a group or in a specific age of time. If you have read this far, those who are not searchers of truth will be tempted to close this book; they fear the spiritual world or the mere mention of a divine plan outside the empirical senses. How utterly sad! It was Albert Einstein who remarked to those who questioned the logic of believing in God with this memorable reply, "Human beings, vegetables, or cosmic dust—we all dance to a mysterious tune, intoned in the distance by an invisible piper."[4] While rumors of God's intervention in a person's life are both possible and biblical, is it probable? I believe so. Would God intervene in a church, an organization, a corporation, even a nation? If we believe the ancient writings of the Bible to be accurate, intervention is both declared and expected. The Psalmist David (a factual king in historical documents) wrote, "The King's heart is in the hand of the Lord, as the rivers of water: he turneth it withersoever he will" (Psalm 21:1). Quoted from the older artistic style of the King James Version, its claim is both sobering and worth remembering. Be assured that significant events or transformations have divine legitimacy if not origin.

Before undertaking to investigate the pivotal turning point in my life, my ministry, the church I revered as a boy, and the men we all trust to lead us, let me offer a note of thanks and respect. Many of our parents, founders of companies, institutions, or the churches we embraced, were nothing short of remarkable individuals. My own parents gave sacrificially to their faith and to the church my father ministered within for more than fifty-five years. Our leaders and teachers were zealous and gave long hours of labor. What a joy they brought to us! What wonderful examples of dedication and sacrifice they made! What glorious praise and excellent works they lifted up to their Creator! These daring Pentecostals or other evangelical believers built notable church organizations or denominations that still carry the gospel to the world. Nor am I am ashamed of their testimony or the curious misunderstood practices in which they tried to honor God. They were trying to live holy according to what they believed was true, and it was, in most cases, better than the "cheap grace" we hear preached, taught, trumped by modern

The Turning Point That Changed Everything

television evangelists, or mega church supermarkets. With humility we should honor past leaders.

There is another explanation required before you read the various chapters of this book. The subject of this book is not exclusively applicable to spiritual matters like ministers, churches, religious institutions of learning, or even to Christians. Since I cannot erase who I am, you will see the influence on my writing of thirty-three years of pastoral experience and thirty-nine years of ministry. But let me begin with one presupposition that, hopefully, you the reader will contemplate. There comes a time in the history of any group, even in a nation, that if you are to survive and be relevant to the world around you, there must be a turning point that sends you in a completely opposite way than you were going. Frightful proposition! Does this mean you may have to reverse and go completely in the opposite way you have gone? Maybe! Could it mean that the turn will require a sudden change that even destroys or severely cripples? Likely so! I base this upon one principle in the field of medicine we call orthopedics. As a lad, I watched a doctor tell my brother one afternoon that his femur bone was healing incorrectly and the next thing we heard to our anguish was the orthopedic surgeon breaking my brother's leg once again. Ouch! Can you believe it? Anyone having knowledge of this orthopedic procedure knows the experienced pediatrician was doing my sibling a merciful act of kindness that would promote correct healing of the bone.

There comes a time when the most merciful thing God can do to intervene in a person's life or in an organization is to literally "break" what we cannot see as leading us to a crippling or debilitating condition. Today, I can understand such a traumatic intervention by God, even if I do not always welcome it as His friendly gesture of love. Therefore, as you move on to the following pages of this volume, I pray some will not be too nauseated by the sounds of snapping bones. Without question, the Great Physician will keep "hands on" this difficult stage of your life. Resurrecting dry and broken bones is possible if you believe in what the prophet recorded many years before modern medicine understood anything about bone renewal.

Ezekiel wrote, "Thus says the Lord God to these bones: 'Surely I will cause breath to enter into you, and you shall live. I will put sinews on you and bring flesh upon you, cover you with skin and put breath in you; and you shall live. Then you shall know that I am the Lord.' So I prophesied as I was commanded;

and as I prophesied, there was a noise, and suddenly a rattling; and the bones came together, bone to bone. Indeed, as I looked, the sinews and the flesh came upon them, and the skin covered them over; but there was no breath in them. Also He said to me, "Prophesy to the breath, prophesy, son of man, and say to the breath, thus says the Lord God: 'Come from the four winds, O breath, and breathe on these slain, that they may live.' So I prophesied as He commanded me, and breath came into them, and they lived, and stood upon their feet, an exceedingly great army."[5]

One last note must be inserted into this introduction. While I desire to offer this writing as a blessing to my own church constituency and more importantly to her leadership, the intent of this book is not directed to them, it is primarily addressed to leaders of all groups whether secular or religious. After the two opening chapters that must contain some autobiography material, we will move to the broader and more central audience-leaders. This will include those from every perspective or vocation of leadership. Having stated such, let me confess that this book is about the drama of life itself. Hopefully, you will be inspired to discover and enjoy it more.

Chapter 1

A Personal Crisis of Faith

The ultimate measure of a man is not where he stands in moments of comfort and convenience, but where he stands at times of challenge and controversy.
—Martin Luther King, Jr.

There was a time when Martin Luther was considered a loyal, highly intelligent and devoted Doctor of Theology in the Catholic Church. But there was an acute anxiety in Luther, and he could never be sure he had confessed everything or that he had not committed some new sin. He was profoundly fixated on Christ as a judge waiting to wreck damnation on him for some involuntary act of impurity or gross sinfulness that occurred in his life. A constant dread weighed him down. The church and its traditions had forced an overwrought conscience on the people. None more than a man like Luther who was thoroughly committed to his vows and to the merit-theology that occupied the masses of the fiftieth and sixtieth centuries.[6]

For those who have watched the 2003 film entitled *Luther*,[7] the real historical books on him probably lack the compelling and entertaining drama of cinematography. But it is obvious from both this excellent film and recorded history that Martin Luther began struggling early in his academia and ministry with both his personal faith and the Catholic Church he served so devotedly. Many scholars refer to Luther's journey to Rome as the turning point of his life, some to the day he nailed the Ninety-five Thesis to the door of the castle church at Wittenberg, still others to the Diet of Worms to defend his writings against the charge of heresy.

Like the author John Todd,[8] I am convinced after years of reading and study that it was his own personal discovery of the meaning and transforming power of the biblical truth of Justification by faith in Christ alone! Aided by his faithful friend Dr. Staupitz, one can witness the opening of Luther's heart to a revelation that completely reversed the course of not only his life, but of those who came into the glorious light this devoted priest was seeing in the book of Romans.

Without such reversals, we are left to continue on in our mundane rut of "crowd mentality" that has taken so many men and women down a dead end path. Realize now that such personal journeys include revelation often affecting others, sometimes many people. Furthermore, these kinds of journeys are not the normal peripety that is dependent on intellect or logic. It is greater than a mindset change. It is a monumental "turning point" initiated by the divine Spirit that calls to men in the dark watches of the night or in solitary places like mountains. These are no ordinary reversals of circumstance!

As I stated in the introduction, some personal experiences must be shared to explain why this subject has intrigued me for so many years. Therefore, it is necessary to take one chapter to share my own journey; indeed, it was a complete reversal, a turning point, and it subsequently was a "change of character." In fact, I believe it was for me an *anagnorisis*—"a learning of something I had been previously ignorant of."

I did not realize or grasp the fullness of this change until a friend named Jack came up to me in a conference in 2004 and said, "Wallace, no one would believe you are the same young man I started college with thirty-six years ago. By divine intervention and necessity, you veered around to the opposite. We have certainly been changed more than either of us ever realized was possible." After

The Turning Point That Changed Everything

we finished our short conversation, he walked down the hall, leaving me standing in deep reflection about my journey.

The Lord helped me so many times through the years to safely pass through so many dangerous pitfalls and temptations that I felt like "Frodo" in the trilogy of *The Lord of the Rings*.[9] Yes, sometimes I got beat up, knocked down, confused by different voices, got angry, bordered on sin, hurt at the wrong people, and even tempted to give up. Like Frodo, I was blessed to have a dear trusted friend like the hobbit Sam.[10] He is my favorite character in this powerful trilogy. His gracious patience, loyalty, strength and forgiveness made him the perfect helper.

Today, I appreciate so much my Helper (Sam), which Christians call the Holy Spirit. There is one passage of Scripture that speaks to me so often about life's journey, but especially my own:

> So I bow in prayer before the Father. Every family in heaven and on earth gets its true name from him. I ask the Father in his great glory to give you the power to be strong in spirit. He will give you that strength through his Spirit. I pray that Christ will live in your hearts because of your faith. I pray that your life will be strong in love and be built on love. And I pray that you and all God's holy people will have the power to understand the greatness of Christ's love. I pray that you can understand how wide and how long and how high and how deep that love is. Christ's love is greater than any person can ever know. But I pray that you will be able to know that love. Then you can be filled with the fullness of God.[11]

Now, it is time to honestly review my changes and my journey. I began my active ministry after leaving my church's Bible College in 1970. At that time, I had only completed my associate degree. But I wanted to pastor and accepted my first parish after getting married in 1971. Thank God, I never stopped learning and would continue to study for years in other colleges and seminaries. During the next fifteen years, Judy and I would serve five different parishes; these short tenures were a typical practice in our church organization well into the 1980s.

My confession here will be strikingly transparent, and some who read it will feel uncomfortable because they have not transitioned through my church's metamorphosis or have remained staunchly refusing of the Spirit's call to continue "walking in the light" (1 John 1:5–10).

The Turning Point That Changed Everything

In the fall of 1986, my Sam (Helper) began to gently speak to me in ways I had never heard Him before. He would speak to me in the nights; He would talk to me while I was hiking in the Rockies, and He certainly lay beside me as I prayed prostrate before the Lord each day. At first, it was just that "quiet, still voice" (1 Kings 19:12), which whispered in my heart and mind so gently. He was there and never pushed very hard, but neither did He go away very long. Later, I shamefully argued and tried to reason with Sam, He couldn't be right because everyone else who was important in my life spoke with a different view.

During these years, the conflict between my father and me intensified over some of the things we discussed. What made it worse was that my oldest brother, who I admired so much, could not hear the rumblings in my heart! I always prayed that he could understand and hear the same voice. He passed away in 1995. Dad passed away in 1999; and even to this day, I miss them and our conversations together as pastoral peers and friends. Needless to say, perhaps, it is hard to hear God's voice when two of the greatest men in your life are speaking something different. Besides, they were holy men who loved the Lord as much as I. My dad and brother were no less spiritual or gifted. But how do you stop hearing Sam (my Helper) when He is always with you?

In May 1989, my father, brother, and I went to a "Solemn Prayer and Fasting" called by our church's General Overseer. The weekend was intense for me, personally, since the three of us spent the evenings in heated exchanges of views about many subjects. Sharing what God was speaking to my heart made matters worse. After coming home that weekend, I confess to wavering and drawing back from some of the things God was speaking to me. Without question, my life and beliefs could have been viewed by some as waffling. It is hard to let go of the past and the beliefs you once thought to be so true.

By 1991, there could be no question that something had to change inside my heart. I knew a "turning point" was coming, but I still was not quite ready to reverse and go the opposite of those two men who were my heroes. But God kept poking his nose in my business. One of my ministerial peers told me that this was spiritual schizophrenia; that will sure make you feel edified! While in the midst of that dilemma, there was a devotional book, *Come Before Winter*, that spoke hope into my struggle. The words were directed right into my heart: "Those who flex with the times, refuse to be rigid, resist the mold, and reject the rut—Ah, those are the souls distinctively used by God. To them, change is a challenge, a fresh breeze

The Turning Point That Changed Everything

that flows through the room of routine and blows away the stale air of sameness. Stimulating and invigorating as change may be—it is never easy. Changes are especially tough when it comes to certain habits that haunt and harm us. That kind of change is excruciating, but it isn't impossible. It is vital—it is essential—that we see ourselves as we really are in the light of God's written Word, then be open to change where change is needed."[12] That night as I prayed, Sam (the Helper) seemed to speak to me until early daybreak. There was no way of going back, and I knew it.

In early August of 1992, I had returned from my parent's home where I shared with my dad what the Holy Spirit was speaking into my heart. He knew that the Word of God was very important to me. He mentioned my hunger over the years to read and study the Bible, even as a child. But He also told me that "he was leaving the church" organization that he had raised me to embrace and serve; it was like my world had come crashing down on my shoulders. How could we go opposite directions? And, yet, that is exactly what "soul stirring" changes can cause in your life. Later that month, I attended International Youth Camp near a place called Monument, Colorado. Things were busy and exciting since I was also serving as the Transportation Coordinator for all who were arriving at the airport in Denver.

Then, early on Tuesday morning, August 18, 1992, I awoke earlier than the campers and staff. During my years in Colorado, I loved to hike the Rockies with my family, friends, and even alone. Sam was calling me, but not like before. There seemed to be urgency in His voice, and there was no doubt that I must go with Him. Since I knew every trail of the small mountain behind the Ponderosa Campground where International Youth Camp was being held, I hiked up in the creeping pre-dawn light to the top. I sat down on a fallen tree and began to talk to the Lord in a simple conversational voice. But it quickly turned to crying, bawling, and confessing my seven years of resistance and disobedience. Sam knew it better than I.

For more than two hours, as the sunrise blossomed on the horizon, it was as if there was no reason to ever leave that place. Peaceful acceptance had come. I looked over to see on the ground part of an old fallen limb that looked just like a harvest sickle. All the bark had been stripped away due to time and the elements. Picking it up, I wrote on it these words that I will never forget: "By your help Dear God, from this day forward, I will go your way!" I kept that treasured stick

The Turning Point That Changed Everything

as a reminder for more than twelve years until the Lord impressed me that it was time to discard it. While God had a temporary purpose for it in my life, it was not to become a Holy relic. By then, He had written it on my heart, and there was no longer danger of turning back (Psalm 119:11). Sam was there with me as always, ready to carry my load that seemed so heavy.[13]

Indescribable is the only word that can describe my life from that moment. This was clearly "The Turning Point That Changed Everything" for me. But I still had to face my immediate family (my wife and two daughters) and my parish I had pastored for more than eight years. My immediate family was understanding and supportive, actually much more than originally anticipated. Confessions, explanations, and forgiveness were necessary and accepted with a few questions. We finished our conversation that Saturday night with tears and prayer for the next morning. On Sunday morning, we left for church as we had so many times before; I found myself praying throughout Sunday School class for the Lord to give me the courage needed for what I was about to do. Please continue to bear with me for a little longer on this critical transition.

On Sunday morning, August 23, 1992, I stood before my congregation to tell them what the Lord had done that past week in my life. As I shared the journey and "The Turning Point" that had occurred that prior Tuesday, many joined me in tears. I asked their forgiveness for things preached or taught that God had now convinced and shown me were incorrect. While I had been taught many of these things and grown up in a home and church that believed such things, it was essential that I take personal responsibility for having contributed to the perpetuating of those traditions, practices, attitudes, and doctrinal errors.

Finally, after speaking for approximately twenty minutes, I stopped to tell them that it was time for me to go to the altar to accept not only God's comfort and direction, but to ask Him to give the church strength and compassion to forgive me. My wife rehearsed for me on our way home that day what had occurred in the altar that I could not see. She told me that the entire congregation without invitation came to the front to pray over me; she could not even see me behind the crush of people. They wept, hugged, and prayed. A ten-year-old girl named Michelle, prompted by no human influence, came to the front and removed our large display flag on a pole out of its stand. She walked over to the altar and stood on top to hold it over me as she glorified the Lord. I cannot express the strong presence of the Holy Spirit in that altar; Sam had to be giggling as He watched this scene. Unexpected is too soft a word. Overwhelmed with emotion is better. I had expected anger, rebukes, disappointments, and even some who might walk out or leave our local church. Thank God, it did not happen!

No one could ever describe the outpouring of love and acceptance I felt that morning and during my remaining year in that church. After having served for nearly ten years in that parish, I did leave a year later because it was better to start new and begin to establish a different type of pastoral ministry. While forgiveness and acceptance had come, God wanted me to do even more to establish a new kind of ministry built on His grace and truth.

Three months later, I was attending a Christian Ministries and Book Convention at the Denver Convention Center. During one of the free breaks, I was browsing the resource booths and came upon a friendly gentleman named Chuck and his gracious wife Cynthia. Our conversation drifted to my recent experience that seemed so necessary to share with him that day. He signed a copy of one of his books that he felt would be good for me to read. I still have that signed copy by Charles Swindoll; without question, I needed to read *The Grace Awakening*. In reading that exposition on grace, there is one statement I underlined that aided my continuing journey in the opposite direction that lay before me: "Grace also brings a freedom to do something else—a freedom to enjoy the rights and privileges of being out from under slavery and allowing others such freedom.

It's freedom to experience and enjoy a new kind of power that only Christ could bring. It is freedom to become all that He meant me to be, regardless of how he leads others. I can be me—fully and freely. It is a freedom to know Him in an independent and personal way. And that freedom is then released to others so they can be who they are meant to be—different from me!"[14]

Meditating over that liberating declaration, the scripture came to mind that speaks to every child of God who has ever had "a legalist" try to force you into their private interpretation. When others are trying to compare you to their perfect idea of a Christian, remember the instruction in God's Word: "We do not dare to put ourselves in the same group with those who think that they are very important. We do not compare ourselves to them. They use themselves to measure themselves, and they judge themselves by what they themselves are. This shows that they know nothing."[15]

How can anyone or any group understand the significance of one person's transformation? Knowing God's Word and understanding what He has spoken to you is not only liberating, it is life altering (Romans 12:1, 2).

Enter into one of the most violent terrains of the ancient world called simply "The Wilderness." Located between three great bodies of water (The Great Sea—Mediterranean, the Red Sea, and the Gulf of Aqaba), it amasses a desert of immense size and challenges. The best and easiest passages to cross this formidable desert lay to the north, either crossing the "Way of the Philistines" or the "Way of Shur." In the ancient times, neither trade route was safe or even remotely recommended for an armed caravan because these convenient short-cuts were constantly under attack by marauding bands of thieves or violent competing armies. To the south lies the Wilderness of Zin and the Wilderness of Paran, which even today are remarkably challenging with modern vehicles. This is where God will take a man facing his mid-life crisis of identity and purpose.

At a remote and forbidding mountain to the far south called Mt. Horeb/Mt. Sinai, the rejected son of Pharaoh named Moses will face his life-reversing drama. No other candidate of the Old Testament dares to be nominated for such a "reversal of circumstances." Imagine not just one dramatic turn in life, but two (at age forty and eighty); it is almost too much to comprehend.

The "Burning Bush" and the subsequent conversation with God became the watershed event of Moses life, and yet in spite of these remarkable miracles that pole-vaulted this Israelite into history, he demonstrates immediately afterward his trepidations about the reversal that was coming: "Then Moses answered and said, 'But suppose they will not believe me or listen to my voice; suppose they say, 'The LORD has not appeared to you.'"[16]

Like Moses, I was not prepared for how far God was taking me on this opposite road—not that my journey is to be compared or was as extreme to this giant in history. I am forever indebted to the scores of wise and mature counselors who tolerated, guided, and aided me in the months and years that followed. Also, as with any metamorphosis, there were the loyal peers who journeyed with me and they had their own issues to resolve. Thank you, dear friends. You see, Moses was discovering, along with manna each day, that sometimes these "turning points" do not mean you will be liked more or that things will be easier. Quite to the opposite, those who often go through these remarkable cataclysms find the road steeper, bumpier, less traveled, lonelier, and more hazardous.

But this does not mean the journey should not be taken. My friends have heard me say this truth more than once: "Transformations change you more than they change others!" That's all right. When I converted to Christ (Acts 3:19), He changed me because He certainly did not change!

Looking at people today in my family, among my friends or within my church organization, there are many who have changed very little over the years. Shall such sameness offend me? Sometimes it puzzles or saddens me, but who am I to judge what God is doing in them or what they have been asked to do. Moses could have taken this approach, but he refused. I want to be like this meek man of God who could give so much and receive so little with such humility.

When God began revealing Himself in ways that beforehand He had never done to me, these conversations with Sam at times were unsettling. Who would believe me, who would listen to me, and what if no one even cared? Those kinds of questions will flatten your pride. I found in Moses something that spoke to me about this quagmire of misgivings. Go to Exodus sometime and just browse around those intimate places like the Mt. Horeb, the Rock of Meribah, the Oasis of Kadesh, Mt. Hor, and, finally, Mt. Nebo.

These were significant steps after Moses' great turnaround that saw him lose loved ones (as I did) who had aided him on his journey. Indeed, these were the places where he faced the consequences of the reversal in his life's calling. God prepares us for why He has decided that He must intervene in our path. Such changes have purpose.

The scholarly A. W. Pink's analysis of the lengthy sojourn on the backside of the desert is applicable to us:

> God dealt personally and directly with the one He was going to honor as His ambassador: there was a manifestation of His holiness, the avowal of His covenant-relationship, an assurance of His compassion for the suffering Hebrews, and the declaration of His self-sufficiency as the great "I am"; in short, there was a full revelation of His person and character. In addition, Moses *received a definite call from Jehovah, the guarantee that God would be with him, an intimation of the difficulties that lay before him,* and the promise that, in the end, God's purpose should be realized. These have ever been, and still are, the vital prerequisites for effectiveness in God's service. *There must be a personal knowledge*

of God for us, a knowledge obtained by direct revelation of God to the soul. There must be a definite call from God to warrant us engaging in His service. There must be *recognition of the difficulties confronting us and a confident resting on God's promise for ultimate success*" (italics added for emphasis).[17]

This analysis brings me back to why the Lord had to bring me through a peripeteia. Some will say I should have shared this earlier, but as with any author, these are my own set of preferences. Frankly, the change was more important than where I had been in the past. Yet for integrity and clarity, this should not be left out of this chapter. Throughout my years of adolescence, formulation of my biblical beliefs and values were being shaped by a myriad of influences that were both positive and negative. Those early lessons, examples, and experiences were shaping the basic presuppositions that would determine my views in life.

Perhaps, you have dealt with these types of influences, too? Whether you are a Christian or an atheist, you interpret Scripture and understand life as an adult based on acquired knowledge and many other influences that have come earlier in your life. This is called a basic presupposition. In this respect, I was normal (which will surprise some). In reality, the ability of the mind to do cognitive thinking can even be invaded by these underlying beliefs. My father was a strong authoritarian figure who rarely allowed his family to be freethinkers. The church organization I was growing up in was even less pliable and was rigid in its pronouncements about good and evil. Believers had no need for the Holy Spirit beyond emotional outbreaks in worship services (there was no reality of Sam's influence beyond speaking in unknown tongues or dancing in the Spirit). Personal revelation was squelched for group submission to a few so-called "holy men" in high positions.

During my childhood and adolescent years, our rulings by our Assembly governed over a multiplicity of everyday activities, clothing, habits, and even attitudes. To me, being a Christian meant anything that was enjoyable or was different from our church's teaching was sin. Not everyone will like or agree with my assessments, but that is my perception. I remember asking my dad only one time, "Why was having fun sinful?" That was a mistake and of course sin itself.

As I entered the ministry, if I thought those restrictions and taboos were abundant, there was more to come. The attitude developed that if the *Assembly Minutes* (that was the book that contained all our rulings) stated something, then we had better interpret Scripture no other way. It took me years to understand the meaning of the verse that said, "Knowing this first, that no prophecy of the scripture is of any private interpretation. For the prophecy came not in old time by the will of man: but holy men of God spake as they were moved by the Holy Ghost" (2 Peter 1:20, 21). Of course added to that Scripture was its twin verse that clenched the deal: "Where no counsel is, the people fall: but in the multitude of counselors there is safety" (Proverbs 11:14). There you have it! The Holy Spirit could not speak personally to me, and, therefore, all those multiplicities of rulings were mine to keep. I cannot tell you how hard it was to understand the distorted interpretations put on these two passages and a host of others.

During the last two years, there has been much in the World News and especially in England concerning the rumor that Mr. Tony Blair was about to convert to Catholicism. Since England has basically been ruled or presided over by leaders and royalty that are all from the Church of England (which is Anglican), this was tantamount to treason. The attacks have been ruthless on this former Prime Minister even though he is no longer in that position. Mr. Blair is going through a horrible situation because many Catholics are saying he is hypocritical since he consistently voted with pro-abortionists while he was in office (a decision with which I certainly would not agree). Yet he also consistently opposed homosexual rights. And he admires the Catholic Church for its worldwide and well-documented humanitarian works. The debate is raging over whether he can receive Holy Eucharist or be baptized and become in reality a Catholic?[18]

Interestingly, a man has announced that he can no longer accept some of the teachings and expected decisions being made in the Anglican Church. He is now ready to convert to Catholicism. This is a big conversion. My point has nothing to do with his past but the huge turnaround from a belief system he embraced so strongly. While I may not understand all his votes, present plans, or his decision to become Catholic principally because of their humanitarian stands, this kind of reversal is worthy to be watched and studied by anyone who has also had to make life-altering decisions.

When the Holy Spirit began to speak to me during those seven years (1986–1992), I had no doubt that something must change. Candidly, I can confess that I had no comprehension in the beginning about how far it would take me, nor how immense the turnaround would be. In this way, I am no different than Tony Blair.

You begin thinking it will only be a slight alteration. But when you submit and finally let the Holy Spirit take hold of your heart and mind, you cannot stop the turning until He is finished. To do so would be disobedience and lead to grieving by Sam: "And grieve not the Holy Spirit of God, whereby ye are sealed unto the day of redemption" (Ephesians 4:30).

With the departure of the fear of "authorities over me in the Lord" and the institutional changes in the church organization I served, it opened up an entire new philosophy of ministry. Later, as I was reading some of the writings by Aristotle, it occurred to me that a person could keep attributing his or her behavior to an irrational element and, thereby, make his or her actions beyond the range of human knowledge or responsibility. It is evident in his writings that Aristotle perceived this drama as most relevant to a Tragedy (more will be written on this in Chapter 3). However, the applicable truth of this philosophy is far-reaching if we stop to think about it. In the same way, many of us exclude actions as something beyond our ability to change.

One particular quote by Aristotle stood out above all others: "Thus a person of a given character should speak or act in a given way, by rule either of necessity or of probability; just as this event should follow that by necessary or probable sequence."[19] I had been guilty of hiding my actions behind the irrational fear of "authority," which excused me from any personal obligation to do anything about what I had been told.

Consequently, Aristotle was correct that some actions are inevitable and must occur out of necessity. Why do we allow this legitimate doctrine of "submission to authorities" (Hebrews 13:7, 17) to be subverted by misinterpretation or inappropriate application? Before I examine this question, let me give a serious warning to those who have lived all their lives under the influence and education of Western thinking. Submission to authority is the last subject we want to talk about since we worship at the ground of "rugged individualism" (I do not know where I first heard this expression).

Millions, everyday, are ignorant or willingly disobedient to this kind of living where submission is practiced. We have been slowly mesmerized into accepting as truth that which is totally opposite of what is right. Hollywood contributed greatly to this hypnotic spell as it entertained us with this diabolical thinking through characters played by leading actors like James Cagney, James Dean, and Marlon Brando. These modern icons have been given the term antiheroes because as a main character in a novel or play, "their idea of the good life is conspicuously in opposition to that of the conventional hero."[20] They have made us feel that rebellion and "doing it my way" is actually our right, no matter how contrary to God's Word or whoever else may be hurt by it. From such examples of rebellion, the Christian and especially leaders should avoid the rejection of all authority whether in the family, church or pertaining to God-ordained secular rulers.

Instead, during those days I was going through my watershed experience, there was a realization that I must identify through three witnesses what was proper authority and what was nothing more than "authoritarian fear." Those three witnesses would be the Bible, Discernment of the Spirit, and a trusted group of mature friends whose understanding of the divine principles of Scriptures I respected.

To this latter witness group, I chose three godly men that I knew would not necessarily agree with me; therefore, they were free to "speak truth" into my life so I would never be the sole determinant of the other two- biblical interpretation and spiritual discernment. For their sakes, I will not include their names, but they know their place and value in my life. Rejecting authority is serious business, and no one can afford to arbitrarily do so.

For me, it is important that I do not claim to hear a discerning voice and at the same time have a rebellious heart. I cannot tell you how many men and women I observed shipwreck their lives because of this kind of excusable disobedience. In the past, many had misused their positions of authority to hold me bound to traditions, institutional practices, and doctrinal misinterpretations.

With this turnaround, I did not want my strong-willed nature to enslave me to my own flesh. Therefore, I kept close to my heart men of integrity such as "feared God" and loved the Holy Scriptures more than life itself. They were my counselors who often quizzed me about what I was thinking and doing. My discernment, at times, was a shade or two off the true color of what was right.

By late 2001, I was reading a valuable and soul-searching book about authority. As I read it quickly, it confirmed what the Holy Spirit had spoken to me more than ten years earlier. Two special excerpts stood out to me. The first one read: "I hear disapproving tones echoed in the voices of many who claim to be discerning, yet have insubordinate hearts. Even as I write this book, I've just received a letter in the past twenty-four hours in which I had to deal with an 'I will submit as long as I agree' attitude coupled with the 'ability to discern.' Those who

The Turning Point That Changed Everything

think like this mistakenly believe they have a sure way out of true submission."[21] This was the very pitfall that I did not want to stumble back into as I tried to find myself walking further into the light. Gratefulness and love fills my heart toward the Lord that He gave me this conviction not to "go it alone." I watched some of my peers do this in the 1980s and 1990s, which broke my heart. They were friends whom I loved and respected.

The second excerpt from that modest exposition on authority and submission was equally reassuring. This strong word from the Lord declared: "Esther had concrete evidence, not just discernment, that her leader lacked the true facts. She went to him in humility and made her presentation in such a way the king was in position to make the decision. She did not belittle, force, or manipulate him. She just trusted in the power of the Holy Spirit to direct her lord's heart."[22] My heart leaped in excitement; this had been the position I wanted to be in before those over me in the Lord. Then as well as now, when I failed to respond like this, I have tried to reach out to those whom I've offended or resisted to ask their forgiveness. But this also meant that I was required to speak up and share with those over me when I had evidence that their beliefs, information or interpretations were incorrect.

This chapter refers to my "Personal Crisis of Faith" and, therefore, at some point, it will be necessary to regress to a period of my life long before the transition began with voices from Sam (the Holy Spirit) in 1986. When I was entering adolescence at the age of thirteen (1963), our family was rocked by news from our father on Thanksgiving Day that he was leaving our mother. He would no longer live with us. The news continued to get worse. Dad had resigned from pastoring after sixteen years. As I sat there with my two other brothers (our sister had married the year before), it was like something was dying. Our mother was crying like I had never seen in my life, and the hurt was unbelievable. Strange, dad was very calm; too calm.

For the next three years, everything that I knew to have been true was lost, shattered, or challenged. I had already accepted Christ four years earlier, but it gave me no consolation for the next two years. It was my mother's prayers I heard every night downstairs after I went to bed that gave me hope in the midst of darkness.

Because I do not want to belabor the point or test your endurance to hear the whole story, those three years were like punishment. People who liked us no longer came to see us. Our extended family was either angry at my dad or my mother. We were ignored by all of our relatives except for my mother. Even our local church seemed to talk about us or around us; certainly, we were looked down upon for something we could not control or understand.

When I was fifteen, I was ready to give-up and asked the Lord to give me direction. Everything I had been taught by my father seemed to be falling apart. The next year would be spent reading the Bible (cover to cover, over and over) and praying many hours each week. I needed answers. When I was sixteen my father came home and was back pastoring within one year (he pastored another thirty years). Mother accepted him back, but I do not think she was ever as happy again. After dad's passing, she privately told me why she accepted his coming back home: "I had to do it to go to heaven." I questioned that logic too many times to count.

When Dad left our church organization in 1993, I was disappointed but not surprised. Being shocked had passed years before and loving dad meant accepting his decisions even when I did not agree with them. We were close friends when he died six years later, and for that I give thanks to God. Like John Eldredge wrote: "God wants to father you. Has been fathering you for some time—you just haven't had the eyes to see it. In fact, even the best father can only take you so far. He was never meant to be your all-in-all. Rather, he was meant to bring you to the Father."[23]

You would think that all this would have fostered a metamorphosis while I was younger, but it did not! What it did do was leave unanswered questions that caused me to want to learn about the Bible and to learn about the world around me. My quest has been going on for years to know God. Perhaps like Frodo and Sam, it takes time to understand your closest companion and friend?

In reading and doing research for this book, I came across a forgotten exposition by a physics professor from several years ago. Let me simply summarize his plea to mankind. While writing on the dramatic change of concepts and ideas that have occurred in physics in the last century, he explores the strange and unexpected reality that tests not only the intellectual mind, but the intense emotional pain of those "turning points" in our world.

Astoundingly, this professor criticizes the overemphasis on scientific methods and the rational or analytical thinking that psychology, physics, politics, corporations, and religion are using today. He speaks about the need of understanding natural balance even in the areas of spirituality and ethics. His greatest counsel is that governments and people must learn to live with more balance in their world. His advice is to stop talking about a Utopia or an eternal place while you ignore the balance required in your own life to bring about such change. He frankly confesses in his own field of study that too many organizations and corporations fear radical change that could bring them more effectiveness and relevance. Therefore, they cling to old ideas, theories, even accepted truths that have long ago proved meaningless. Exploitation in any name or cause leads to excess.[24] He is so right on it. Who among us cannot confess to seeing such refusal to bring balance literally stymie groups and organizations? I've enclosed this thought for a specific reason. Years have come and gone in my life. I do not fully know why I was born in a specific place, to specific parents, and in a specific time. But having seen where I've been, reviewed what has happened to me, and others, and appreciating where I am today, helps me put it all into clearer perspective. I'm trying to find a balance in my faith (not for self-actualization) but realizing that the Lord rarely works in the extremes of man's fanaticism.

My first bishop (supervisor) when I began pastoring would say to me, "Wallace, avoid extremes and seek moderation in all things (Philippians 4:5). Believe and preach the Bible with the same measure that God spoke through His Word to us. Do not let others push you to either side; those two sides will hinder and nullify your work for Christ." I never forgot those words from my early mentor. Bishop C. J. Cunningham was wiser than I knew back then; so tragic that we learn those lessons so slowly and painstakingly.

I believe my changes have been essential for both natural and spiritual balance in my life. Now, I'm trying to communicate that message to my peers and to a younger generation that follows. Hopefully, they will not be satisfied to duplicate my same revelation, but may they find the reversal required in their own life to bring balance. Whether it comes suddenly as it does in literature and theater or slowly as it does in religion and science, may your transformed life bring you as much satisfaction and enlightenment as it has brought to me.

God's drastic reversal in my life was not to send me careening into some oblivion of destruction in the opposite direction. Not so! My "turning point" was to rescue me from the extreme of doctrinal legalism and the ritualistic practices that hindered my worship of God. "But the hour cometh and now is, when the true worshippers shall worship the Father in spirit and in truth: for the Father seeketh such to worship him. God is a Spirit: and they that worship Him must worship him in spirit and in truth" (John 4:23, 24).

Besides my personal change, the Lord desired me to be an influence to help others to change. And, for myself, He never wanted me to become a liberal philosopher or a sin-living heathen; He wanted balance like He gave Adam and Eve in the garden until they desired the extreme of demonic self-indulgence.

Getting balance is a challenge and rarely do most people want you to go there; it makes them very uncomfortable. Like Paul, you will have to press to find that place in your life. He did: "Not as though I had already attained, either were already perfect: but I follow after, if that I may apprehend that for which also I am apprehended of Christ Jesus. Brethren, I count not myself to have apprehended: but this one thing I do, forgetting those things which are behind, and reaching forth unto those things which are before, I press toward the mark for the prize of the high calling of God in Christ Jesus" (Philippians 3:12–14).

As such, I continue to press on with a thirst to come more into His image. Like Paul, with the veil of ignorance that once covered my eyes gone, my change must daily continue: "Nevertheless when one turns to the Lord, the veil is taken away. Now the Lord is the Spirit; and where the Spirit of the Lord is, there is liberty. But we all, with unveiled face, beholding as in a mirror the glory of the Lord, are being transformed into the same image from glory to glory, just as by the Spirit of the Lord"[25]

Before closing this chapter on my personal transformation, I must to some degree confess a longing that I will explore much later in this book. So many times God begins a series of changes in our lives, and somewhere along that difficult climb the noises or distractions around us get so intense that we falter in the journey. It becomes easier to stop climbing and just run along a parallel course. You know it is very hard to have people disappointed or angry at you! Pitifully, we are tempted to start descending again to find more ease or comfortable air. Several times in my life these times have come around to beckon me like a "forbidden lover." I recognized their allure and entertained them quite frequently much longer than I should have. Dismissing their soft and pleasant invitation, the Lord would call me again to begin the ascent to the next higher level in my relationship with Him. Thankfully, these enticing persuasions were rebutted after a time with Sam's trusted friendship. The result was that I found the need to keep drawing closer to God.

A couple of years ago, I read the following words that strengthened my resolve to keep climbing upward:

> My experience—confirmed by the stories told to me by many men—is that God mostly wants to do our initiating directly, personally, Himself. He wants the same relationship with us that Jesus—as a man—experienced with Him during his journey on this earth. Remember, you are the son of a kind, strong, and engaged Father, a Father wise enough to guide you in the Way, generous enough to provide for your journey, offering to walk with you every step. Whatever else might seem true, this is what is most true.[26]

Chapter 2

Unbelievable Events vs. Uncertain Future

The dogmas of the quiet past are inadequate to the stormy present. The occasion is piled high with difficulty, and we must rise with the occasion. As our case is new, so we must think anew, and act anew. We must disenthrall ourselves, and then we shall save our country.
—Abraham Lincoln

In 1974, one of the most notorious and disgusting prisons in the world closed for business. Called Humaita, this dark and foreboding prison in the state of Sao Paulo, Brazil, had a reputation for not only violence but a huge recidivism rate. By early 1970's, criminal rehabilitation programs were no longer seen as effective vehicles for reducing recidivism.

Most research studies of a wide variety of programs indicated meager or unfavorable results in reducing the number of convicts returning to prison. The future looked bleak for not only Humaita, but throughout prisons worldwide. Not only was the individual impact of this penal institution tragic, the cancerous result of this stale and archaic system effected families and the entire nation of Brazil. Then, in a remarkable peripeteia, there was a reversal of circumstances so profound that criminologists and penal institutions around the globe took notice of the remarkable transformation.

Humaita was taken over that same year of 1974 by the urging of two men associated with the Cursillo movement, a Catholic evangelization program. They told the authorities of Brazil that their group would take over running the prison as a Christian institution; the plan was for the state to provide only the food and the facility. It was to be run with volunteers only. But it was considered by most a dangerous gamble.

However, this group of dedicated Christians immediately changed the entire atmosphere of this penal institution. Soon, brightly colored walls, gardens maintained by the inmates, manicured and well-kept walkways, even clean grounds and cells met all arriving guests. Positive posters encouraging moral living were placed everywhere. The inmates smiled and cheerfully did their duties. They recited the Lord's Prayer before their meals. The chapel services each day were filled to capacity with prisoners singing, clapping, and joyfully worshipping and testifying about God's grace. Priests and ministers had transformed Humaita into a Christian culture where, every night, the Bible was taught.

Now, the recidivism rate is more than two-thirds less than other prisons that operate under the old paradigm of punishment and deprivation. Even more, the cost to the Brazilian government is so drastically reduced that other places of incarceration are now being raised up to emulate the success of this incredible turnaround.[27] Unlike Humaita, how many other institutions limp along or die because no person or group will take on responsibility to change the status quo?

In this chapter, I want to candidly rehearse and examine another institutional turnaround that occurred in my church organization. Let me begin by offering a simple and sincere disclaimer at this juncture. I do not think or claim to be an expert on change, nor do I write as an authority or historian of my beloved church.

The Turning Point That Changed Everything

My goal is simply to bring to light the transformation that occurred within my church body. Many wonderful leaders have blessed this beloved group and could certainly offer their own personal or positional insights.

At this point, I humbly beg their forgiveness if they do not see the past or the future as it unfolds in this chapter. These are my observations and thoughts for others who hopefully will be encouraged by them.

Lastly, I honor, highly, those faithful pioneers and warriors who paved the way to make my church a great place in which to grow up. You have my lifelong admiration and thankfulness. Read with patience, read with tolerance, and read with hope for tomorrow. As the wise king Solomon wrote long ago, "I returned, and saw under the sun, that the race is not to the swift, nor the battle to the strong, neither yet bread to the wise, nor yet riches to men of understanding, nor yet favour to men of skill; but time and chance happeneth to them all" (Ecclesiastes 9:11).

In the Scriptures of the Bible, there is a unique term called *peripateo* that is used several times in the New Testament. While some references pertain to "the physical action of walking," it is also used figuratively, "signifying the whole round of the activities of the individual life, whether of the unregenerate or of the believer . . . all figurative applications of this term generally appear in the Pauline Epistles and are used primarily for the function of the plan of God in the Church Age (i.e. Romans 6:4, Galatians 5:16, 17, and Ephesians 5:1, 2)."[28] In the spiritual sense, a church body is under the same decree and must be walking in conjunction with the plan of God. This is, undoubtedly, the instruction of Paul to the church in Ephesus where he writes: "I therefore, the prisoner of the Lord, beseech you that ye walk worthy of the vocation wherewith ye are called, with all lowliness and meekness, with longsuffering, forbearing one another in love; endeavoring to keep the unity of the Spirit in the bond of peace" (Ephesians 4:1–3). Rightfully so, I inject this word study for a specific purpose.

A peripateo is not limited to us as individuals but can apply to local churches, the general church, and even to a corporate institution or nation. God has included all of these in His plan.

As with most dramatic turns to opposite in literature or theater, there are strange and subtle whisperings heard by the keen observer that signal the coming reversal of circumstances. Within my church organization, "The Turning Point That Changed Everything" began in 1984. While the quote that follows is lengthy, it may be the most important reading within this chapter because it was the significant point of turning for thousands and eventually millions of people.

On a Monday morning, September 10, 1984, the following statement was read by a simple committee assigned for the purpose of bringing important questions or subjects to the attention of their worldwide constituency:

> Although we feel that all the matters to which we have given attention during the course of our meetings this year are important, one matter, in the opinion of this Committee, eclipses them all. It is a subject that the Holy Ghost brought very forcefully upon us in our first meeting of the Assembly year held in January. Its need finds expression in the second Chapter of Joel: "Blow the trumpet in Zion, sanctify a fast, call a solemn assembly: Gather the people, sanctify the congregation, assemble the elders, gather the children, and those that suck the breasts: let the bridegroom go forth of his chamber, and the bride put out of her closet. Let the priests, the ministers of the Lord, weep between the porch and the altar, and let them say, Spare thy people, O Lord, and give not thine heritage to reproach" (v. 15–17). *This Committee knows of no greater need to bring to this Assembly's attention than the need for repentance—the need to fall on our faces before God, confessing that we have drifted in many ways from a vital relationship with the Holy Ghost, confessing a self-centeredness lacking in deep compassion for a world of people who are living now under the judgment of God to eternal damnation, rededicating ourselves to being the Church of God of the Bible.* God's message to the church in this Assembly has been a call to repent, and we must not ignore His voice. We cannot afford to continue the pursuit of our mission without convincing evidence of His presence and approval. There is no acceptable substitute for repentance when that is what God is calling us to do. With the moderator's permission, we suggest that this portion of our report be accepted, not by a motion and a second to the motion, but by those present in this Assembly falling down before the Lord, thus setting the pace for *a church-wide repentance to follow when these recommendations are ratified in our local church conferences around the world, where every local church at that time will likewise confess their*

The Turning Point That Changed Everything

failure in sincere repentance.[29] [italics added in this quote for emphasis and attention of the reader.]

This bold declaration was humbling and far-reaching to any sincere believer in the Holy Spirit. Never before had I heard or seen such honesty and humility from our leadership in such an important global setting. Since I knew all these godly men who stood there reading this confession of repentance that day, I was profoundly moved by this action.

When I went back home to my church in Denver, Colorado, I could not sleep. The next Sunday I would bring the same plea to my local congregation. What surprised me about that Sunday service was the lack of response. A few came to the altar and were restored to their once vital relationship with God, but the overall response was disappointing. All that week, I remember the tugging on my heart by the Holy Spirit. Yes, even then Sam (the Holy Spirit) began to speak to me without my complete understanding. But throughout our organization there seemed to be a prevailing attitude that said, "Repent of what?" I was brokenhearted, yet I was irrefutably weak also.

After a few months and events, work would take me away from the urgency of the Spirit's call, but it never went away completely nor did it lack significance in my life. I suppose the same was true in my general church organization, yet only a few ministers or people spoke about it. Haunting fears in the night and endless hours of prayer became my constant bedfellows. I would awaken to the thought, "Why hasn't there been more of a drastic change in my church; no, in ME?"

Questions were now emerging more than answers. From late 1984 to early 1989, there was a vast emptiness that I sensed and yet, candidly, I confess that most of us tried to ignore it very successfully. Five years ago, I read a book that reminded me of those unsettling days and nights.[30] Writing this book has caused me to reflect on the questions and feelings that stirred about in my soul during those agonizing years.

Undeniably, the "Whys" became more abundant and unbearable! Why so few miracles? Why not more people harvested to Jesus? We claimed to be preaching and teaching powerful truths, so where were the results? If we had repented—all of us truly repented—why hadn't the windows of heaven been opened and our lands healed? I would like to compare those days in our church as a giant "Pause," but in reality there was no rest, no relief, and certainly no evidence of the changes forthcoming. Reflecting back, it was part of the shift without the visible evidence. Like the Titanic, warnings and actions were taking place below decks among some of our leadership, but would real change come in time to save us from a fateful termination of our voyage?

In 1989, hope of the reversal in our church's journey came from an unexpected voice. Our aging General Overseer of our church made an announcement that was like a maternal cry of good news when a family is about to experience new life. He called on the worldwide ministry of our church to come to our International Headquarters for a three-day "Solemn Assembly of Prayer and Fasting." Something remarkable happened in my soul; the voice of Sam was awakening from my long, summer's nap in the Shire. The excitement and hope that preceded that late May 1989 event was unparalleled for many of us. Surely the "Call of Repentance" from 1984 was being heard and, perhaps, there was hope that our church organization could still repent and change its course. One can describe this development best in the language of *The Lord of the Rings* and the characters that portray so vividly a people's search for eternal life. A few years back, a Christian author took J.R.R. Tolkien's allegorical tale and gave us better understanding into his monumental novel. Through his insights, we can understand God's plan a little better, including how hope was springing forth in my beloved church:

> Many Christian believers at the beginning of the third millennium feel as if they have a great deal in common with the Elves at the end of Middle-earth's Third Age. Our world is changing for the worse. Many fair things are passing away; indeed, many are already long gone. The pall of evil is spreading, growing, and engulfing everything. The post-Christian era has arrived and established permanent residency. A few islands of sanity and goodness remain, of course, a Rivendell here, a Lothlorien there, but soon they too will be swept away. We kept up a brave front as long as we could, but the eve of our departure is at hand. Let's bar the doors, batten down the hatches, and get out while we can. The end is near. It's at moments like these that we're arrested by a whisper in our ear. A small voice from behind says, "Sam Gamgee's old Gaffer was right: where there's life, there's hope." We turn our head, glance to one side, and

suddenly, in some obscure corner where no one would have expected to find it, we discover fresh new evidence of burgeoning spiritual life—fragile, perhaps, small and tender, but tenacious and unconquerable. This has been the experience of the church over and over again throughout the long centuries of its history. Just when death seems to have triumphed at last, up through the cracks of the hard, dry earth springs a tender curl of green, crowned with silver and gold. Suddenly we remember: Christ lives. And because He lives, the enemy's defeat is certain. It's just a matter of time.[31]

This is what happened in my church organization in May 1989, and it is worth repeating part of that quote again: "We turn our head, glance to one side, and, suddenly, in some obscure corner where no one would have expected to find it, we discover fresh new evidence of burgeoning spiritual life—fragile, perhaps, small and tender, but tenacious and unconquerable. This has been the experience of the church over and over again throughout the long centuries of its history."[32]

I could feel and see the life was returning; waiting now became easier, but the turning was still a struggle to come. Legalism, institutionalism, and autocracy had entrenched itself so strongly in our heritage that breaking it fully would require great effort, sacrifice, and losses. No single person could do it, but no single person would be exempt from the struggle. If spiritual life lay ahead, we must recognize that going in the same direction is not always going in the right direction. As 1990 approached, many of us began to come to terms with the reality that if a real transformation was in the process, making a turnaround in the complete opposite direction was far from being accomplished.

Like the wise Gandalf in The Lord of the Rings, there comes a time when the fortress that holds us captive must be breached so we can stop the increasing darkness around us.[33] We have indeed reached a better place, but the journey is not over. Without reservation, I can say that it was during this 1989 "Solemn Assembly" of prayer and fasting that it occurred to me for the first time how much this turnaround would cost the church I loved and the family I loved even more. While sitting next to my father on the flight home in 1989, our trip was filled with much silence and some tears. Both my father and I knew that we were going in different ways.

The Turning Point That Changed Everything

Then it happened, the unexpected "reversal of circumstances" so unlikely that none could imagine. It was the beginning of the visible turnaround; the invisible turning point of 1984 had prepared us so that God could usher it in. In early 1990, the International Presbytery of our church was called to come to the International Offices for a meeting with the General Overseer. After a brief song, a corporate prayer, and a few secretarial assignments, a statement was read by the General Overseer where he informed them of his plan to resign his official position as soon as they were able that week to choose a successor. Several statements in that "open letter" from this ill and aging leader revealed the powerful change that was about to take place. They were glimpses into our ideology of the past and future that require your careful examination:

> For over forty years I have . . . let me say that again, for over forty years, for forty-six years, I have served as the General Overseer for the Church of God. This high calling of God has been both a labor of love for God and His church and a heavy burden of responsibility, and I have felt that not to fulfill this office and this calling was to risk my very relationship with the Lord. In all things, I have wanted to be a servant who was found faithful, and with Paul I want to say, "I have fought a good fight, I have finished my course, I have kept the faith," and I know, as Paul, there is laid up for me a crown of righteousness which the Lord, the Righteous Judge shall give me one of these days. That's what we're working for. Praise God.
>
> I've only felt the call to the office of General Overseer was without repentance. I have never wanted to fall short on what the Lord or the General Assembly have asked me to do. However, I now find myself in a difficult place. My body, which has served me well for over eighty-three years, is now failing me, and I do not want the work of the office of the General Overseer hindered in any way by my health and needs. And as you know, the General Assembly has given this office a great deal of responsibility and authority over the years. The smooth operation of our Headquarters Office and the church work in Headquarters Office . . . no, wait a minute, I got . . . General . . . let's try that again—A smooth operation of our Headquarters Office and the church work . . . generally depends on the involvement of the General Overseer. More than

anything, I do not want my physical limitations to impede the work of the last days Church of God. I want you to understand that my spirit is very willing to continue on, but my body is very weak.

Since we have no precedent set for the leadership crisis we now face, asking you brethren to search the Scriptures and see the face of God in prevailing prayer before making my declaration. I have but one monumental concern regarding the task that's before you. I do not want us to do anything that would not be in God's perfect will. God's will for my life, for the Church of God, and, uh, and for the office of the General Overseer, has always been at the forefront throughout all my years of service. In this special meeting that convenes today, God's will, and His alone, must govern all decisions. I charge you, brethren, to find His perfect will. After you have prayed, listen to the Holy Ghost, and, uh, determine as did the early church brethren in Acts 15 "what [seemeth] good to the Holy Ghost, and to us." You may advise the General Overseer when the full Presbytery is ready to reconvene at the end of your Overseer's session. To your interim selection, I will then pass the mantle of this sacred office.[34]

In three days time, a dramatic transformation was unfolding. The new leader chosen that week was a slender man of recognizable character. But even more, his mind and heart was throbbing with new directions, new life, new ideas, and new hope for the future. His voice had arisen among us like the meadowlark in the morning announcing the first glimmer of sunrise. He did not come to this moment without struggle—like Lazarus he still needed the "grave clothes" of the past to be removed by others waiting to rejoice in his coming forth (John 11:44). A monumental turnaround in the drama of literature carries with it a noticeable upheaval of circumstances and the passionate change in the main characters on the stage; this reversal in our church contained these elements of upheaval and, furthermore, a cast of characters that would exit and enter the scene. Alone on that illustrious stage, the main spotlight having quickly faded on the old character and illuminated again to refocus on the new, the distinguished gentleman stood to address those who feared this revolution and the central role this new character would play. Courageous words he spoke:

I feel sometimes that, that we're in a spiritual battle and, and the devil is seeking so hard to divide us. And he is succeeding in some ways. Some people see the solution as simple. Cut off all these irrelevant questions. Get rid of them. I, I, I can't go along with that. I have had, I have had questions, and I have questions. I have many questions right now that I'm struggling with. But I am submissive to the church. But I want to know, know about what He really meant the Church of God to be. I don't think we have arrived at that perfect understanding, so there's a need for the church as a body to seek better understanding, even about this very office that we're talking—the office of General Overseer. I feel that the man who fills that office is going to need to lead the church, the Assembly, into taking a new look at that office. It is, and I speak this just as a personal conviction, it is my feeling that we have over inflated that office. Our former General Overseer . . . he did a great deal to elevate that office. Some elevation probably was proper and necessary. But he used terms in trying to build esteem of that office that are beyond the scriptures.[35]

This man named Billy Murray was boldly saying what so many had privately thought for years and spoken of only in the most private of conversations. With those humble and risk-taking words, the stage rumbled as both old and new characters struggled during the change of scenery. Not only would the following acts of the play be altered, careening at times into the opposite direction they once had been played, but even the dialogue and cast would be momentously redirected. I watched as my church met for its Annual Assembly gathering on Monday, August 13, 1990. The official *Assembly Minutes* that day record the acceptance of a new leader in my organization. In a simple few lines it says, "There was much praise to God and rejoicing as many came to the platform, surrounding Brother Murray and the Committee. A time of singing and worshipping the Lord occurred as many greeted Brother Murray on the platform."[36]

I was among about 200 people who gathered spontaneously on that stage that day to lay hands on our new temporal leader (not spiritual, since we view Christ Jesus as the Head of the church). No one could have stood on that stage that day without realizing that we were witnessing more than a new leadership. We were witnessing the beginning of an entire reformation of our unique Christian movement. Frankly, I was not up there because of the man we were accepting and blessing, but more because of what this represented to my generation and to many others who called this movement our "home" this side of heaven. As I've said before, I do not intend for this book to be an autobiography or even a history of the organization I minister within, but a true study of what in Chapter 3 is called a *peripeteia*. Having stated such, this eyewitness experience has created in me an appreciation for what it is, what causes it, and what are the lasting results of dramatic reversals. As such, this example holds great credibility for study.

Abundant writings and studies by various parachurch organizations reveal that churches, institutions of higher learning, and secular corporations tend to drift away from their original purposes and roots. In almost all such cases, a genuine revival will be required to discard the old status quo and bring a shift in the paradigm that once seemed so irreplaceable. Several sources are worth noting that examine the complexities that befall such organizations.

Ed Silvoso writes about the need to broaden a group's concept of ministry. His observations include the need of Christians and organizations to realize that giving people truth without giving them authentic expressions of love can become self-serving. He cites how many churches have exalted the ministry or their churches at the expense of not recognizing kingdom ministry beyond the clergy or building. His clarion call identifies four lethal misbeliefs that minimize the impact of believers: "A division between clergy and laity, churches operating primarily inside a building, people in business not viewed as spiritual like those in pulpit ministry, and that the primary purpose of people in business to make money to support those in traditional ministries."[37] My church in many ways had regressed into this inept mindset.

Even the family has not escaped this institutional drift that allows ideas about the family to move away from God's intended purpose and design. Chuck Colson has strongly opposed the relativistic idea that children are the responsibility of schools and governments to shape. Over the last three generations, he declares that America has allowed an emergence of a bureaucratic mega state that saps family rights and interferes with legitimate civil liberties. This non-Christian effort has resulted in a society where families are no longer the vestige for truth, discipline, and moral values.[38] In my family of origin, the church had greater influence than godly parents who sought out the truth from the Word of God to use in teaching their children. If honest enough, many other families would confess this similar malady.

Finally, we have witnessed this not only in my church organization but in many others affected by a slow slide into legalism and institutionalism. Within my group, this elevated a once genuine need for an international director into a position (General Overseer) that grew increasingly more powerful. Not only did we become a strong centralized government with ever expanding administrative authority, but the focus turned to the annual assemblies, headquarters, and universal compliance. In the 1990s, a study released on the office of the General Overseer (within the Church of God of Prophecy) revealed this steady decline into an oligarchy or bureaucracy that left many local churches little more than dying and dwindling "piggy banks."[39] The phrase may seem offensive, but the perception mirrored reality.

All the aforementioned examples demonstrate the evidential fact that we have all witnessed this decline in every aspect of life. More often than not, great movements and organizations have suffered these twisted paradigms. This being said, if a change has occurred in an individual's life or in a group, the action and characters on the stage may not move in the opposite direction as fast as we like. In theater, there is a limited amount of one to three hours that can show the activity that may in real life take years. Therefore, the playwright and the director work to abbreviate the events into three to five act dramas. Such brevity does not always represent the true timeline of a transformation. Like the metamorphosis of a caterpillar into a butterfly or a tadpole into a frog, Shakespeare or Aristotle could whisk away a character in a few minutes through the portals of time. In my own life and in my beloved church, the Lord would patiently move us forward toward His intended goal. Having confessed this reality, I am sure that more changes will come in my life and in my church. The same can be said about your life and those groups you have encircled within your life's experience.

Certainly, there are those who will resist my analogy and purpose in using my church organization in such candid ways, but such comparisons help us learn and hopefully even improve. If this writing accomplishes that for even a few, it would have served its purpose. For others, may this serve as a caution that life holds many surprises! Indeed, my audience is not intended to be those who belong to my religious body, but to both "leaders of leaders" and to those who lead any group of people.

The Turning Point That Changed Everything

I confess to loving the films of Alfred Hitchcock. While some flock to his horror films, it is such blockbusters as *North by Northwest* and *Vertigo* that intrigue me. Recently, my wife and I curled up in front of the fireplace to watch his classic called *The Rear Window*; our first opportunity to see this 1954 masterpiece since we were first married. Every minute of it was worth viewing. In case you're not a fan of old films, let me rehearse the plot. Jimmy Stewart plays a professional photographer (Jeff) who gets his leg broken while attempting to take pictures at a car race. Confined to a wheelchair in his apartment for more than six weeks, he has nothing much to do since reading is not his favorite hobby. Therefore, he tactlessly takes up an interest in watching his neighbors through his binoculars and camera. From the rear window of his "flat," which overlooks a shared courtyard, he watches into the other apartments.

After awhile, not even the visits of his nurse Stella (Thelma Ritter) and his girlfriend Lisa (Grace Kelly) can thwart him from his obsessive pastime. Late one night as Jeff is watching outside his rear window, he sees something that makes him think that his neighbor (Raymond Burr) has murdered his sick wife. With the help of his nurse and girlfriend, he rushes to get the police to investigate with no success. They lack a little detail named evidence. Adapted from a short story by Cornell Woolrich, the film now begins the sudden and astonishing peripety (as modern cinema would call it). The suspected neighbor across the courtyard discovers Lisa snooping around in his apartment and the "reversal of circumstances" becomes full blown. Before the movie ends, both Jeff and Lisa almost become homicide victims of an unintended outcome they never anticipated.[40] Like so many people who have stumbled through a reversal of circumstances, this couple's amateur voyeurism had changed them and the strength of their relationship is tested to the limit.

Let me return to the remarkable changes that were occurring in my church organization. If the past transformations had been difficult and amazing, the subsequent actions of our International Assemblies would be even more incredible. In a series of major changes in structure, hierarchy, polity, and even doctrinal interpretations, our leadership and delegates to our new biannual assemblies were bringing us into line with the roots of our forefathers and the New Testament faith we embraced. It is not my intent to defend or advocate any of these adjustments from our past positions or practices. Rather, it is my purpose to illustrate the profound reversal of the past. To understand the gravity of the change that had taken place as early as 1984 with "The Call for Repentance," this next series of documented dates and decisions must be included to properly sense the transformation that was taking place:

- 1991—Our church passed to allow a study of relocating the Assembly from Cleveland, Tennessee, where it had been held for more than seventy-two years (with the exception of 1923). In the same meetings, they repealed the taboo on wearing wedding rings initiated in 1952.[41]
- 1992—Our church passed to allow a study of restructuring the office of our General Overseer, which held such incredible power or influence over every facet of ministry and doctrine.[42]
- 1994—Our church passed the first major restructuring of our "General Assembly Procedures" that affected the bottleneck that had hindered or prevented most important business and doctrinal matters from being adjusted. In the same year, the office of General Overseer was revamped and a plurality of leadership began implementation. In addition, there was a dramatic reversal on the past ban on the use of jewelry by our membership.[43]
- 1996—Our church passed to allow women for the first time to speak in the local church, state or national and Assembly business sessions. They also allowed women who had been serving in the role as pastor for the first time to the same rights as their male counterparts in performing weddings, sacraments, and moderating business meetings.[44]
- 2000—Our church doctrine committee went on record for the first time refuting the belief that we were the exclusive body of Christ and embracing in harmony with the Scripture that all those who are truly converted are added by the Spirit into His body (1 Corinthians 12:13).[45]
- 2004—Our church passed to change the criteria of membership from a specified list of four arbitrary prohibitions to the New Testament truth that the only litmus test was "such as should be saved" (Acts 2:47). Also, a new proxy system replaced the old delegate system that allowed only those who could physically come to the Assemblies to have voice in church matters. The tradition of those present as the only official delegates negated the input of most of the nations outside the United States.[46]

- 2006—Our church passed a comprehensive marriage document that prohibited any same-sex or polygamous marriages. They also went on record opposing abortion, euthanasia, and child or spousal abuse. Also, they removed the restrictions that had prevented anyone (regardless of the circumstances) who had ever been divorced and remarried from being members of this church. This was done by recognizing the forgiveness of Christ to a sinner, which makes them eligible for membership after they have repented to God.[47]

When a person studies the social dynamics of groups, large institutions, and especially the history of religious denominations, the turnaround described above could be unparalleled. Certainly, this fits the definition that Aristotle attached to *peripeteia* ("the dramatic change or transition"). There was definitely a necessity for this reversal, but the chance of its probability would have been seen as impossible in 1984. Looking back is easier than looking forward, and, therefore, it is convenient for people to do so. I would confess in 1984 that my hopes and beliefs were alive that things could change, but I absolutely did not envision the degree to which the *turning point* would change EVERYTHING! Resolving my heart to find answers in the Bible, the Lord has consoled me and caused my faith to soar upward. When a young man came to Jesus with a desire to follow him, the Lord leaves us an indelible lesson on His ability to do the impossible with our lives: "The young man said, 'I have obeyed all these things. What else do I need to do?' Jesus answered, 'If you want to be perfect, then go and sell all the things you own. Give the money to the poor. If you do this, you will have a treasure in heaven. Then come and follow me!' But when the young man heard this, he became very sad because he was very rich. So he left Jesus. Then Jesus said to his followers, 'I tell you the truth. It will be very hard for a rich person to enter the kingdom of heaven. Yes, I tell you that it is easier for a camel to go through the eye of a needle than for a rich person to enter the kingdom of God.' When the followers heard this, they were very surprised. They asked, 'Then who can be saved?' Jesus looked at them and said, 'This is something that men cannot do. But God can do all things'" (Luke 18:21–27).

The essence of this last question and the answer by Jesus is the key to life. Having been a party to some of the changes aforetime mentioned in this chapter, the words of another have come true for me: "We are ruled by what we believe, whether it's true or not."[48] I believed long ago that things could be altered and that we could have affect on the future. But little did I know what all God could do! Do you comprehend the enormous opportunity afforded through faith if you, your group, or church would only believe the impossible?

Subsequently, looking back on all that has happened both in my life and in my own church organization, there have been mistakes. These usually involve putting on garments that later had to be discarded because we had not yet changed the attitudes of many of our people. We broke one of the laws of Christ who taught us the danger of "putting new wine in old bottles" (Matthew 9:17). Many rushed in such haste to make changes in personnel, structures, programs, policies, and even doctrine. Being swept up in this wave of change, my mistakes were many.

Although I was often chided because some felt we should have moved faster or farther in transitioning to the future, my confession today is that we moved too swiftly. In retrospect, the leadership in the 1990s may have moved very quickly in too many areas at one time. Yet when dramatic reversal occurs, the characters move under the orders of the director of the play. But, experts on change could have served us well in those early days of transition. I find myself frequently wanting to apologize to our War Generation (many who have already passed away) for the swiftness by which we moved in those early years of transition. We absolutely needed a turnaround, and the change should have started earlier; but the methods and speed was terminal to those unable to cope with the abruptness of it all. This is not an indictment of any, for I too would be guilty and would confess this openly. If any of them are reading this, I love you and ask you to forgive us for lacking understanding of how to implement and manage the change! On the other hand, most historical examples of turnarounds (even when divinely ordained) do not run smoothly from their inception to their completion. Just ask the biblical Jacob or Joseph and his eleven brothers. Best of plans often go awry when the *enemy* awaits them.

In the introduction, I mentioned a splendid work entitled, *The Human Side of Change*. While there are many books on implementing change and understanding transitions in both an individual's personal life or in the life of an organization, this one is my favorite from the volumes I've read. Here is one passage in this writing by Timothy Galpin that is so applicable to this process:

The Turning Point That Changed Everything

A clear vision for change helps people to see where the organization seeks to go. In addition, a vision helps communicate the value of change to the organization. The vision should be expressed in a way that allows all people in the organization to understand it, relate to it, and see their roles in achieving it. Moreover, the vision for change should stretch the organization and the people within it while at the same time be perceived as attainable. Which people are involved in developing the vision depends on the scope of the change. . . . A number of methods can help establish buy in, ranging from announcements to an interactive and personal approach. There are advantages and disadvantages to each approach. A combination of the two approaches—or cascading the vision of change—often works well. The greater the buy in and the more entrenched the ideas to be changed, the slower and more incremental the changes must be.[49]

Perhaps now is the appropriate place to deal with the uncertain future. Having witnessed the past and confessed the miscues along the way, we must now turn toward preparing for what lies ahead of us. Whether it is a personal experience, a corporate turnover, an organizational restructuring, or changes within a church dynamic, someone must take up the challenge and respond with positive actions. Realizing that it is impossible and fatal to go back to the status quo (which is usually either gone, embittered or passed away), it is now necessary to launch into presenting new products and finding new customers. For those in the biblical-thinking mode, these are simply generic terms, but even churches must emerge from their past with new inspiration, new methods, and new prospects. There is a still a living gospel and multitudes of people who need Jesus Christ.

Drawing from a wonderful illustration from the world of early television, there is a marvelous case in point of this kind of retooling and revisioning for future growth: "Descending from the serious to the comic, the contemporary television sitcom grew out of the original *I Love Lucy* show, which was itself a response to a challenge that might have doomed a less responsive crew. Lucy and Desi didn't want to live in New York City, where all the TV comedies were filmed and broadcast to relay stations. Instead, they decided to film the show on 35 mm film in Los Angeles and distribute the show like movies through CBS affiliates. Not only did their response work, but it also changed network distribution patterns and (for better or worse) created the possibility of TV reruns. It was revolutionary because the movie film kept its quality much longer than did the then-current kinescopes."[50] The negative mindset thinks that you can either remain entrenched by fighting the inevitable future or mourn the past by simply refusing to move forward. The longer this posture is maintained, a group loses the impetus to search for new venues and people who they can enlist in their new adventure.

What if all leaders, executives, administrators, and even employees or members of a group could have the spiritual outlook of the apostle Paul? He could foresee things with more clarity than many of his contemporaries. Pressed by unpredictable events, changing environment, hostile opposition, and deteriorating health, he refused to be bitter over a reversal of circumstances. Writing back to his friends in the ancient city of Philippi, he penned these insightful words: "Not that I have already attained, or am already perfected; but I press on, that I may lay hold of that for which Christ Jesus has also laid hold of me. Brethren, I do not count myself to have apprehended; but one thing I do, forgetting those things which are behind and reaching forward to those things which are ahead, I press toward the goal for the prize of the upward call of God in Christ Jesus. Therefore let us, as many as are mature, have this mind; and if in anything you think otherwise, God will reveal even this to you."[51]

As you meditate on this chapter, much appreciation and recognition should be given to the many individuals who aided my organization in its season of change, such as Bishop Billy Murray, whose insights, inspirations, and courage caused a generation of Christian leaders to rise up to stand by his side while they pursued new vision and a fresh enthusiasm to reach many new people for our organization. His leadership will forever remain stamped on the hearts of ministers and other Christian workers who needed a shepherd-like David to take on the "Goliath of Despair" that hung over a spiritual encampment longing for someone who would challenge the "institutional paralyses." When David, who many considered an undeserving shepherd boy, came upon this stalemate in the valley, his words sounded like an approaching thunderstorm in a dusty valley: "And David spake to the men that stood by him, saying, 'What shall be done to the man that killeth this Philistine, and taketh away the reproach from Israel? For who is this uncircumcised Philistine, that he should defy the armies of the living God?' And the people answered him after this manner, saying, 'So shall it be done to the man that killeth him.' And Eliab his eldest brother heard when he spake unto the

The Turning Point That Changed Everything

---

men; and Eliab's anger was kindled against David, and he said, 'Why camest thou down hither? And with whom hast thou left those few sheep in the wilderness? I know thy pride, and the naughtiness of thine heart; for thou art come down that thou mightest see the battle.' And David said, 'What have I now done? Is there not a cause?'" (1 Samuel 17:26–29).

Even so, this man who stood in the gap was not alone. David had his four hundred men (1 Samuel 22:1, 2) who stood with him through those difficult times and remained loyal to the cause of the "anointed one." Names would fail me to list all those who partnered in making this transition through the wilderness of change. Perhaps identification is not as essential as the sense of love and duty for a cause worth fighting for. As you learn more about peripeteia in Chapter 3, you will learn how it often involves more than the main player on the stage. To each of the supporting cast members who sacrificed the spotlight, the leading role, and the comfort of the box seats, we must stand in applause for their brilliant performances. God is not always smiling just on the David's, but also on the unnamed men and women who made his short tenure of servanthood both meaningful and liberating to so many.

When the overall perspective and impact of the turnaround is evaluated by outside and unbiased observers of this change, history will record that there were many sacrifices made to bring this reversal of such magnitude. Furthermore, many congregates and their offspring stayed the course and made the necessary adjustments to allow such a worldwide transition.

Here in Salem, Oregon, I have a close friend named Peter, who serves as youth pastor for a large Slavic church. While sharing lunch with him in the spring of 2007, he made a encouraging and complimentary comment about my church's incredible redirection. What he shared was too important to leave unrecorded. Worthy to be quoted here, it remains the best testimony I've heard from someone who has studied most of the major Pentecostal churches:

> Wallace, you have much to be happy for. Your group has never been the biggest fish in the ocean, neither has there been a world renowned person from your ranks, yet you have no parallel in the kingdom of God today. My Belarusian people around America call your leaders *innovative, inclusive, likeable, and spiritual* (italics added for emphasis). No religious denomination or institution has been able to match your will-

ingness to change. Not one church I know has ever so publicly repented and asked for forgiveness of what they did wrong in the past. I tell my pastor we need to learn more about how you were able to do this. But, my church is rigid and won't change. We are a big church, but we are dying!

As I drove home that day, I was happy for a while. Then it dawned on me that I needed to pray for Peter and his church elders. He was telling me they needed to do something immediately. Later, I went back to talk to his senior pastor and his two elders; they listened but made no changes. Peter told me after a few months during another visit that they once had over a hundred adolescents in their youth ministry, and they had lost nearly half of them in the last three years. When I think what the consequences are to a group of people who wait to change until its gets too late, I remember in my church a generation of Baby-Busters and even much of Generation X and begin to weep. May we all seek the Lord to give us courage to move when He whispers that there is a need to move out beyond the comfort and security of the Shire!

While I have addressed my church and the changes we went through, I want those who read this book from my church, the Church of God of Prophecy (COGOP), to know that they are not my primary audience because the picture is bigger than us. Rather, I want to direct the heart of this writing to those leaders in our communities who are responsible to lead in their respective fields during difficult yet exciting turnarounds. I trust you will find both wisdom and encouragement.

Chapter 3

Between a Peripeteia and a Peripety

History fades into fable; fact becomes clouded with doubt and controversy; the inscription moulders from the tablet; the statue falls from the pedestal. Columns, arches, pyramids, what are they but heaps of sand, and their epitaphs but characters written in the dust?
—Washington Irving

At this juncture, let me ask for your indulgence as I find it necessary to examine some key terms that we will refer to throughout this book, but especially in the remaining chapters. All will agree after becoming familiar with the subject at hand that these necessary definitions or explorations are essential. Your indulgence is appreciated.

The Turning Point That Changed Everything

The origin of the term *peripeteia* comes from the Greek theater and was used to indicate a "reversal." It is the turning point in a drama or comedy that was first elaborated on by Aristotle in the *Poetics* as "the shift of the protagonist's fortune from good to bad. It is often seen as an ironic twist, as found in Sophocles' *Oedipus Rex* (the King) when he receives news about his parents that he thinks will cheer him but in reality leads to something quite the reverse. In comedy, it is used to explain a hero's shift from bad fortune to good. Therefore, the term *peripeteia* has come to be defined as "a reversal of circumstances, or a turning point." Aristotle defined this term as "a change by which the action veers round to its opposite, subject always to our rule of probability or necessity."[52]

An English form of peripeteia developed in later years called peripety. *Peripety* is "a sudden reversal dependent on intellect and logic." Not all dictionaries even recognize this word as existing separately from peripeteia, but its definition most certainly distinguishes it as unique even if not totally different. The impetus within this term indicates something the subject has done to help bring about the turnaround or eventual reversal. For instance, Alfred Hitchcock, whom we mentioned earlier, is often seen as the modern master of this variation called peripety.[53] Most drama books include this term but are not complete in one volume and, therefore I will indulge in using a convenient Web resource. Regardless, the ancient source, the modern definition of peripety does have a slight variation from the original Greek root of *peripeteia*.

Now, imagine you are in a grand London or New York theater watching an English Shakespearean play; better yet, dream of being present at an outside amphitheater in Athens watching a Greek drama written by Sophocles. I've been in those settings and the atmosphere would lend itself well to watching a peripeteia. There is something exhilarating and also suspenseful to realize that your heroin is being impacted by a life-changing event or situation. You watch knowing you can do little to intervene and even if you could, it was too mesmerizing with which to interfere even if it were permissible. Anyone having enjoyed *The Phantom of the Opera*[54] has witnessed this "sudden reversal of circumstances" that has pinned you to your chair with eyes wide open. Judy and I watched a "live" theater production and were moved by the passion demonstrated by the characters.

In the story, the leading female character, Christine, becomes enamored by "OG," who she believes to be the musical ghost of her dearly departed father. She is enraptured by his charm, his voice, his music, and his caring understanding of her longing heart. Then, in a powerful crescendo of sudden events, she is transported into his lair and held captive by someone who instead pictures her as his eternal spiritual possession. He loves her, and she is not ready for this smothering captivation he has lured her into. After all, "OG" is not the opera ghost of her beloved father, he is a hideous creature who bears the bitterness of bygone events and longs to be accepted. He has lived with loneliness as a deformed orphan adopted by a dance choreographer. In the end, Christine overcomes her grief of losing her father and realizes the danger of this demented man's thinking. She turns her love toward the true hero that loves and wants to save her from "OG" and his obsession.[55] This is the dramatic form of turning from good to bad that the depressed Victorian Era playwrights loved to produce to appeal to an oppressed religious society that did not know the joy of God's grace and love for mankind. But in this production, there are two reversals that are unusual in Greek tragedies.

On the other hand, there is the peripeteia that symbolizes what we are speaking about from this point forward. It is not a tragic form of peripeteia, but the positive life-changing and corporate transforming kind. In biblical history, we have several of these special "reversals of circumstances." One of those recorded in Genesis concerns a colorful figure named Joseph. It takes place when Joseph reveals his true identity to his brothers who years before had sold him into Egyptian slavery: "And Joseph said to his brothers, 'Please come near to me.' So they came near. Then he said: 'I am Joseph your brother, whom you sold into Egypt. But now, do not therefore be grieved or angry with yourselves because you sold me here; for God sent me before you to preserve life. For these two years the famine has been in the land, and there are still five years in which there will be neither plowing nor harvesting. And God sent me before you to preserve posterity for you in the earth, and to save your lives by a great deliverance. So now it was not you who sent me here, but God; and He has made me a father to Pharaoh, and lord of all his house, and a ruler throughout all the land of Egypt.'"[56]

Unlike the Victorian Era negativity that emphasized the harsh legalistic banishments of both Catholic dogma and Protestant creeds, we are only now discovering in Christianity the liberty and joy of divine peripeteia—how that people can literally encounter a life-changing reversal and go the very opposite way they have gone before. This kind of wonderful turnaround is not only possible because a person is a Christian, but because God is a benevolent Father who loves to make "all things new" (2 Corinthians 5:17). I am intentionally speaking about non-religious elements of life because so often the "children of darkness are wiser than the children of light" (Luke 16:8). Observation has taught many of us that many corporations, institutions, and even individuals have literally been able to experience a complete reversal in the direction they were going. They have recognized the needs of people, the times that face them, and the mediocrity that has made their products, service, or message irrelevant to the needs of people today. Their quickness to reverse their methodologies, their old paradigms and structures, even long established traditions or policies were worthy of any playwright. The business world does not reward ineffectual efforts or banal sameness no matter how much it is enjoyed by those who can "go through the motions" in their sleep. Rightly so, most churches would go out of business in a year if they depended on results rather than comfortable sameness.

The twentieth century saw a host of corporations, schools, and institutions flourish as they learned the importance of seeking and welcoming those "turning points" that determine the continuation of relevance that leads to continuing growth. This past century also left us a remarkable trail of businesses and institutions that declined into irrelevance or just died out. Names that were once household words like American Motors, F. W. Woolworth, and Gulf Oil Company have ceased to exist! A man on an air flight coming out of Atlanta recounted to me how his former company had failed. Many of his fellow peers in middle-management field positions refused to change their standard "modus operandi" that doomed their prospects to turn their market share around. Most churches like most corporations are led by a small, control group that intentionally, whether consciously or not, has taken root in that organization to keep things as they have been for many decades. Sometimes their biggest fear is that something will occur or come in among them to dislodge the "exclusive club" that has yielded them their favored status. To such controllers, any kind of peripeteia would be equivalent to the greatest Greek drama tragedy. Sadly, many innocent players on the stage of that institution, corporation, or church would be wielded like weapons to prevent the turnaround even if God Himself orchestrated it. Why? Because God's voice no longer is heard by such controllers since they have long ago learned to use a "voice-over" that sounds like godliness, but it does not contain His awesome life-giving power (2 Timothy 3:5).

Laid aside by many modern gurus of leadership, it was the Consulting Director for Overseas Missionary Fellowship, J. Oswald Sanders, who wrote a classic entitled *Spiritual Leadership*. After reading many books on leadership, none have come close to the simplistic truth and the practical application of this small publication. While reading one day Sanders' inspirational thoughts about improving one's leadership potential, it became apparent to me that much of our chaotic modern organizations were caused by a mistaken notion that a group could be led by a committee or specialized oligarchy. I was ashamed at my own contributions to this folly. Here was the counsel that pricked my heart: "One more way in which leadership potential can be improved is to refuse to submit to what has been termed 'leadership from the rear.' True leadership comes from the top down, not from the bottom up. It was leadership from the rear that led Israel back into the wilderness. Many churches and organizations are stalemated because the leaders, instead of giving a strong lead, submit to a form of blackmail from the rear. No small dissident or reactionary element should be allowed to determine the policy of the group when the consensus of the spiritual leaders is in the opposite direction."[57]

God blessed me to have a very minute part in a notable peripeteia that occurred near the end of the twentieth century, but I will speak of this later on. This awesome peripeteia began on March 11, 1985, in the old Soviet Union after the death of political leaders Yuri Andropov and then Konstin Chernenko. Former KGB (secret service) chief Mikhail Gorbachev emerged as the new General Secretary of the CPSU (Communist Party of the Soviet Union). His policies of Perestroika and Glasnost brought a new openness to the Soviet Union. It also exposed the many failings of the communist system, exasperated by the failed Russian invasion and occupation of Afghanistan. Gorbachev would oversee the eventual breakup of the Soviet Empire that escalated by allowing first Poland and then many other communist satellite nations to secede from the Soviet Union bloc. In the secular sense, this was a peripety because the humanistic mindset that dominates education and politics today would say this was "a sudden reversal dependent on intellect and logic." If you listened to the "think tank" headed by Mikhail Gorbachev in 2007, this is what they wanted everyone to believe. But this was not just a political and social revolution called Perestroika or Glasnost; it was in reality a divinely guided response to thousands of Christians praying in places like Romania, Hungary, Poland, Ukraine, Czechoslovakia, East Germany, and Belarus.[58]

The Turning Point That Changed Everything

My own experience of this unique peripeteia is closer to what Aristotle's writings describe as an anagnorisis. I will write in much more length about this in Chapter 8, entitled "The Arrival of Anagnorisis." But for now, let me define it simply as Aristotle would demonstrate in the Poetics. It occurs when a character learns something he had been previously ignorant of and is, therefore, normally distinguished from peripeteia as an anagnorisis or discovery."[59] In 1989, I approached a gentleman named Felix Garcia who served as the World Language Director from my church about a desire my wife and me had about helping to plant churches in the Soviet Union. Felix was a passionate missionary who loved people beyond words. We had become good friends several years before and neither of us realized how our friendship would develop so strongly. He assured me that if the doors opened for us that I could accompany him on a short-term mission trip to Russia. Big events were occurring by now in Moscow and other hot-beds of discontent in many major capitals of the Soviet satellite nations. Unexpectedly, Felix died of cancer before he was ever able to see the fruition of all his dreams about evangelizing the Soviet Union.

In August 1991, another very special friend named Henry O'Neil came to me at our biennial International Assembly to invite me to join him and others that were forming a team to make an investigative mission trip to Russia and the Ukraine. He explained that Felix had mentioned my interest in such a mission trip before his untimely sickness and subsequent passing. Of course, I was elated and humbled that we would get this very unique opportunity. We left on our first trip in March of 1992 without realizing that in the following sixteen years that we would visit the Ukraine, Russia, Hungary, Poland, and Belarus at least thirty times. Most of these short-term, mission trips would last from ten days to a month in duration. I will forever be thankful for my dear friends John Doroshuk and Clayton Endecott who gave me so many numerous opportunities to minister to such wonderful people. Since this is not meant to be a journal, I will not linger on the many stories that could be retold.

Peripeteia is best understood in the context of what occurred in what is now the former Soviet Union. Nations that had been completely engrossed in the communist doctrine of atheism for fifty to seventy-five years were about to witness the most phenomenal philosophical and spiritual change in history. During those harsh and oppressive years of communism, there had been a strong and vibrant underground church. Although sometimes very loosely formed in the context of

The Turning Point That Changed Everything

structure or ecclesiastical identity, they had prayed for decades for the fall of communism and religious freedom. They held secret meetings, prayer services, and Bible studies even if it meant threats, beatings, imprisonment, torture, and even death.[60]

Who could imagine such a sudden turnaround where the very opposite of what had been done before with such intensity and dynamic result would now occur with equal fervor for Christianity. Unless a person has actually been in the villages, churches, and political offices of the former Soviet Union, it is impossible to grasp the radical reversal of circumstances that have taken place. I've been in villages where the entire population came out into the street to hear the gospel, in churches where so many came to give their lives to Christ that you could not count them, and in a capital building or a mayor's office where they allowed you to talk to them about Jesus. I've been in a communist youth camp or a public state-sponsored school where the director/principle allowed us to share the gospel. Where once communism ruled for seventy-five grueling years of hatred, Christianity embraces both young and old with a new hope and excitement. If Aristotle could have seen what was unfolding, he would have written a new set of *Poetics* that may have saved the world from the selfish ambitions of generals, kings, potentates, and other dictators.

It would be impossible to write this chapter without recognizing one person, whom I have never met, that has had more profound impact on my mindset than anyone other than Jesus Christ. I began reading the books of Charles Colson about twenty-five years ago. Since then, I wait to hear or read about any new book he might be releasing. Chuck has blessed my life, and I thank him for his boldness and truthfulness in a society that worships relativism. Conversely, churches remain silent too much about societal illnesses and spend too much conference time debating finances. Having confessed the impact of Chuck's writing, any honest observer would have to admit the peripeteia that is so historically obvious in his life. Chuck served as special counsel to President Richard M. Nixon from 1969 to 1973. In 1974, he pleaded guilty to charges related to Watergate and was incarcerated seven months in prison. By his own confession, he says: "When I was in the White House, I was a complete secularist and confirmed conservative; and though I didn't know it at the time, I was also a social utopian. I really believed that government being changed could change people. I never looked beyond the structures and the institutions and the legislation into the hearts of people. But

The Turning Point That Changed Everything

when I became a Christian, I gained a new perspective on the actual influence political structures have over the course of history. I began to see that societies are changed only when people are changed, not the other way around."[61]

Sometimes a person enters into a stage of their life when the mundane must come to a hard-hitting thud of reality. You cannot continue to pursue your life with the same matter-of-fact existence, regardless how comfortable and convenient the past or present might be. At times a person discovers it without fanfare, it is simply an aching in the heart that keeps whispering, "There is more, there is more to life than this." Sometimes the realization that things are about to go in the opposite direction is visibly and brutally confrontational. Like a lava-spewing volcano you see, hear, and feel, the movement that makes you hold on for survival.

One realizes how far reaching this kind of peripeteia phenomenon is felt when he reads how various professions and spectrums of life are encountering such experiences. In movies like *The Lord of the Rings* by J. R. R. Tolkien and the *Chronicles of Narnia* by C. S. Lewis, the children's fiction writer Stephen R. Lawhead discovered an extraordinary revelation: "There is a paradox of sorts at work here. . . . How does one illustrate the invisible? I came to realize the artist does not have to paint God directly. Instead, the artist paints the Creator's reflected glory—paints the objects God has touched, the visible trail of his passing, the footprints he leaves behind. . . . What is more, I am convinced it was no accident. I discovered a new way to live and write that would send me off in an entirely different way of composing stories."[62] Yes, even a storybook writer can experience a turning point where he no longer can write or view his work in the same way he once approached it. In my profession, we ministers like to feel occasionally that we are the only professionals who have these life-altering incidents. Nothing could be farther removed from reality.

Corporate bodies and institutions whether out-rightly Christian or not have come to this same juxtaposition. They lay out the path of their past performance—activities, priorities, and current direction—only to discover that it does not align with their original values, goals, and mission. If they are brave and true to this conscious-raising revelation, they know they must begin to change and rediscover the founding principle they have lost.

Recently, the news was full of stories about how Harvard University had come to this kind of radical inspection of their purpose. With a 26 billion endowment and 370 years of history, Harvard University says that it can afford a gamble that could shake up the world of elite college admissions, Harvard announced plans Tuesday to drop its "early action" admissions round—and urged rivals to follow. Under early action, applicants get word by late fall if they've been accepted to a college, but can still apply elsewhere in the spring. Unfortunately, few really do since it requires heavy upfront investment. Some other schools have "early decision," meaning accepted applicants usually cannot apply elsewhere. Harvard said such early admissions programs have two harmful effects: they may hurt schools' diversity because poor and minority students are less likely to use them, and they create anxiety for the typically more affluent applicants who take advantage of them. If others follow Harvard's lead, it could noticeably change the college application experience of high-achieving students. Applicants would face less pressure to identify a first choice early in their senior year of high school but would also lose the chance to put the process behind them. "There's no question (losing good students) is a risk," Fitzsimmons said. "We just felt it was much more important to do the right thing."[63]

Can powerful institutions come to the reality that something must be changed? This is precisely what happens if we believe in divine intervention. But it is also a mark of integrity that helps a corporate and personal conscience from thwarting critical turnarounds that would preserve the original intent with which they started.

Nowhere is the necessity of peripeteia more evident than in educational institutions and churches! We humans have come to expect everything to be the way we want it to be. And many Christians are even more set in their ways than the worst of sinners. I always say, "At least the sinner can be converted!" Often times than not, many Christians see change as an "enemy of the gospel." People are missing daily the amazing transformations that God wants to make in their lives because they have already dismissed as impossible anything that does not fit inside their own doctrine of life. By the way, before any unbeliever gets down too hard on all those Christians, stubbornness and "rut living" is not just a social disease that affects the church-going kind. The political theater is far more tragic and often affects decidedly more people by its pathetic sameness and retention of the "status quo" at the peril of progress.

Jesus had to confront the religious kind as He journeyed around Judea, Samaria, and Galilee. Later on, one of his dearest apostles (Peter) spoke about the inherent danger of believers becoming skeptical and thinking that things will never change. Regretfully, some will lose their faith so much that they will willfully refuse to see that something quite opposite to what they have come to expect is occurring or repositioning itself to change. The Apostle Peter cautions believers about this failure to discern a peripeteia: "Beloved, I now write to you this second epistle (in both of which I stir up your pure minds by way of reminder), that you may be mindful of the words which were spoken before by the holy prophets, and of the commandment of us, the apostles of the Lord and Savior, knowing this first: that scoffers will come in the last days, walking according to their own lusts, and saying, 'Where is the promise of His coming? For since the fathers fell asleep, all things continue as they were from the beginning of creation.' For this they willfully forget: that by the word of God the heavens were of old, and the earth standing out of water and in the water, by which the world that then existed perished, being flooded with water. But the heavens and the earth which are now preserved by the same word are reserved for fire until the Day of Judgment and perdition of ungodly men. But, beloved, do not forget this one thing, that with the Lord one day is as a thousand years, and a thousand years as one day. The Lord is not slack concerning His promise, as some count slackness, but is longsuffering toward us, not willing that any should perish but that all should come to repentance."[64]

One does not have to undergo the Deluge of long ago to comprehend the effect of sudden change. I read several years ago about a guy who loved to call himself, Charlie Tremendous Jones. A friend often reminded him that there were only two eternal things—people and the Word of God. Later, after a devastating flood in Youngstown where he lived, Charlie Tremendous Jones retold how he walked down the stairs in his house to find thick mud and gunk waist deep. He walked among the trophies, awards, and all the plaques he had in the room to display his many accomplishments. They had all been covered by at least four feet of mud. As he stood there in disbelief, he said he heard the voice of God say to him, "Charlie Not-So-Tremendous Jones, don't worry about all this, I was gonna burn it all up anyway!"[65] Seriously, dear reader, you can do everything you want to avoid facing a day when you will have to deal with a monumental turn to the opposite in your life, but be assured that you will face sooner or later (to some degree) a peripeteia.

As a marriage counselor, I came face to face with this kind of phenomena after speaking to a couple in my office a few years back. The husband shared

The Turning Point That Changed Everything

with me that he and his wife had good jobs, two beautiful children, a nice home, loved playing softball together, and going to church. I was certainly impressed at their apparent happiness. Then, his wife began to cry and tell me that things had to change in their home. She wasn't abused, neglected, or unloved. What could be the problem? Her words are memorable and cautionary to every couple. She felt bored! The routine and the sameness of their lives were driving her crazy. He wanted the same foods on the same nights. He wanted always to do everything "together." And she told how he constantly "smothered" her by not wanting to alter their hectic schedules or lifestyle (even though she was worn out from working long hours). The more I listened, the more it occurred to me that there was a major peripeteia coming into their lives. Their divorce was postponed for three more years, but it came just the same! This husband could not deal with the reality that their little utopian world was going to change; he resisted adjustments or further counseling to examine and correct those things he perceived to be so perfect.

Like many of you, I've read many books, periodicals, and attended scores of growth conferences and seminars. But simple truths have always spoken to me more than volumes written with slick programs or tons of endorsements. During those years when "growth institutes" were popping up faster than the gospel was spreading in America, I was inundated by my own deep questions. Why was there so many "mega-churches" emerging in America at a time when the "churched" population of our nation was declining? Why were there so many teachers or experts on "church growth" yet so many dying churches? And why did I get the impression that pastors with bigger churches were thought to be more successful than pastors of smaller churches?

Then, while reading another one of those books on change, someone wrote five simple questions that others had left unanswered. First, "Why should an organization change at all?" Second, "Who will benefit from this change?" Third, "Are you prepared for the resistance to change and how will you deal with it?" Fourth, "Will there be a lasting transformation that achieves the desired outcome and allows people at all levels to see the change as positive?" Last, "When will the change effort be stopped or adjusted if it isn't working correctly?"[66] If these are not paramount questions worth exploring by individuals or groups, then any consideration of change or a turnaround is ill advised. In the last twenty years, these thoughts became increasingly persistent in my heart and mind. Even in the face of a major peripeteia, we must test ourselves with this sobering investigation of where we have been going, what we have been doing, why we need the turnaround, how such a change will affect us, and when we will know we have turned enough. It doesn't have to be a puzzle, but it should be a truthful pursuit!

Let me share the supreme exercise you can undertake as an individual or organization wanting to take ultimate advantage of your past or forthcoming peripeteia. Back in the 1990s I was privileged to travel with a friend named Clayton Endecott to visit some historic German landmarks. One of them was the famed Wittenberg church. As I thought about this recently, it sparked a favorite historic reminder. When Martin Luther nailed the famous Ninety-Five Thesis to the Wittenberg church door, it would be noteworthy to read the very first one on the list. It reads, "When our Lord and Master Jesus Christ said 'repent,' He willed that the entire life of believers be one of repentance."[67] If you read only this one chapter of this book, I pray you will not miss the last portion of it. Why? No person, organization or church has ever had a significant peripeteia without experiencing this important characteristic or action- repentance. Charles Colson capsulated the truth of this when he wrote: "This begins with what the Greeks called metanoia, which means a 'change of mind' and is translated in the New Testament as 'repentance'. Repentance is commonly thought as simply an acknowledgement and confession of sin. Surely we as individuals need to repent of our disunity, our moral laxity, our hard hearts—indeed, we need to repent of the sins in the society of which we are a part. But the repentance God desires of us is not just contrition over particular sins; it is also a daily attitude, a perspective. Repentance is the process by which we see ourselves, day by day, as we really are. . . . It is the essential manifestation of regeneration that sets us straight in our relationship to God and so radically alters our perspective that we begin to see the world through God's eyes, not our own. Repentance is the ultimate surrender of self."[68]

Yes, repentance! A word almost exclusive to religion and courts of law today, but a term the common man would have known quite well a hundred years ago in most Western societies. In the next two chapters, I will revisit this term more than once. In the beginning of this chapter, I spoke about the ancient Greek usages of the term peripeteia. The common usage in literature was used more frequently in the negative sense of a "turning point or a sudden reversal of circumstances." In the positive sense though, this term referred to "a change around to the opposite" that greatly influenced a person toward a better direction. Most always it involved an internal change of character that may or may not include the influence of a peripety, which was determined solely by intellect and logic. Therefore, the most far-reaching, positive and complete reversal includes repentance—a turning point so profound and complete that the character learns something he had previously been ignorant of. This is the distinguishing mark of real change.

As I was finishing the original first writing of this manuscript, another Presidential Election was just concluded in the United States of America. For many of us, this was a tough endurance that involved listening to thousands of media ads and endless promises that will never be fulfilled. One of those candidates, whether you are a Republican, Democrat, or Independent, included a real American hero. Although he prefers not be called such, most Americans do consider him just that kind of person even if they do not accept all of his political views. Senator John McCain, who was a prisoner of war under the North Vietnamese during the Vietnam War, tells the story of a prisoner who refused to let the enemy break his will during his imprisonment. His recollections help us to understand the nature of how traumatic events can have far-reaching impact on how a peripeteia sometimes changes everything:

> In the early years of our imprisonment, the NVA (North Vietnamese Army) kept us in solitary confinement two or three to a cell. In 1971 the NVA moved us from these conditions of isolation into large rooms with as many as thirty to forty men in a room. This was, as you can imagine, a wonderful change and was a direct result of the efforts of millions of Americans on behalf of a few hundred POWs 10,000 miles from home. One of the men who moved into my room was a young man named Mike Christian. Mike came from a small town near Selma, Alabama. He didn't wear a pair of shoes until he was 13 years old. At 17, he enlisted in the US Navy. He later earned a commission by going to Officer Training School. Then he became a Naval Flight Officer and was shot down and captured in 1967. Mike had a keen and deep appreciation of the opportunities this country and our military provide for people who want to work and want to succeed. As part of the change in treatment, the Vietnamese allowed some prisoners to receive packages from home. In some of these packages were handkerchiefs, scarves and other items of clothing. Mike got himself a bamboo needle. Over a period of a couple of months, he

created an American flag and sewed it on the inside of his shirt. Every afternoon, before we had a bowl of soup, we would hang Mike's shirt on the wall of the cell and say the "Pledge of Allegiance." I know the "Pledge of Allegiance" may not seem the most important part of our day now, but I can assure you that in that stark cell it was indeed the most important and meaningful event. One day the Vietnamese searched our cell, as they did periodically, and discovered Mike's shirt with the flag sewn inside, and removed it. That evening they returned, opened the door of the cell, and for the benefit of all of us, beat Mike Christian severely for the next couple of hours, and then they opened the door of the cell and threw him in. We cleaned him up as well as we could. The cell in which we lived had a concrete slab in the middle on which we slept, four naked light bulbs hung in each corner of the room. As I said, we tried to clean up Mike as well as we could. After the excitement died down, I looked in the corner of the room, and sitting there beneath that dim light bulb with a piece of red cloth, another shirt and his bamboo needle, was my friend, Mike Christian. He was sitting there with his eyes almost shut from the beating he had received, making another American flag. He was not making the flag because it made Mike Christian feel better. He was making that flag because he knew how important it was to us to be able to pledge our allegiance to our flag and country. So the next time you say the "Pledge of Allegiance," you must never forget the sacrifice and courage that thousands of Americans have made to build our nation and promote freedom around the world. You must remember our duty, our honor, and our country: "I pledge allegiance to the flag of the United States of America and to the republic for which it stands, one nation, under God, indivisible, with liberty and justice for all."[69]

This is a pointed story with real application to the dramatic reversal of circumstances that would have made even the great Aristotle applaud. John McCain's life was so altered by events like this that he was forever changed. By his own admission, he would never live or think the same way again. His life since that time has been one of outstanding service to his beloved nation. "Through the witness of many political figures who represent the opposite party as McCain, he is a person that symbolizes authority and yet humbleness. His own testimony brings to the surface his transformed nature: 'I was not a hero; I was a witness to a hundred, thousands of acts of courage, compassion and love by men who remain my heroes to this day.' His spirit and attitude reflect a determined will that refuses to quit."[70]

Profoundly held in awe, I have and shall continue to realize everyday this definition of a turnaround. While Senator McCain and I do not have identical views on every topic, he deserves every person's respect and admiration to undergo such inhumane torture and cruel imprisonment for five and one-half years.

Before I conclude this chapter, Shakespeare's tragedy *Othello* comes graphically to mind. Indeed, some readers will find the Old English difficult to understand, but this example is too good to avoid. Thank God, the King James Bible we use today is not the original English Version of 1611; most could never read it. There are those who will describe the drama of Othello as a peripety ("a sudden reversal dependent on intellect and logic"). I will withhold judgment on this matter and simply retell the middle of this play and leave you to discern which term is applicable.

Whether you have read or been an audience member to *Othello, the Moor of Venice*, Act III, scene 3, is where we will pick up the action. Othello is slowly deceived by Iago's rhetoric, persuasiveness and imagery, yet it is in this scene where a change takes place. Iago begins to toy with Othello and challenges his intentions of love toward Desdemona. He asks Othello whether her other love interest Michael Cassio was informed of his intentions to marry Desdemona. Iago says, "Indeed" with strong emotion, where after Othello replies: "Indeed? Ay, indeed. Discerns't thou aught in that? Is he not honest?" Iago keeps using rhetorical emphasis to corrupt Othello: "Honest my lord? . . . Think, my lord?" Othello, who is of weak character and easily persuaded, replies: "Think, my lord! By heaven, he echoes me, as if there was some monster in his thought too hideous to be shown." This corrupting conversation continues (which you cannot see the deceptive plot here) until the peripety occurs.

Othello has recently gotten married to the beautiful Desdemona, whom he seemed unlikely to marry due to his ethnic background; nevertheless he has been very lucky he thinks. Then, the sudden reversal takes place. Othello filled with doubt and suspicion exclaims, "Why did I marry? This honest creature (Iago) doubtless sees and knows more, much more, than he unfolds." Then the change of his character continues as he says, "This fellow's of exceeding honesty and knows all qualities with a learned spirit of human dealings." Now, the audience can see the peripety. Othello degrades mentally, and the transition in his character is evident in his accusatory language. He is no longer eloquent and using skillful metaphors. He now speaks with a diabolical tongue and uses degrading physical descriptions. He confirms now his uncertainty about everything. In fact, he has now taken on a darker role and joins in the devious game of questioning even the intent of his wife. The conversation involving *trickery* with the dangerous Iago will continue.[71]

The turning point in the play of *Othello* is both initiated and heightened by the influence of a clever fellow. Iago is both scheming and determined to create a situation that causes the main character to change into something he never wanted to be and might not have ever become. Who knows? Again, I would leave the probable to other minds to ponder or debate. This is the way life comes at us; we rarely get to choose what day, event, and circumstance will confront us on this journey that is so much like a vapor that quickly vanishes away (James 4:14). But, I am also convinced that we will all experience a peripeteia or peripety at least once in our lifetime (if not more). And I am convinced by observation, experience, and learning that each of these will either be of a positive or negative impact. Much depends on how we handle such reversal of circumstances.

The turning point for some will cause them to go another direction that changes character, location, profession, or even their faith in a positive way. While others, feeling life or others are unfair, will feel sorely betrayed and set off in a direction that brings the most negative experiences or results. Like the epic routes of two men who were caught in a peripeteia of biblical proportions like Jacob and Esau, almost everyone will be given a choice. The reversal of circumstances, the change by which the action veers round to the opposite, we cannot avoid; even though many have tried only to become frustrated and bitter. On the other hand, we can look upon the events and circumstances to say it was both inevitable and meant for our good. We can take the route of faith and watch as God does amazing things in our lives. This is what Esau did as he met his brother Jacob after many years of separation and fear. In this beautiful reunion, both men discover a great future:

> Then, in the distance, Jacob saw Esau coming with his 400 men. Jacob now arranged his family into a column, with his two concubines and their children at the front, Leah and her children next, and Rachel

The Turning Point That Changed Everything

and Joseph last. Then Jacob went on ahead. As he approached his brother, he bowed low seven times before him. Then Esau ran to meet him and embraced him affectionately and kissed him. Both of them were in tears. Then Esau looked at the women and children and asked, "Who are these people with you?"

"These are the children God has graciously given to me," Jacob replied. Then the concubines came forward with their children and bowed low before him. Next Leah came with her children, and they bowed down. Finally, Rachel and Joseph came and made their bows. "And what were all the flocks and herds I met as I came?" Esau asked. Jacob replied, "They are gifts, my lord, to ensure your goodwill. Brother, I have plenty," Esau answered. "Keep what you have." "No, please accept them," Jacob said, "for what a relief it is to see your friendly smile. It is like seeing the smile of God! Please take my gifts, for God has been very generous to me. I have more than enough." Jacob continued to insist, so Esau finally accepted them. "Well, let's be going," Esau said. "I will stay with you and lead the way."[72]

Many like to preach or talk about the splitting of these two adversaries, but I love the reunion. Jacob and Esau see in this second peripeteia between them the opportunity to make something new and better than it ever was in the past. They were certainly born as adversaries, but they end up as friends (Proverbs 17:17). Now, you have begun a journey with me, and I pray you will continue to read. It matters not if you are a Christian or an unbeliever, a businessman or an educator, a busy housewife or a pastor, may you read the following pages with a passion to see life differently. May your heart and mind be opened to the new possibilities for your life, marriage, family, ministry, church, and even your corporation or institution. There may be some unusual and unexpected days ahead for your life. I know there will be for me. If your past has been like mine, it has been very interesting. Yet I am sure the future will hold new adventures and challenges we have not seen. Any peripeteia can be quite shocking and unnerving, especially as we get older and grow more comfortable with our routines and the sameness that makes us feel very secure?

I suppose if Moses can have a major peripeteia at age forty and again at eighty, then all of us can survive and thrive whenever any of those abrupt changes decide to make its appearance on the scene. Be expecting them!

Chapter 4

Resistance and the Control Factor

If a great change is to be made in human affairs, the minds of men will be fitted to it; the general opinions and feelings will draw that way. Every fear and hope will forward it; and they who persist in opposing this mighty current will appear rather to resist the decrees of Providence itself, than the mere designs of men. They will not be so much resolute and firm as perverse and obstinate.
— Edmund Burke

Consider the life of John Wilkes Booth. Simply said, he was the iconoclastic symbol of the resistance to the abolition of slavery. On January 1, 1863, President Abraham Lincoln issued the Emancipation Proclamation freeing all slaves in the United States, including the areas still in rebellion. This single defining act of his presidency would cost him his life at the hands of John Wilkes Booth and a handful of men dedicated to preventing a peripeteia. Lincoln's presidential action forever changed the outcome of the Civil War, the popularity of the President himself, and the future of millions throughout America and the world. Prior to this Proclamation, slaves had only been freed by the August 1861 Confiscation Act if they had supported or would actively support the rebellion against the Confederacy.[73] Less than twenty years prior to this monumental milestone in history, no politician, scholar, historian, or preacher would have foretold of such a dramatic reversal of circumstances for this young emerging nation.

Although the British Empire had outlawed slavery in 1833 under the inspirational and persistent leadership of William Wilberforce, the passage of the Slavery Abolition Act required 46 years of consistent parliamentary struggle.[74] Besides all the decades that slowly led to the turnaround in England, the United States was uniquely more difficult in three distinct ways. First, many of the disgruntled slave traders and owners of England had simply switched their investments into the Americas where it was permissible by law to have and trade slaves in the Southern states. Second, America was fashioned differently in political terms from Great Britain. States' Rights were cardinal to the principles of America's independence and self-rule that initiated their rebellion to the British Empire. Third, the conservative religious establishment in the South actually supported slavery while in England they had long opposed it. Many other educational, cultural, and economic obstacles stood strongly to hinder the emancipation of slaves or even the abolition of the slave trade, but none matched the power of "state codes" that assured that America would never become a King's pawn.[75]

For you who find history tedious or boring, forgive the necessary inclusion of this example. Even so, there is no single act of history that illustrates peripeteia and the resulting resistance as the decades that followed the Civil War of the American States. Within the framework of politics, culture, education, and religion, the Emancipation Proclamation in 1863, along with the defeat of the Confederate States in 1865, had left an indelible imprint on society. Tragically, the Great Emancipator, President Abraham Lincoln, could not have seen the resistance that followed nor by those abolitionists who often tolerated the dangerous use of child labor in the North. While they had fought so tirelessly for slavery's defeat, the victory they presumed had been won was not as perfect as it seemed at the time. As many of us can attest to, changing political laws, educational policies, business practices, and church doctrines are easier than transforming the attitudes of people that can restrain and minimize a peripeteia for many decades.

Few observers ever realize the control factor that subverts some of the most noble and righteous causes of mankind. None other than Pastor Henry Ward Beecher and the ageing congressman Daniel Webster had warned President Abraham Lincoln about this subversive attitude. They both realized that the battle would go beyond sermons and laws; it might take generations to finish the "reversal of circumstances" that Lincoln so desired.[76] In a lecture originally scheduled for Henry Ward Beecher's church on February 25, 1860, (moved at the last moment to accommodate over 5,000 people), Lincoln challenged the likes of Stephen Douglas and Roger Taney with the voting records of the 39 men who signed the original constitution of the United States. These Founding Fathers had repeatedly voted to outlaw slavery from Federal Territories and demonstrated through their speeches the intent of these Founding Fathers to stop slavery as "an evil not to be extended."[77] Even so, long after President Lincoln's assassination, those same forces of resistance and control fought the causes of "Equality" and "Compassion" in our society by attempting to preserve racism, exclusivity, and protectionism. Their subversive tactics hindered progress for another century in our courts, schools, and churches.

Indeed, the major obstacle to any peripeteia is the ego-centric attitude that causes people to resist change. They are fearful of losing control of something they perceive to be their exclusive domain or property. Nowhere was this more apparent than in the institutions that remained virtually unfazed by the results of the Emancipation and the American Civil War. Schools remained extremely segregated and un-proportionately provided for in the South. As the twentieth century unfolded, white students in the North also headed off to parochial or private schools in distant suburbs where they could sequester themselves away from black students under a veil of equality in the public school system. Education became one of the major forces to impede the progress of equality for blacks.

The Civil Rights Bill of 1964 finally became essential to stop discrimination of blacks in four distinct ways: 1) promoting freer registration of voters; 2) forbidding discrimination in such public facilities as hotels, restaurants, and stores; 3) authorizing action by the Attorney-General against school segregation and other discriminatory practices; and 4) creating a federal agency for the enforcement of equality in job opportunity.[78] Incredibly, it took one hundred years to overcome the resistance and the control factor that impeded real civil rights.

During the year of 2008, we watched in the United States as a woman, a black man, and a white man campaigned vigorously to see who would be the next President of the Republic of the United States of America. While none of them held my moral values and neither would I endorse any of the three, it is interesting that this race for the White House came down to three issues that speak to the problem of resistance to change and the control factor in our society. Immigration, the economy, and the Iraq War took the center stage and fear gave the power of this election to those who advocated radical change over those who wanted to pursue a more gradual transformation in our nation. In actuality, there will be much resistance or control in whatever the outcome may be in the future. Unless God chooses intervention, mankind will most likely receive something far less than required to bring a true spiritual transformation in America. Even so, religion is just as perplexing when it comes to how it deals with changes.

During my childhood and early adolescence, I witnessed this same discrimination in my church. At our International General Assemblies, which were held annually in Tennessee, the bathrooms were clearly marked "Whites Only" and so were the water fountains. My brothers and I used to slip away from my parents and go up in the balcony to sit among the blacks where we enjoyed their worship and excitement for the Lord. In retrospect, they never made me feel white, but loved; and they took care of us boys like their children. When I was a small child in Alabama, men in white gowns and white masks came to our house very angry and set a cross on fire in our front yard. My dad stood on the porch defying them in the Lord's Name. They threatened to burn our house down with the family inside if my father did not stop letting blacks come worship in our church building. The shotgun in my dad's hand may have helped, but there were a lot of those men with torches. Dad sat us down later and tried to help us to understand, but we were still very scared until our father made the decision to move our family the following year to Wisconsin. Some will doubt this could have happened in the early 1950's, but my mother who is still living at 84 is a witness to the integrity of my recounting of the facts.

As one can see, Henry Ward Beecher and other Christians may have long ago encouraged and promoted abolition of slavery, but in the 1950's and early 1960's, discrimination and hatred hung over most American churches of almost every denomination. Like education, religion was married to the past and those who wanted to retain control and not allow their institutions to change staunchly opposed the transformation. Thankfully, my church organization has been a leader in the last forty years in both race and cultural amalgamation and opportunity. Sadly, some vestiges of the "old attitudes" linger in some places, but this too will pass as we transition to the future.

There are those who will proclaim righteously that this was the past and we need to move on. I wish this was altogether true. My response would mirror the spiritual revelation of Paul when he says, "O foolish Galatians! Who has bewitched you that you should not obey the truth, before whose eyes Jesus Christ was clearly portrayed among you as crucified? This only I want to learn from you: Did you receive the Spirit by the works of the law, or by the hearing of faith? Are you so foolish? Having begun in the Spirit, are you now being made perfect by the flesh? Have you suffered so many things in vain—if indeed it was in vain?"[79] What Paul is writing about has much to do with true change.

Frequently someone starts out on a journey of transformation to live in the opposite manner they once lived. Subtly, the culture around them and the temptation of evil sucks dry their desire to act, talk, or think differently. Like the Galatians, many are bewitched to return to their old prejudices, negative habits, and their once comfortable environment. Can you remember a character named Archie Bunker on the old television sitcom *All in the Family*? Whenever something threatened what he viewed as the status quo, he would push the intrusion out the door or mutter unintelligible verbiage as he retreated to his comfortable big chair. Like so many people, when something challenged his "safe world" or his presupposition that kept him feeling smugly better than another person, his reaction was to resist any change. Most especially, he acted out this behavior when someone of a different color, ethnicity, religion, or class entered into his "small world" where he felt he controlled everything as king.

While reading a recent magazine interview with a Yale Law Professor named Amy Chua, I was intrigued by her grasp of what has caused the demise of so many great civilizations. The interview came as a result of a compelling nonfiction book she had written entitled Day of Empire. It speaks about the rise and fall of the major empires in history and ushered in a warning to the United States about their future. She spoke about America's rising lack of tolerance! Before you think she was talking about the current trend of tolerance toward sin and immoral lifestyles, she was not! In her exhaustive studies of these famous world empires and their institutions, she has examined their governments, schools, and religious bodies. In doing so, there has emerged a similar pattern of intolerance toward less desirable immigrants, certain religious types, and perceived threats by fast-growing ethnic groups or people from a different linguistic origin. Amy Chua also cites the serious growth of racism and economic deprivation to attack some and how it is justified by a society as they falsely blame their current troubles on another distinct group of people. This leads them into a protectionism that causes them to feel smugly vindicated in passing unjust laws or taking biased measures toward this targeted group. In the end, this shortsighted approach backfires into rebellion and further deterioration of the empire.[80]

Reading this article made me grasp the current maladies of our own society and the popular myth that people of Hispanic origin (Latinos) are growing too fast in America. Ironically, this was the identical "fear message" concerning black slaves that was spread by Senator John C. Calhoun from 1850–1860 before the Civil War.[81] Contrary to such negativity, a nation like the United States has benefited culturally, economically, intellectually, and spiritually from the infusion of immigrants fleeing financial poverty, horrible wars, religious persecution, and totalitarian states. Anyone reading history would soon realize the benefits that legal and illegal immigration has brought to North America people of diverse languages, skills, religion, ethnic food, music, art, and scientific or medical knowledge. With the peripeteia that has "completely reversed" Canada and the United States from homogenous societies to multi-cultural nations, there has also come stronger and more vocal resistance to more immigration. Why? Higher crime rates, over-population, disease, rising unemployment, strange new religions, and economic worries have all been used as reasons for severe persecution, harsh laws, open racism, and fierce opposition to more immigration. Am I speaking solely about Hispanics in America today? No. Amy Chua points out that these were the arguments and subsequent actions used in the second century Roman Republic, in the Dutch Republic in the eighteenth century, and in German Republic prior to World War II in the twentieth century.[82] It should not surprise us that this same spirit is being resurrected again in North America as we have entered the twenty-first century!

The churches, synagogues, and temples of America have not escaped the "hate scourge" that has gripped our world. Many hate anyone or anything that causes them to have to change. A very serious article speaks to this deep-rooted problem called "R U Serious"?[83] It talks about how churches in America, after years of rhetoric about being relevant to their community and the needs of people, have instead reverted back to old paradigms and have become more deeply entrenched in the past. If you go into many churches in America this Sunday, it won't be just the plants that are stiff and the donuts stale; you will also find outdated sermons, ineffective methods, irrelevant music, and the same control group that has kept that church paralyzed and stagnant for years.[84] Furthermore, the growing economic factors causing high property values and inflated building costs have left many new, innovative, vibrant, and growing multi-cultural churches left out in the cold, while many old church sanctuaries are scarcely drawing anyone. Prejudice, pride, fear, and the mine mentality is forcing fast-growing and healthier congregations into renting shopping centers, store fronts, or starting house churches (which are now illegal in many cities). As one elder told me, "We built our church years ago with sweat and toil; let them do the same." His church will hold 120 people, but it will have six to eight in attendance next week. The aging of many local church congregations is proof of the resistance that has hindered the joy of true peripeteia.

A great article appeared recently with an "in your face" pronouncement entitled, "The American Church In Crisis?" Throughout this bold study that faulted Gallup and Barna polls for over-stating church attendance and faith in America, it unearths the little known fact that these estimates relied on self-reported information. In reality, *The Cold, Hard Facts* done by observation of independent analysts revealed that there was not a forty percent U. S. population attending church regularly, but only seventeen percent. What is even more troubling is that at the beginning of the twentieth century, religious leaders and Pentecostal pioneers were blazing the trail with new approaches to evangelism and garnering changes in "How to do church?" To the contrary today, most American churches at the beginning of the twenty-first century are doing the opposite (with a very few exceptions) and failing to make necessary adjustments and the overhaul required when the culture or trends of society call for new innovative ways of doing church and connecting to the new youth generation.[85] On the other hand, growing churches, cutting edge schools and profitable corporations around the world are discovering, reinventing, or rebirthing their earlier vision as their paramount key to surviving this new globalization.

While Christians of the early twentieth century were finding the needs of people and reaching out to them, their actions became a catalyst for a new peripeteia that caused a reversal of past redundant and dead liturgical practices that had held the church bound. As we move farther each year into the new twenty-first century, the church (all denominations) must confront cultural changes. This will require adapting words, images, music, and art forms to express the true essence of the gospel message. While the content of the message must be retained if it comes from Scripture, the packaging must reflect an attractiveness missing in many churches today. The existing or established churches have become sick and require "intensive care" (sometimes radical surgery) to make them better. Until these churches once again begin to love one another, including the emerging ethnic groups, and serve the needs of their community, they will continue dying at unprecedented rates. New churches must be planted with purpose and with a well-designed intent to minister to specific, targeted groups. Personal evangelism must be renewed in relational settings instead of congregational settings.[86]

Finally, the American church must get off the psychological or therapeutic habit of trying to solely help people with practical living advice and include radical "gospel transformational proclamation." People don't need another Dr. Phil or Oprah with a clergy collar; people need a God of miracles who can restore their life. To accomplish this critical reversal of circumstances, both the resistance and control factor must be addressed before they euthanize the lingering ones still left in our pews. Frankly, too many do not see the hindrance they cause to spreading the gospel. They are hampered by the crusade banner of "standing for truth" that has blown across their faces to blind their eyes so they cannot see the reality of where they are today.

Near the end of the first century, the aged apostle John saw the beginning of this *resistance* in the church when he wrote: "He who has an ear, let him hear what the Spirit says to the churches. And to the angel of the church of the Laodiceans write, 'These things says the Amen, the Faithful and True Witness, the Beginning of the creation of God: I know your works, that you are neither cold nor hot. I could wish you were cold or hot. So then, because you are lukewarm, and neither cold nor hot, I will vomit you out of My mouth. Because you say, I am rich, have become wealthy, and have need of nothing—and do not know that *you are wretched, miserable, poor, blind, and naked*—counsel you to buy from Me gold refined in the fire, that you may be rich; and white garments, that you may be clothed, that the shame of your nakedness may not be revealed; and anoint your eyes with eye salve, that you may see. As many as I love, I rebuke and chasten. Therefore be zealous and repent. Behold, I stand at the door and knock. If anyone hears My voice and opens the door, I will come in to him and dine with him, and he with Me'" (italics added for emphasis).[87] John's writing could never be more applicable, the Lord grows increasingly impatient with the sickened state of too many churches in the Western world.

Let me move away from this train-of-thought and draw back nearly two hundred years. A story begins in the Atlantic Ocean on a slave ship named the *Amistad*. In 1839, in the waters off the coast of Cuba, a group of forty-nine Africans ensnared in the Atlantic slave trade struck out for freedom. They had been captured, sold into slavery, carried across the ocean, sold again, and they were being transported on what was, for millions of Africans, the last leg of the slave trade when they found the chance to seize the initiative. One of them, a man the world would come to know as "Cinque," worked loose from his chains and led a shipboard revolt. The vessel they won was a schooner that had been named, in a grim bit of irony, the *Amistad* ("Friendship"). The Africans tried to force two of the Cuban crew survivors to sail them back to Africa, but the *Amistad* wound up instead in U.S. waters, just past Long Island Sound, where the Africans were again taken into custody. Spain promptly demanded their extradition to face trial in Cuba for piracy and murder, but their plight caught the attention of American abolitionists, who mounted a legal defense on the Africans' behalf. The case went through the American judicial system all the way up to the Supreme Court, where former president John Quincy Adams joined the abolitionists' legal team. Finally, in March 1841, the Supreme Court upheld the freedom the Africans had claimed for themselves. Ten months later, in January 1842, the thirty-five *Amistad* Africans who had survived the ordeal returned to their homelands.[88]

The movie about the *Amistad* is a saga directed by the cinematic genius of Steven Spielberg. Morgan Freeman plays the leading abolitionist named Theodore Joadson who was once a slave himself in Georgia. The young ambitious and persevering lawyer who defends the slaves is named Roger Baldwin, played by Matthew McConaughey. And, it is the powerful actor Anthony Hopkins who plays the venerable former President John Quincy Adams. But it is Cinque (a Mende tribesman from Sierra Leone), played brilliantly by Djimon Honsou from Benin, who makes this movie a must for anyone who cares to understand the resistance and control factor that rises up to hinder a true peripeteia. The entire epic unrolls like a thunderous applause by God who is standing in the shadows as he watches the incredible spirit of man to live free and turnaround the worst of circumstances.

After you view the film as I have done several times to catch every meaningful twist that usually accompanies a peripeteia, you feel like you are watching a theatrical masterpiece. Characters like the governmental prosecutor, Senator John Calhoun (the leading anti-abolitionist from South Carolina), and the self-serving President Martin Van Buren, are all classical examples of those who resist change and fight tenaciously to retain their control over institutions, schools, and churches. Throughout the dialogue, they expose their racist masquerade by arguing over "property rights" rather than human rights. Frankly, these blatant racists were not the only ones who hindered the turnaround in attitudes that held institutions captive to the past.

In the story, two very subtle actions betray even the slaves' attorney Roger Baldwin and his part in prolonging the reversal of past biases. Every time he enters the prison to talk to Cinque, the two black gentlemen (abolitionist Theodore Joadson or the translator Lewis Tappan) who accompany him will bring the white lawyer a chair to sit in and subsequently these black men both stand or crouch down in the floor. Watching this several times, it is obvious he unconsciously expects them to serve him this way. There is another situation that bears observation. In a carriage ride one day, another abolitionist named Professor Josiah Gibbs shares how it might be more advantageous that these slaves be convicted so they can become martyrs to the cause of the abolitionists. He then tells his fellow abolitionist that the eventual overthrow of slavery is paramount above these thirty-five surviving slaves. Appalled by this callousness to simply "use" them and allow them be convicted to push along the cause, Theodore Joadson replies that their lives are the primary objective of their mission and expresses surprise that the professor could brush aside their immediate fate. That is when the most cleverly concealed prejudice of the movie creeps out in the professor's mean retort toward Theodore Joadson, reminding him (as a black man) to be careful how he talks to him and never let it happen again. This is more than anger; he is speaking down to Theodore to remind him of his place even in the new society that is coming.[89]

One additional illustration in the film gives a brief glimpse of the struggle that will confront anyone who dares to journey the road that begins with a peripeteia.

The Turning Point That Changed Everything

Earlier in a meeting between the slave prisoner, former President John Quincy Adams, his attorney Baldwin, and abolitionist Theodore, Cinque tells them a story of how he became so respected among his fellow tribesman. A lion had attacked his village and he instinctively grabs a big rock and throws it at the beast. Amazingly, the rock hits the lion squarely in the head and kills him instantly. He carries not only a tooth from the lion that he had used to unloose the chains that held him prisoner on the *Amistad*, but the respect of his people. Later on, the wise John Quincy Adams uses this analogy of the lion to keep Cinque balanced as he prepares for the final outcome of the Supreme Court's decision. That statement is important for every person who struggles with people who are part of the resistance to change: "There comes a time when even a king cannot always kill the lion. That's just the way things are, but we must keep trying!"[90]

It would be derelict for me to leave this graphic picture of struggle without giving attention to the penetrating looks given by Cinque throughout the movie. One tantalizing scene above all others captures the emotions of people forced to deal with lengthy resistance that never seems to end. In the face of horrible injustice and careless disregard for what is right, a turnaround is often perpetually "put on the back burner" to cruelly torment those who fully know that justice is being derailed. Certainly, the haunting stare of Cinque as he stands in court to spontaneously cry out, "We want free,"[91] pierces the heart with utter sorrow. Those eyes say it all. Frustration, anger, betrayal, confusion, hurt, and hopelessness are all voiced like a grand chorus of an opera into those three words. Echoing over and over through the courtroom, both protagonist and antagonist are caught in one moment of divine connection. They all know the transformation must and will come, but they are all caught transfixed on those suffering from the agonizing delay. Yes, I've seen those same eyes in many of our hurting young people and disillusioned families who grasp that a group of resisters are holding their future hostage. God give us all the courage of Cinque who will not be silenced by gavel or chains! Like Cinque, many are weary from the legalistic wrangling and the fears of prejudice that bind institutions to keep them tethered to the past.

Exactly one hundred years after the Emancipation Proclamation by Abraham Lincoln, the late Dr. Martin Luther King rose up to address a crowd estimated by the Federal authorities between 200,000 and 250,000. This followed the March on Washington when they walked from the Washington Memorial to Lincoln's Memorial where a Baptist preacher would address a nation. I was watching this

The Turning Point That Changed Everything

event on television and my eyes were wide with amazement at this never-before-seen spectacle. I feared even then he would be shot. Little did I realize such a fateful moment would come later to shatter a nation still hurting from the assassination of President John Kennedy! King's words that day set the tone for everyone who has wrestled with the status quo and the forces of control. His speech entitled "I have a Dream" still rings out through every generation who are tired and frustrated. Here is an excerpt that challenges us to persevere in the face of inequality and resistance:

> So we have come here today to dramatize a shameful condition. In a sense we have come to our nation's capital to cash a check. When the architects of our republic wrote the magnificent words of the Constitution and the Declaration of Independence, they were signing a promissory note to which every American was to fall heir. This note was a promise that all men, yes, black men as well as white men, would be guaranteed the unalienable rights of life, liberty, and the pursuit of happiness. *It is obvious today that America has defaulted on this promissory note insofar as her citizens of color are concerned.* Instead of honoring this sacred obligation, America has given the Negro people a bad check, a check which has come back marked "insufficient funds." But we refuse to believe that the bank of justice is bankrupt. *We refuse to believe that there are insufficient funds in the great vaults of opportunity of this nation.* So we have come to cash this check—a check that will give us upon demand the riches of freedom and the security of justice. We have also come to this hallowed spot to remind America of the fierce urgency of now. This is no time to engage in the luxury of cooling off or to take the tranquilizing drug of gradualism. *Now is the time to make real the promises of democracy.* Now is the time to rise from the dark and desolate valley of segregation to the sunlit path of racial justice. . . .
>
> *Now is the time to make justice a reality for all of God's children.* It would be fatal for the nation to overlook the urgency of the moment. This sweltering summer of the Negro's legitimate discontent will not pass until there is an invigorating autumn of freedom and equality. Nineteen sixty-three is not an end, but a beginning. Those who hope that the Negro needed to blow off steam and will now be content will have

a rude awakening if the nation returns to business as usual. There will be neither rest nor tranquility in America until the Negro is granted his citizenship rights. . . .

But there is something that I must say to my people who stand on the warm threshold, which leads into the palace of justice. In the process of gaining our rightful place we must not be guilty of wrongful deeds. Let us not seek to satisfy our thirst for freedom by drinking from the cup of bitterness and hatred. We must forever conduct our struggle on the high plane of dignity and discipline. We must not allow our creative protest to degenerate into physical violence. Again and again we must rise to the majestic heights of meeting physical force with soul force. The marvelous new militancy which has engulfed the Negro community must not lead us to distrust of all white people, *for many of our white brothers, as evidenced by their presence here today, have come to realize that their destiny* is tied up with our destiny and their freedom is inextricably bound to our freedom. We cannot walk alone (italics added for emphasis).[92]

As I read this famous speech again last night, my thoughts leaped forward to the racism and evils that still exist forty-five years later and are now being poured out on the Hispanics in America. Like 1963, they have endured harsh words, discrimination from even Christian brothers, and intolerable laws or regulations passed to exclude them refuge and freedom in this nation. It is sad to witness the misled zealots of our nation again trumpeting "fear" and "laws" to deprive a despised people from their rightful "pursuit of happiness" in this land of opportunity. The old argument grows thin about their illegal entry to this nation, especially when for almost two hundred years a great many Irish, Scots, Germans, Italians, Africans, Haitians, and a host of others have also come here illegally. In 1998, an American right was stripped from us, without even a "whimper," by the President of the United States in an "executive order" that removed an American citizen's right to have his/her spouse from another nation given legal residence in the United States. Democracy, liberty, and freedom have historically had notorious resistance from the control factor that wanted to preserve these opportunities for their exclusive race or specific class of people.

Under the Displaced Persons Act of 1948 only a select 415,744 people were allowed to emigrate from out of Europe, but complaints were rampant that most if not all of these were given to aristocratic and wealthier citizens who were white. Objections flew through the media and other sources that Jews, blacks, and gypsies were routinely rejected while communist, fascists, and former rich Nazis were quietly slipped in through the screening process because of the money they could pay lawyers or legislators. Later, legislation called the Immigration and Naturalization Act of 1952 was enacted to correct this abuse. Craftily, it became even more notorious for arbitrarily assigning quotas to various nations; even worse was adding to the INS Code provisions allowing some favored nations "refugee status" by an influential congressional caucus or by a Presidential whim based on so-called "national security." Those who received this arbitrary "refugee status" also received full monetary assistance that often included housing accommodations, living allowances, and setting them up in business. This has been used to allow millions of Bosnians, Serbs, Croatians, Nigerians, Vietnamese, Koreans, Filipinos, Laotians, Salvadorians, Russians, and Iraqis to be given "favored status." Intentionally absent from fair representation and quota was our neighboring border country of Mexico and other Latino nations to the South.[93]

As you study the laborious rules and regulations designed to exact fairness in the process, an honest observer realizes the notorious deception and inequality birthed by our entire Immigration and Naturalization Service for adopting aliens into our nation. Critics' charge that this has been done to keep "cheap labor" firmly entrenched in Mexico for rich American corporations to readily use for bigger profits. If the Mexican or Latino people ever needed a Martin Luther King, it was in 2009. It is puzzling that many more African-American political and religious leaders have not been more zealous and persistent to take up the defense of another persecuted ethnic group.

While many citizens of the United States are consumed with fear of the twelve million illegal immigrants in our nation today, our greatest concern should be this control group that has always offered resistance to our transformation as the greatest nation on earth. Ethnicity, minorities, immigration, and cultural diversity will never destroy this nation; it will be the hate-mongers and egocentric idealists who believe they can live in a utopia where there are no problems, adjustments, or allowances. There comes a pivotal time in history when Christians must realize and audibly make known our belief that the moral laws must override legal laws!

Anyone who believes in the Second Coming of Jesus Christ cannot hold to such illusions that this world can remain our perfect playground where we can control who comes into our backyard. Some of you may be having trouble reading such thinking and you may even consider me "un-American," but I am a Christian who believes that the moral laws of God have preeminence over any other man-made laws. Having been to places like Russia, Belarus, Israel, and Venezuela, I have seen first-hand the mistaken notion that all laws must be kept regardless how unjust!

The Apostle Paul gives us a very astonishing insight into how we should view those different from us and from those we consider having no rights to enter into or remain in our nation. The early first century Jewish Christians were struggling over the acceptance of other people whom they considered had no rights to inclusion into the nation of their dear Lord. Regarding these mistaken Jewish believers, Paul wrote to the Ephesian Christians: "You were born non-Jews. You are the people the Jews call 'uncircumcised.' Those who call you 'uncircumcised' call themselves 'circumcised' (their circumcision is only something they themselves do on their bodies). Remember that in the past you were without Christ. You were not citizens of Israel and you had no part in the agreements with the promise that God made to his people. You had no hope, and you did not know God. Yes, at one time you were far away from God. But now in Christ Jesus you are brought near to God through the blood of Christ's death. Because of Christ we now have peace. Christ made both Jews and non-Jews one people. They were separated as if there were a wall between them. But Christ broke down that wall of hate by giving his own body. The Jewish law had many commands and rules. But Christ ended that law. Christ's purpose was to make the two groups of people become one new people in him. By doing this Christ would make peace. Through the cross Christ ended the hatred between the two groups. And after Christ made the two groups to be one body, he wanted to bring them back to God. Christ did this with his death on the cross. Christ came and preached peace to you non-Jews who were far away from God. And he preached peace to those Jews who were near to God. Yes, through Christ we all have the right to come to the Father in one Spirit. So now you non-Jews are not visitors or strangers. Now you are citizens together with God's holy people. You belong to God's family."[94]

I want to appeal especially to those sitting with this book right now to consider carefully what you are reading. The great peripeteia started by President Lincoln's

The Turning Point That Changed Everything

Emancipation Act is somewhat congruent to the Atonement Act of Jesus Christ on the cross. These two acts are similar in five distinct areas:

1. It will cost the life of the man who sponsored the magnanimous act. His blood will be spilled to assure its lasting impact on us.
2. It will liberate men from slavery and give them freedom.
3. It will mean bitter resistance by those who even profess to be Christians.
4. While the impact of his action is immediate, the complete reversal of circumstances will take centuries to fully accomplish.
5. Each will make his sacrifice to bring unity among all people who live in his nation.

The similarity is more than coincidence; for sure, the intent without question was ordered of the Lord. Plainly, Christians must reconsider their mindsets and feelings of their heart that are being manipulated through the media of this world. This propaganda is having a detrimental effect on their words and actions. Prior to the Scriptural injunction above by the apostle, he relates this tender and fatherly warning to the people he once had pastored: "Yes, in the past you lived the way the world lives. You followed the ruler of the evil powers that are above the earth. That same spirit is now working in those who refuse to obey God. In the past all of us lived like them. We lived trying to please our sinful selves. We did all the things our bodies and minds wanted. We should have suffered God's anger because of the way we were. We were the same as all other people. But God's mercy is great, and he loved us very much."[95] Is it not strange how we, who have been given so much mercy and blessings, can become so calloused toward others who are trying to find for themselves a better life?

As I was writing elements of this book, there was a movie slowly progressing its way across the theater screens of my nation. Actually, according to most estimates, most Americans will never see the film and fewer people around the world. Although highly acclaimed, people don't usually swarm to movies that deal with too many details and complicated plots. But, *Charlie Wilson's War* is a stupendous study into one of the greatest peripeteia of all time. Recently, the retired Congressman Charlie Wilson sat down with his acting counterpart Tom Hanks to discuss the movie with feature writer Meg Grant. It seems that Charlie Wilson was a congressman from the Second District of Texas during the Cold War years. He

The Turning Point That Changed Everything

had been watching carefully the Afghanistan War that had embroiled the Soviet Union in a major military operation for years. The Communists had installed a puppet government in this nation and they were using their full military might of over 200,000 troops to enforce their harsh rule on Afghanistan. But a stubborn group of insurgent fighters had held them neutralized in the mountains for years, and this cost the Soviet Union tens of thousands of lives and billions of wasted dollars. The CIA advocated that the United States should give up on this struggling nation and its insurgents who sought independence, so we could divert more funds to fighting the Sandinista rebels in Nicaragua. But Congressman Charlie Wilson did not agree. He believed that if we let the Soviets off the rope, then this victory would pave the way for Soviet expansion and raise morale among communists everywhere. Behind the scenes, he steadfastly fought from his powerful position on the House Defense Appropriations Subcommittee to get millions of dollars to help the insurgents grind the Soviet army into ruination. In 1988, the Soviet Union finally acquiesced and conceded publicly its defeat. Withdrawing from Kabul, the great "Bear" appeared weak and vulnerable, perhaps even dying. In 1989, the falling of the Berlin Wall and Perestroika were all spawned by this silent war beneath the surface. Throughout military and diplomatic circles today, Charlie Wilson is recognized along with President Ronald Reagan as two allies in bringing down Communism. Although one a Democrat and the other a notorious Republican, both were strong patriotic chaps who worked secretly together to bring down the Soviet Union.[96]

On the other hand, there is another side to the Afghanistan War. The insurgents that fought the Russians were none other than the notorious Taliban. One of the staunch supporters of the Taliban was a Saudi Arabian named Osama Bin Laden. He was there all through the Afghanistan War not only to support the insurgents against the Soviets, but to exploit the situation to train his terrorist forces known as the "Al-Qaeda" (or Al-Qaida). In an exhaustive interview by Peter Arnett in eastern Afghanistan, Osama Bin Laden ". . . thanked the United States for helping us to get rid of the atheist Communists." However, during the same time period Osama was doing this, he was training insurgents and masterminding the 911 Plan to strike at the heart of the United States.[97] Sometimes in an attempt to control a peripeteia, those attempting control like Charlie Wilson or the CIA can actually unleash a change that brings about an outcome they never intended or desired.

The Turning Point That Changed Everything

Unquestionably, *Charlie Wilson's War* was a part of a larger peripeteia associated with the fall of Communism and the crumbling of the Soviet Union. But this chapter deals with two components that can hinder any type of peripeteia; therefore, we must investigate the components that became part of the control factor and the resistance. Certainly, advisers both within the first Sr. Bush Administration (1988–1992) and the Clinton Administration (1992–2000) later nullified the turning point of 1988. Congressman Charlie Wilson also lost much of his influence at this point, retiring in 1996. Later, CIA insiders following the destruction of the Twin Towers on 911 influenced a nation and other critical parties toward Iraq as the target for a military response.[98] By now, I trust you have picked up on the ominous clouds that gather swiftly when anyone and any nation, institution, or church begins the turnaround in an opposite direction. Before the proverbial "dust settles," the results may be historically or philosophically poles apart from their past. Like the sudden jerk of a weather vane in the wind, the smells, sounds, and sights that begin to fill the air will also generate an opposing force that goes undetected or underestimated in the beginning.

This phenomenon is not new; the impressive deliverance of the Children of Israel from Egyptian bondage under their charismatic leader Moses is a colossal illustration. Within days of departing the land of Goshen, the spirit of resistance rose up quickly under an influential control factor who decided that the predictability of the Egyptian pharaohs and the established order of the past was better than the uncertainty of the future. Men like Korah, Dathan, Abiram, and others opposed the sudden reversal of circumstances. Later on, even Aaron and Miriam were voices that offered resistance to all that was changing Israel from a people of "comfort with bondage" into a great nation (Numbers 16:1–3). They, like so many today, when a great peripeteia takes place, assume that if it is of the Lord, there will be no struggle or difficulty when a person or institution is going in the direction God wants it to go. Nothing could be further from the truth. How can we forget Jesus when He put His face straightforward to the cross? He encountered every opposition a man could face. This opposition included His own family, His disciples, leaders of Israel, religious scholars, and His own human flesh. Peripeteia does not mean smooth sailing; it only means the wind that fills the sails are sometimes instantly coming from a different direction, and we must set the sails accordingly. It is no time for timidity or comfort. Rather it calls for diligence and perseverance that Someone beyond us has whispered a different command.

The Turning Point That Changed Everything

It is informative to read the story of the rebellion against going in the opposite direction of Egypt. The Lord sees the sorrow of the dynamic leader Moses who was attempting to lead Israel in a completely radical way than they had lived or gone before. As resistance often does, they were bold in their declarations against Moses, and Aaron and even declared themselves to be "men of renown also." Such control groups often assume to be spiritual and have equal voice with God. The response by the Lord will be difficult for unbelievers, but its message cannot be dismissed by any:

"Then the Lord said to Moses, 'Tell everyone to move away from the tents of Korah, Dathan and Abiram.' Moses stood and went to Dathan and Abiram. The older leaders of Israel followed him. Moses warned the people, 'Move away from the tents of these evil men! Don't touch anything of theirs. If you do, you will be destroyed because of their sins.' So they moved away from the tents of Korah, Dathan and Abiram. Dathan and Abiram were standing outside their tents with their wives, children and little babies. Then Moses said, 'Now you will know that the Lord has sent me to do all these things. It was not my idea. If these men die a normal death—the way men usually die—then the Lord did not really send me. But if the Lord does something new, you will know they have insulted the Lord. The earth will open and swallow them. Alive, they will go to where the dead are. And everything that belongs to them will go with them.' When Moses finished saying these things, the ground under the men opened up. The earth seemed to open its mouth and swallow them. All their families, all Korah's men and everything they owned went down. They were buried alive, going to where the dead are. And everything they owned went with them. Then the earth closed over them. They died and were gone from the community."[99]

This chapter about resistance and the control factor could scarcely close without an observation by Harvard political philosopher Michael Sandel. His weighty study of the dynamics of group change and the ascension of individualism in the Western culture is worth consideration by anyone seeking to understand the actions and attitudes of people in the twenty-first century: "This is the philosophy of the 'unencumbered self,' a worldview that depicts the isolated self as prior to all commitments or moral obligations. In traditional societies, a person's identity was found in and expressed through the social roles he or she played in the family, church, village, trade, tribe, and ethnic group. Today, however, roles and responsibilities are regarded as separate from, even contradictory to, one's essential identity, one's core self. The self can either accept or reject them in the process of defining itself."[100]

Dr. Michael Sandel has hit the bull's-eye on target. I've witnessed scores of people within churches, institutions, schools, and other avenues of life that support something as long as it meets their primary "core self." Some of those who once insisted so passionately their obedience to the church and those over them in the Lord (Hebrews 13:17) think nothing of scandalously attacking leaders today because the ship is now sailing on a different course than they interpreted or preferred. Their identity was never intricately entwined with the institution or the people they embraced so enthusiastically; it was the concept of who they were and their own self-centeredness that they loved so dearly. Their "inner self" was made uncomfortable by a sudden turn in how and where God was now leading. They chose to preserve their "essential identity," that makes them comfortable with their "inner self," even if it was a mistaken presumption. It is a dangerous folly to think that resistance or even a control factor can be avoided under such primitive conditions where we worship the ME as more important than a community. Individualism sacrifices others to preserve its idol worship of self. Even so, this does not explain the actions or feelings of many who were confused by a sudden reversal of circumstances.

Having made this striking observation above, I must in good conscience love and reassure the many innocent adherents within churches and other organizations who were simply uninformed, undervalued, or neglected as change took place. There is no doubt that many voiced disapproval or refused to go along with changes because they were bewildered, hurt, and were never given sufficient time or information to accommodate their understanding during the transitional stages. To each and every one of these sincere workers in churches, corporations, and educational organizations, we who serve in leadership owe them an apology for our lack of understanding concerning the nature of change that often caused such distress to them. Yet if we are forthright, there were also many others who knew acutely very well the need of the peripeteia and deliberately fought the inevitable for their own selfish reasons. They are the catalyst of opposition who owe the innocent ones the deepest apology for their sin of intentionally misleading others and acting as if they were doing the divine will of God. On the surface, their self-effacing attitude seemed commendable and attractive. But in reality their ambition and deceit can and does leave untold masses of people, as Jesus described, ". . . scattered abroad, as sheep having no shepherd" (Matthew 9:36).

I will explore more about this resistance in a later chapter entitled "If Bishops Become Kings, So What?" But at this juncture, there is no more ominous note than a comment made by the writer of the Book of 1 Kings from the Bible. Many scholars attribute the writing of 1 Kings to a later prophet called Jeremiah. Whoever wrote this commentary in one indelible phrase catches not only one of the most impacting peripeteia in history, but explains that even in resistance that Providence of a divine nature may play out in the eventual outcome of events: "So the king did not listen to the people; for *the turn of events* was from the LORD, that He might fulfill His word, which the LORD had spoken by Ahijah the Shilonite to Jeroboam the son of Nebat" (italics added for emphasis).[101] Indeed, not even the artistic Shakespeare could have written a more dramatic tragedy or a more intriguing summary than the one included in this verse. For it contains not only the unpredictable outcome of the fall of the main character Rehoboam, but brings to light the implausible rise of a king called Jeroboam, whose reign is noticeably unimpressive and without moral character. This is without contradiction the litany of too many situations where *resistance* has rarely ended in the promise that justified its birth. At this point, we will leave this to a later delineation.

Chapter 5

Unmanageable Change

To-day is not yesterday. We ourselves change. How then, can our works and thoughts, if they are always to be the fittest, continue always the same—Change, indeed, is painful, yet ever needful; and if memory have its force and worth, so also has hope.
—Thomas Carlyle

I've already confessed to being a history buff, but I am also a person who loves the out-of-the-mainstream magazines or news articles. Recently, I was reading the most captivating article about a little known car called the Morgan Motor Car. No, it is not an MG, nor an automobile built from a kit, and not just an antique car. The Morgan Motor Cars are still built and sold as they have been since 1912 when they moved from a family hobby to an actual company. The Morgan is a motor industry phenomenon. In a small town in Malvern, Worcester, England, there is a factory run by Peter Morgan and his son, Charles, where the Morgan 4/4, +8 and

+4 are still built. They, and the workforce of just fewer than one hundred, lovingly produce about ten of the hand-built, ash wood-framed cars per week. And, the waiting list of customers continues to grow. At last count, it was five years to acquire one. Matter-of-factly, they have only made three major changes in the history of their industry. The first came in 1932 when they went from three wheels to four. Later, in 1954, they changed the radiator grill from square to rounded corners, and, finally, in 1974, they introduced a Ford 1600 cross flow engine—the same as a Lotus 7. Now, they had a sports car.

There is no question that the Morgan family has succeeded in making a living at building a few cars each year. But even to their own admission, they made a choice against the Assembly-line process in the 1950's, and the result is a very controlled atmosphere of obscurity and inaccessibility that only the most avid car connoisseur desires to pursue.[102]

Well, you can't say that Morgan Motor Company is an example of the danger of change. I doubt from the way they run their firm that a peripeteia would ever be welcomed or allowed, since they had the opportunity to make adjustments in the 1930s and 1950s and flatly refused even to the loss of some of their innovative minds and much greater revenues. They have done an excellent job of managing smallness. Now that is not necessarily a negative, unless you are an organization, institution, or church whose basic philosophy and mission is to advocate growth. Subsequently, sameness and smallness are neither attractive nor desirable. In such cases, what happens if a society, an educational institution, or even a church makes a decision that opens up floodgates to wholesale changes without any checks and balances? What happens when the wind that we rely on to make stronger trees, to spread seeds, and to carry rain and heat becomes a raging tornado that destroys everything in its erratic path? As a boy growing up in southern Wisconsin that sits at the end of "tornado alley" in the heartland of America, I've witnessed my share of these winds that are normally essential get out-of-control and do more destruction than good. So it is with a peripeteia—sometimes even that which has been divinely approved (although not predestinated) can get "hijacked" or "misdirected," leaving in its wake a swath of littered dreams and frustrated hopes for a better life.

The Easter Islanders, a Polynesian people, settled on an island that was originally forested, and whose lush greenery included the world's largest palm tree. The Easter Islanders gradually chopped down the forest to use the wood for

The Turning Point That Changed Everything

canoes, firewood, carving, building small dams, transporting and raising statues, as well as for housing. Eventually, they cut down all the forests to the point where all the tree species were extinct, which meant that they ran out of canoes, they could no longer erect statues, there were no longer trees to protect the topsoil against erosion, and their society collapsed in an epidemic of cannibalism that left 90 percent of the islanders dead. The question that has intrigued most anthropologists and sociologists throughout the last several decades has been this one question: "How on earth could a society make such an obviously disastrous decision as to cut down all the trees on which they depended?" In fact, what did the Easter Islanders say as they were cutting down the last palm tree? Were they saying, "Think of our jobs as loggers, not these trees?" Were they saying, "Respect my private property rights?" Surely the Easter Islanders, of all people, must have realized the consequences to themselves of destroying their own forest. It wasn't a subtle mistake. One wonders whether—if there are still people left alive a hundred years from now— people in the next century will be equally astonished about our blindness today as we are today about the blindness of the Easter Islanders.[103]

Jared Diamond's example was not the first time I had read about the notorious events on Easter Island, but his descriptions were much more exhaustive. One very clear truth emerges since the decline of the Easter Islanders—few societies have learned much from their gruesome tragedy. Too many groups continue to proceed on a self-destructive path without taking definitive steps to understand what it is they are changing, why they are shifting internally, and what are the group's intended goals. It is remarkable how that progress or advancement can get out of hand before a person or a group of leaders can fathom the degree to which the situation has become unmanageable. Frankly, a peripeteia rarely gives you advance notice as to when and how it will occur, but once underway the transition must be managed where possible and appropriate. Such insight came early enough in the Wilderness Crossing of Israel from an external source named Jethro, who intervened in his son-in-law's dilemma. Moses, overwhelmed by the enormous task of leading what Bible scholars call "the church in the wilderness," was trying to micromanage the daily affairs of almost two million people. Jethro's advice was straightforward and wise:

> And so it was, on the next day, that Moses sat to judge the people; and the people stood before Moses from morning until evening. So when

Moses' father-in-law saw all that he did for the people, he said, "What is this thing that you are doing for the people? Why do you alone sit, and all the people stand before you from morning until evening?" And Moses said to his father-in-law, "Because the people come to me to inquire of God. When they have a difficulty, they come to me, and I judge between one and another; and I make known the statutes of God and His laws." So Moses' father-in-law said to him, "The thing that you do is not good. Both you and these people who are with you will surely wear yourselves out. For this thing is too much for you; you are not able to perform it by yourself. Listen now to my voice; I will give you counsel and God will be with you: Stand before God for the people, so that you may bring the difficulties to God. And you shall teach them the statutes and the laws, and show them the way in which they must walk and the work they must do. Moreover you shall select from all the people able men, such as fear God, men of truth, hating covetousness; and place such over them to be rulers of thousands, rulers of hundreds, rulers of fifties, and rulers of tens. And let them judge the people at all times. Then it will be that every great matter they shall bring to you, but every small matter they themselves shall judge. So it will be easier for you, for they will bear the burden with you. If you do this thing, and God so commands you, then you will be able to endure, and all this people will also go to their place in peace." So Moses heeded the voice of his father-in-law and did all that he had said. And Moses chose able men out of all Israel, and made them heads over the people: rulers of thousands, rulers of hundreds, rulers of fifties, and rulers of tens. So they judged the people at all times; the hard cases they brought to Moses, but they judged every small case themselves.[104]

Perplexed, by this illustration in the life of Moses, I cannot begin to explain my past feelings about this event. I've asked the following question as a boy in Sunday school and almost got myself a rebuke for such brazen audacity. But I will ask it here and wince if I think I hear the sound of a preacher or teacher coming to thump me for it. "Why hadn't Moses learned this simple truth of management in the House of Pharaoh where he lived and was taught during the first forty years of his life?" That sounds as if I doubt this story! No. Quite the contrary. It proves the weakness of human nature even in God-called leaders. The Egyptians were masters at construction, management, engineering, and organization. Surely Moses had observed this order and sharing of responsibilities! One day, growing up in my church, it dawned on my little mind an incongruous discovery. You see, when we call something a "God Program," church, or school, many feel they are exempted from reasonable accountability, leadership principles, and proper management skills. Moses had received those Ten Commandments cut out by the finger of God into stone; yes, he had seen the hinder part of God, and he opened the Red Sea with his rod. Why would he need the counsel and help of others to make this transition in the wilderness? There is no greater danger to transitions or changes than the "anointing" we leaders claim upon our ministry. The danger is not the Holy Spirit (which we desperately need more than ever), but the mistaken notion or, in some cases, doctrinal misconception that causes us to believe we are infallible in leading or making decisions for a group of people.

Unmanageable Change is directly linked to human ambitions, extreme dogmatisms, and what Charles Finney called antinomianism, "the impulse of feelings rather than divine illumination."[105] One cannot separate from an examination of peripeteia (in the sense of a group or corporate dynamics), the indelible imprint made by ambitious individuals who see such turnarounds as an opportunity to thrust themselves into the main circle of leadership or influence. This axiom is applicable to educational institutions, corporate businesses, church denominations, or even in government. We can all see this in political parties and in the corporate board rooms, but why do so many blindly ignore it during transitional periods of churches or schools. History is littered with hundreds of cases in church archives and institutional libraries where major leaders emerged during a crisis of change that had lingered hungrily for several years around the old guard that would soon be replaced. Some will be surprised at such candid admission of human maneuvering in divine affairs. Actually, the only surprise is the unwillingness of so many to confess that these opportunists have existed, do exist, and will always exist until Jesus comes (Acts 20:28–30).

As a sincere student of the causes of Unmanageable Change, the discoveries are grimly clear that there have always been people standing close off-stage waiting for a leading player to foul up their lines, stumble and fall severely, disappoint the director, or find disfavor with the audience. In real life dramas, the parallels are too overpowering to ignore! It is my intent to delve into only four primary areas where Unmanageable Change has some of the strongest examples to explore: Religion (Holiness and Pentecostalism), Business Corporations, Educational Institutions, and American Politics. I will launch this exploration with an understanding that my own area of experience must draw upon that which I know best—religion. In the following cases, several names will be listed with no intent to dishonor any of them but only to illustrate the powerful personalities and forces that will later cause upheaval to incredible institutions and groups of sincere people.

The Holiness Movement developed in America during the nineteenth century subsequent to the Second Great Awakening. The potential of these movements that birthed the Holiness Movement were profound, but lacked the ability to completely unify this strong religious base of believers. Careful observation uncovers the impact of several movements that were at the root of Holiness experience. First, there was the highly contagious Methodism that sprung out of the teaching and work of John Wesley. Second, most reliable religious scholars also credit Revivalism and its emphasis on "perfectionism" by Charles G. Finney. Third, there was the lay evangelist Phoebe Palmer from New York City who fanned the flames of the Holiness Movement phenomena into major metropolis areas of the nation.[106] No other religious belief in the history of Western world struck the life-chords and crossed all the lines of racial, social, and academic barriers that heretofore had existed. Even today, it remains the heartbeat of several seminaries, church denominations, and newly founded churches around the globe. Without contradiction by even reputable media journalists and secular historians, the rise and influence of Holiness Movement during the nineteenth century was the second hottest news story after the Slave Issue prior to and following the Civil War between States.[107] As you can read, the Holiness Movement was in fact a literal peripeteia in both the church and the emerging cultural psyche of America. There are many other historical documents to verify the weighty effect of this new religious movement on the moral landscape.

Reading the pages of history refreshes the heart to see the budding spirituality this movement offered for centuries to come. Yet what hindered and subsequently slowed the rapid spread of the Holiness Movement within the American States and to the rest of the world? The movement mushroomed, thrashed, debated, and divided into more than 150 groups. Some of these later amalgamated into denominations, but a larger part have maintained a separate existence even to this day. Cracks developed over Perfectionism, Higher Christian life, radical and conservative associations, "entire sanctification," gospel music, and later on the differences over the acceptance of *glossolalia* (speaking in other tongues as the Spirit gives the utterance).[108] Pouring over numerous articles and documents from various veins of Holiness tradition and history that covers more than one hundred years from the 1830s through the 1930s, the record unravels a litany of missed opportunities by the early leaders to stop the bleeding that was weakening the Holiness Movement. Because they failed to put away often-petty differences and personal interests for their own place in the spotlight on the stage, their motives and actions became more self-serving and more antagonistic toward each other. Not all were to be blamed, but far too many contributed to the fracturing. An excerpt from a letter written by Charles G. Finney to a group of pastors on June 4, 1845, indicates this:

> Indeed some revival preachers appear to me to have forsaken the right way without being aware of it, and really to have become highly fanatical in their spirit, preaching and general bearing, until God has manifestly been obliged to rebuke them by withdrawing his Spirit and closing the doors of the church against them. If revivals of pure religion are to be preserved from fanaticism, the utmost pains should be taken to preserve the leaders from this spirit. It is one of the great devices of the devil to infuse this spirit stealthily into the leaders and thereby poison the revival (of holiness) to death.[109]

Uncontrolled change is not always God-ordained change. Finney could see this danger that was causing the Holiness Movement to spin out of control right at the time it had the golden opportunity to bring about a worldwide transformation to all of Christendom. But everyone in the holiness tradition did not always welcome his admonitions. In gracious contriteness, every leader who guides an organization, religious or otherwise, big or small, must refuse to succumb to this folly that puts on the mask of divine origination on the slightest deviation that simply promotes a personal agenda. Without steadfastness to the task of bringing about a successful transition, a selfish motive can become a "time bomb" to the best church, movement, or institution.

Let's take another peek into the camera of time and ask, "What caused the incredible splintering of Pentecostalism into so many ideological fissures?" During the early rise of Pentecostalism, the abundance of characters upon the stage at the beginning of the twentieth century appeared to have been a great drama of biblical unity and spiritual victory. It did not remain so. Human ambition joined ranks with extreme dogmatism to tempt the main characters of God's grand drama into following their own newly devised scripts where each would have their own cast of players. There is no doubt that early Pentecostal leaders had strong intricate ties to the previous Holiness Movement of the nineteenth century that we have mentioned heretofore, but the division that followed was neither holy nor solely doctrinally motivated.

As the opening scenes of the twentieth century began, you can see standing on the bright stage of the restoration of Pentecost several great characters that would be instrumental to the divine plot. To study the lives and writings of key Pentecostal leaders such as William H. Durham, Thomas Hampton Gourley, Charles Harrison Mason, Ida B. Robinson, William Seymour, and A. J. Tomlinson, there was no doubt a Spirit-endued zeal, innovation, and dedication. Each of them would contribute enormously to the explosion of Pentecostalism that swept from the East to the West Coast (or West to East, depending on your view of Pentecostalism). From the inception, many of these key players acted in a masterful and divinely orchestrated drama that brought the glossolalia movement from a small band of outcasts to the center of the religious stage.

As Holiness had rocked religion in the 1800s, Pentecostalism would thunder upon the scene of the 1900s. A supernatural peripeteia was happening. Christian and secular historians are only now beginning to agree on the impact of these early Pentecostal believers. Today, Pentecostalism is the only religion increasing at a faster rate than Islam. Places like Africa, South America, Mexico, Ukraine, Russia, and China are being swept into the presence of this "rushing mighty wind" (Acts 2:2). The Pentecostal Movement was more ethically, socially, racially, and theologically diverse than any period of Christian history since the third century. The youth and vigor of this new movement was broader than the Holiness Movement that had preceded it. This radical wing of the earlier Holiness Movement had not yet reached the numbers of its predecessors, but it was evident that it would eventually surpass the movement that birthed it.[110] With so much spiritual momentum and charismatic leadership, no obstacle seemed too insurmountable for this new Pentecostal Movement. Even Peter's prophetic sermon on the Day of Pentecost was being fulfilled: "Then Peter said unto them, 'Repent and be baptized every one of you in the name of Jesus Christ for the remission of sins, and ye shall receive the gift of the Holy Ghost. For the promise is unto you, and to your children, and to all that are afar off, even as many as the Lord our God shall call'" (Acts 2:38, 39). This awesome turnaround in Christianity would now hopefully succeed instead of repeating the divisiveness of the Holiness Movement. But the elements of human ambition, strong personalities, and extreme dogmatism were waiting in the wings to come on this electrifying stage.

In a series of missteps and well-intentioned decisions, the implausible reversal of circumstances that had reawakened the once buried "Gift of the Holy Spirit" was within twenty years beginning to split apart. The main supporting cast had often parlayed for the leading role. Severe doctrinal interpretation on everything from spiritual gifts, glossolalia, and the church's role in governing this new power were bringing major divisions. Into this volatile mix, racial integration became a disruptive issue to many. None of the participants intended evil, most never sought personal gain, which was lacking anyway, and some felt issues relating back to holiness had never been settled. More subtly, success and money sowed deadly seed also. All of these contributed to the unmanageable change that resulted. This new, fiery and watershed experience had enough to overcome already. With so many unwilling or ignorant of the necessary understanding required to manage this potent force, fleshly gravitational habits pulled away at the unifying exhilaration that this newly revived doctrine had brought to Christianity.

Individuals emerged as inspired seekers of deep religious experience with an evangelistic fervor to spread this new message. They were united and willing to move as evangelists wherever doors opened in America, Mexico, or overseas. But there were also conflicts highlighted by their writings and actions to incorporate into specialized associations, missionary societies, church organizations, or with a few to remain unfettered by any formal group.[111] William H. Durham seemed almost inspired and blossomed when embattled into a controversy with others.[112] Thomas Hampton Gourley mistrusted organizations and sought to be independent while maintaining loose ties to various groups.[113] Charles Harrison Mason trumpeted the interracial freedom found in the Church of God in Christ. While William Seymour emblazoned by the Azusa Street Revival in 1906 chose the itinerant path. Ida B. Robinson began a ministry directed toward the "nurturing of family-like relationships."[114] Finally, A. J. Tomlinson, perhaps the most charismatic in personality and leadership, slowly evolved into an "organizational man" who

The Turning Point That Changed Everything

loved politics and founded the Church of God.[115] Regardless of their wonderful efforts to restore the first century church's spiritual power and manifestations of the Spirit, all of them may have not known that their personal or shared actions would make this amazing new peripeteia increasingly unmanageable.

Before leaving this example, it is vital that I make note that these humble, self-sacrificing, and highly gifted leaders did more than they would see in their lifetimes. As the late twentieth century rolled into its final three decades, the Pentecostal fire hit believers all around the globe with new zeal and fervor for evangelization that had only occurred in the first two decades. It reopened the door for the first real opportunity in sixty years or more for evangelicals to reunite. As the Yearbook of American and Canadian Churches recently stated, "The Holiness-Pentecostal churches as they entered the 1980's are the new churches flexing their muscles as they enter maturity riding a crest of fantastic growth."[116] As one who was birthed in this Pentecostal heritage, I am grateful for those dedicated leaders of the early twentieth century Pentecostalism, but I also want to be one of those who are forthright about our past and willing to learn from the causes of the unmanaged change that hindered and delayed even so great a cause. This being stated, the secular culture has had even a higher rate of failure to count the cost of change, as seen in the following example.

In April 1962, Walter Cronkite took over the anchorman's position from Douglas Edwards on the CBS Evening News. Less than a year later, the program was expanded from fifteen to thirty minutes. It was also ironic that Cronkite's first thirty-minute newscast included an exclusive interview with President John F. Kennedy. Almost two months later, Cronkite was the first on a newscast to report Kennedy's assassination; and in one of the rare instances when Cronkite's journalistic fortitude deserted him, he shed tears. Cronkite's rise at CBS was briefly interrupted in 1964 when CBS News was overtaken in the television ratings by NBC's Huntley and Brinkley. CBS executives hastily decided to replace Cronkite as anchor at the 1964 presidential nominating conventions with the team of Robert Trout and Roger Mudd. Publicly accepting the change, but privately fuming, Cronkite contemplated leaving CBS. However, more than eleven thousand letters protesting the change undoubtedly helped convince both Cronkite and CBS executives that he should stay on.

In 1966, Cronkite briefly overtook the Huntley-Brinkley Report in the ratings, and in 1967 took the lead. From that time until his retirement, the CBS Evening

News was the ratings leader. He was to become an American icon for trust and reliability. While he had critics like anyone in the public eye, his credibility and fatherly approach to the Evening News or "crisis reporting" caused viewers to tune in by the millions. Some referred to his time in the spotlight as "the magic." In 1981, in accord with CBS policy, Cronkite reluctantly retired.[117] But the decision incensed television land and many vehemently disagreed with this convenient policy the network had used to disguise their underlying motive. In reality, the move was a reaction taken to give Walter Cronkite's anchor chair to a hot young reporter who CBS feared would leave to take a position with their network competition.

In the beginning, CBS appeared to be the winner regardless of the temporary spike of 18,000 letters from unhappy viewers. With the forced retirement of Walter Cronkite, the CBS News was destined now to make a revolutionary change from Cronkite's style and thinking. Executives had criticized him because of his preference for short "breaking stories," many of them originating from the CBS News' Washington Bureau, rather than longer "enterprisers," which might deal with long range and non-Washington stories. In addition, many executives felt that Cronkite's demand for center stage—averaging six minutes out of the twenty-two minutes on an evening newscast—took time away from more in-depth coverage of the news.[118] This was the genesis of a massive peripeteia that began within the CBS network.

Moving in a completely opposite direction from their past, they went to more exhaustive journalistic reports from various locations, they elevated a younger Dan Rather to the anchor chair, and they switched to sharing their newscasts from multiple locations on one televised program. Critics who called their decision futuristic and the model of "the changing face of global news" hailed CBS. They were at first the envy of other networks. Then the other side of the coin flipped up! Critics complained that Dan Rather was very Harvard-like in his presentations, impersonal to the regular viewer, and could often demonstrate his temper on screen. Dan had a great reputation as a news-hound for being gutsy and willing to do anything to get the story, as he had showed in Afghanistan when he went underground. But over the next ten years, viewers left in droves from this once-dominating news network. So much so, that CBS after awhile was running third behind other rival networks like ABC and NBC. Not to be blamed for all the editorial decisions being taken to reinvent the evening broadcast, Dan Rather became the poster child of liberal ideology and of "failed policies" that had made CBS no longer a comfortable and trusted friend in the homes of many more conservative Americans who liked to call Cronkite "Uncle Walter."[119]

Although I've cited this single illustration, space does not permit scores of other debacles in the corporate world. In a litany of documents about corporate transformations over the last one hundred years, there is a pattern of Unmanageable Change that usually surfaces from underestimating the demographics of the targeted audience, customers, or fan base. Even more precarious is that many of these organizations have a similar "Achilles' heel." Far too many in top management often assume they have worked to get where they are and it's their turn "to rule." Some see themselves by their own inflated estimation as the ones who know best what they now control. To study the history of CBS and a host of comparable corporations, you will dig up two dangers that are equally destructive to their future: 1) lack of planning to avoid the unmanageable change, and 2) refusal to turnaround the present course when it is not profitable or successful.

Educational institutions have no doubt suffered the most from the rejection of a peripeteia that surfaces from generation to generation in the academic world. Nothing is a greater example of this than the decrepit and corrupt worldwide system of college and university accreditation, especially in Europe and America. The elite system is egotistical, full of contradictions, and simply outdated in the age of the Web and the information highway. A few years ago, I had a friend who was a genius who came to the United States from the Ukraine. He had earned highly distinguished degrees in both physics and chemistry, but his academic honors were considered unaccredited in the U.S. He had to start over again and earned degrees in Computer Engineering and Computer Networking over the next six years. I was embarrassed in our nation as I realized the inequity of our archaic accreditation system. Even so, accreditation is just the tip of the educational iceberg where learning institutions are imperiled.

One educator calls the failure of the academic community to address virtues, character and tenure another major malady in education today. Schools or universities have abandoned the task of teaching "moral literacy" and forming character. Educators have allowed their political interests to sterilize academia today from any presuppositions, absolutes or morals. From the earliest intelligent and advanced cultures, there was a united and understood belief that education must never be void of character training. In fact, educators felt they had an obligation to offer instruction to all young people on the importance of good character.[120] Unfortunately, since 1962, we have seen the perpetual erosion of Unmanageable Change in the educational halls of society who have opposed God, morals, prayer, charter schools, home schooling, and parental authority. Yet educators have simultaneously embraced evolution, humanism, relativism, monism, and toleration of any belief system or religion other than Christianity. On the opposite spectrum, the teacher's union has stubbornly resisted any real reform to cull out bad teachers. Subsequently, violence has mushroomed in classrooms; immorality has multiplied like a plague while academic excellence in every grade has been steadily declining. While there are some oases of learning, the desert spans out evermore vast in America.

Life is very unpredictable. So are we. This being true, why has the academic world fought major change in their arena more than any other group? To look at how organizations can become so intolerant of real change, you only need to read a few books about the world of academia written by their own peers. Many see organizations or educational institutions that have become so entrenched that they fight to avoid any real lasting transformation. If a major turnaround is attempted, intense underlying forces begin to aggressively attack the character or motive of the person or group advocating change. Unmanageable Change usually spirals out of control until it returns an organization or institution into a latter state that is worse than where it was before the peripeteia began. But as we will see, there is a more common enemy of all groups when it comes to transitioning into something higher, better, or more meaningful than they have been before.

During an educational forum I attended in Phoenix, Arizona, two educators introduced some insights from a book they had written thirteen years before. Their research uncovered some drastic information about educational organizations. Unbelievably, educators ignored their discovery on the whole as we can observe by the abundance of the same problems still existing in schools and universities. They wrote about executives and institutional leaders who ignore systemic hindrances by blaming individuals whenever an organization fails. Rather than seeing what remains to be changed in the institution or in the transitional methods being employed in the reversal, most simply point fingers at those they deem to be the opponents or weak links to the turnaround. As they pointed out, people are not always the problem. Here is their excellent observation that any "leader of leaders" should not ignore:

Because we haven't understood organizations, we have hurt one another deeply. We joined together to accomplish a purpose, we spun intricate webs of relationships, and a system emerged. But then, what happened if we disliked what emerged? How did we respond? Usually, we turned on one other. We singled out one leader, one team, a few troubling individuals. We thought that if we changed them, or got rid of them, our problems would be solved. How many people have been terrorized by this endless search for scapegoats? For all of the terror, how often have we succeeded in transforming organizations by changing individuals? This approach to change is yet another dark Darwinistic shadow. In classic evolutionary thought, change occurs within individuals. Each of us invents our own survival strategies as we struggle against the environment. When we apply this thinking to organizations, it leads us straight to individuals. If a distasteful situation develops, or we don't like where the system is headed, we just pluck out the bad genes. We look for the mutants in our midst and expel them."[121]

This brings us to the last area we will examine in correlation to Unmanageable Change. As I've mentioned before, as I began writing this book, we were in a Presidential election year in America, and the political world was once again on the front pages of every newspaper or magazine. Nowhere has there been more dysfunctional behavior than in government and politics. Just the time you believe that real change is beginning to take place, and there can be a complete reversal of the "politics as usual" motif, the same polarizing forces arise to tear down the advances of new leadership or pundits of change. How often we assume that some political leaders were bad and some leaders were good is dependent on political interests that do not want a complete or radical reversal of circumstances. Generally, most want only a change in who is in command, or they are interested in limited invested alterations. That is why in any genuine peripeteia that occurs, you will witness shortly following this divine or spectacular event an attempt by a "control group" to manage the degree of the turnaround or the subsequent end results of this reversal of circumstances. This not only applies to politics and government, but also to education, business, and religion. Tragically, when these "control groups" or an influential person attempts to manage for personal gain or interest a peripeteia, it interferes with the healthy reversal of peripeteia causing then a less-than-desired Unmanageable Change.

Let me offer you a splendid case in point. With the close of the Civil War between the American States in 1865, it was clear that President Abraham Lincoln had no desire to punish the South (the former Confederate States). Even in his Second Inaugural Address of 1865, when events in the Civil War clearly began to reveal the outcome, President Lincoln wanted reconciliation, healing, and restoration of the Southern states. He had already appointed provincial governments in all but three states where there were political leaders who had remained loyal to the Union. He also had plans for Reconstruction and reparations to those in the South that had been unfairly treated and their property illegally confiscated or destroyed.[122] When Vice-President Andrew Johnson assumed the office of President following the assassination of Abraham Lincoln, he had been from Tennessee (a state that had seceded from the Union) and many Northern politicians thought they could control him for this apparent weakness. In the next three years, they would find out that Andrew Johnson was not as feeble as they had hoped. Instead, he believed in Abraham Lincoln's plan of reconciliation and restoration of the South. He did not embrace the attitude of the politicians and businessmen, who were "carpetbaggers" wanting to take advantage of the South to build their own power or fortunes. Johnson's plan called for these southern states to have their own conventions with only three stipulations:

1. To invalidate their old ordinances of succession,
2. To abolish slavery in their states,
3. And repudiate all debts contracted to support the Confederacy. Other than this they were free to write their own state constitutions.[123]

President Johnson's Plan for Reconstruction was designed much the same as Lincoln's idea, but the mood of unscrupulous politicians in the North was not conducive to such forgiveness and healing. President Johnson did make one serious mistake because he feared freed slaves were not ready to vote or govern, so he advocated, mistakenly, what was called "black codes" or "black laws." His administrative decision was not only rebuffed, but met with the seeds of discontent and a later attempt to "impeach" him. Radicals in the North saw President Johnson as a Southern sympathizer and pushed through under Senator

Thaddeus Stevens of Pennsylvania what eventually became known as Radical Reconstruction. Henceforth, one of the greatest opportunities to turnaround past divisions was lost and seething resentment continued in the South for almost one hundred years. This Radical Reconstruction was designed around three laws that caused the South to "lose face" in the Union:

1. Punishment of Confederate rebels by allowing none of them to serve in Congress and, thereby, effectively having no qualified persons in the South who could really represent them effectively.
2. Military Rule over the South was divided into five regions where corrupt politicians and their business cronies could place "carpetbaggers" in high positions for their own profit. These profiteers raped the Southern States for their own personal gain.
3. Moving of "County votes" by blacks to an area they did not live in to control the outcome of local elections where whites dominated the population. The "Negro Suffrage" allowing blacks to vote was controlled by invested political appointees from the Northern states who used propaganda to persuade former slaves to elect them and not Southerners.[124]

I have painstakingly given such details not to give you a history lesson, but to completely lay bare the minefield waiting any who dare to tread into a genuine peripeteia. Neither President Lincoln nor President Johnson could have fully comprehended the attitudes that would hijack Reconstruction in the American South. As President Lincoln worked to preserve the Union, he also tirelessly fought for reconciliation without malice or retribution. So it was with his successor; and to this day; Johnson has never regained the stature he deserves as "one who meant to do good in a chaotic time." Remarkably, even the United States Supreme Court after the Civil War remained in fear of the radical deconstructionists who actually wanted to punish the Court. These deconstructionists were bitter at the abuses of the "carpetbaggers" and tried for years to refuse new court members or to remove their authority to do whatever they wanted.[125] When Unmanageable Change gets unfettered, it is hard to restrain its hunger to devour anything in its path that threatens what it perceives to be its divine mission. In every institution, whether secular or spiritual, men and women of honor should remember this sobering lesson.

The Turning Point That Changed Everything

Earlier in this chapter, I referred to a great professor of geology and physiology at UCLA. During his study of societies and their decision-making, he discovered some simple and amazing categories to divide their actions into. They are not only single actions, but they are directly related to one another. He calls these The Four Factors that Cause Societies to Make Bad Decisions:

1. A group may fail to anticipate a problem before the problem actually arrives.
2. When the problem arises, the group may fail to perceive the problem.
3. After they perceive the problem, they may fail even to try to solve the problem.
4. Sometimes, they may try to solve it but may fail in their attempts to do so.[126]

This leads me to one clear eye-opener for which I am grateful to Jared Diamond for assisting us to identify. There are times during or after a peripeteia that a "turning point" has happened, and there is nothing you or anyone else can do anymore to prevent or alter the events that are occurring. I've been a part of institutions where no matter what others or I did, it was impossible to change the outcome of what had already taken on a synergy of its own. Things spiral out of your control at such a rapid pace and on an undefined course that you are simply trying to comprehend the dynamics of it. Such explosive elements make you glad that you have confidence that the Lord God has direction over the entire path of your life (Psalm 37:23). I offer you this counsel for encouragement when you realize that there has come a moment in time that you are not able to grasp, to alter, or undo. Learn not only to forgive yourself in those moments, but also others where we tend to be much more judgmental and less able to forgive!

In October 2007, my wife and I were traveling with three other couples from a short-term mission trip to Belarus and Hungary. We had changed flights in Frankfurt, Germany, for a non-stop flight to Portland, Oregon. This eleven-hour flight is quite an adventure in itself. The flight ended up taking more than fifteen hours. Why? Well, taking the curvature of the earth, we passed over the North Sea, Scotland, and Iceland and were just starting to cross Greenland when a woman suffered a heart attack. Incredibly, there were two doctors on board the flight who, thankfully, were able to finally revive her. Then, the pilot announced that we would have to turn back to Iceland where it would be only two hours to land and get her better treatment. So we made an about face and went back to Iceland. Coming into Reykjavík International Airport was an experience. It really looked like we were going to land on the North Atlantic. As we finally saw land and flew over this island only fifty miles across, I was stunned by the topography. You see, there is a familiar saying that goes like this: "Iceland is really Green and Greenland is really Ice." Well, erase my memory card! Iceland was incredibly barren, and we saw some vegetation that was no taller than a tiny bush. We saw no trees! Well, it was late October, and almost everything was covered in white frost or snow.

Emergency resolved, we took back off again headed west for our long flight still to come until we reached Oregon. Afterwards, I became interested in reading Iceland's history and studying topography maps of this island nation. Well, like Paul Harvey used to say, ". . . now, for the rest of the story!" Beginning in the year A. D. 871, Norwegian Vikings began to immigrate to Iceland. Their beloved homeland of Norway has heavy clay soil ground up by glaciers. It is abundant and thick. Those soils are sufficiently weighty, and the vegetation covering them is thick. When this vegetation is cut down, the soil is too heavy to be blown away. Sadly, the Viking colonists who settled in Iceland did not know that the soils covering Iceland are as light as baby powder. This soil covering does not come from glacier grinding, but through winds that carry light ashes blown out in volcanic eruptions over thousands of years. Unknowingly, as the Norwegian Vikings cleared the forests and other large vegetation off the soil in order to create pasture for their animals, the winds then blew out again the light soil where vegetation had grown to protect it. Within a few generations of the Vikings arrival in Iceland, half of the Iceland soil had blown away or eroded into the ocean.[127] They did not intend to destroy Iceland's abundant "green" covering, but with trees gone, the lesser vegetation then became vulnerable to further destruction as storms year after year pound relentlessly on Iceland.

Unmanageable Change is not a cute phraseology to entertain or use as a "catch-all" for this chapter; it is a harsh consequence of those who undertake changes without fully appreciating the dynamics of modifications to institutions of every kind or size. The next opportunity you have to be involved in the transition of an organization, church, or corporation, you should consider this chapter carefully. There are many books worth reading on managing change or understanding the nature of human groups. But it will take more than a study of sociology or psychology; it will necessitate biblical theology, which society loves to criticize but rarely attempts to grapple with. Ignoring biblical revelation about a peripeteia is like trying to decide how to guide a boat to another destination while abandoning the use of its sails. Not just improbable, but impossible. No wonder men like Daniel were left as our example in the Bible. He had to deal with more than one major peripeteia, both in Babylon and Persia. We also must learn to call upon the Lord when faced with new challenges or old problems to see what wisdom God will reveal to us:

"Daniel said:
Praise God forever and ever.
He has wisdom and power.
He changes the times and seasons of the year.
He takes away the power of kings.
And *he gives their power to new kings.*

He gives wisdom to people so they become wise.
And *he helps people learn and know things.*
He makes known secrets that are deep and hidden.
He knows what is hidden in darkness,
And light lives with him.
I thank you and praise you, God of my ancestors.
You have given me wisdom and power.
You told me what we asked of you.
You told us about the king's dream" (italics added for emphasis).[128]

As you will see in the next chapter, the wisdom shared by the prophet Daniel about "kings" is gravely important. Remember these insightful words!

Chapter 6

If Bishops Become Kings, So What?

Since nothing is settled until it is settled right, no matter how unlimited power a man may have, unless he exercises it fairly and justly his actions will return to plague him.
— Frank A. Vanderlip

At the close of the thirteenth century in Europe, the papal power of Rome exceeded that of any prime minister, prince or king. When Boniface VIII ascended the exalted throne of St. Peter in 1294, he had every reason to believe that the prestige and authority of Rome gave him the unparalleled power to do as he desired. Often stating his claims to supremacy over all rulers of the earth, more than any of his predecessors, he aspired to chasten even kings who dared to stand up to his magnificence. Caught up in his thirst for preeminence, he set out to challenge King Edward I of England and Philip IV (called the Fair) of France. First, he declared the King of France unable to tax or to collect any monies from

The Turning Point That Changed Everything

the priests of England, since only the Pope had authority to force them to pay allegiance or dues to a higher power. He even issued a Papal Bull, called the Clericis laicos, which forbade any monarch or other ruler from exacting tribute and taxes from any clergymen in his or her realm. This divisive and self-indulging church law incited the people to rebellion and even the priests in England sided with their king. Subsequently, the Pope was forced to withdraw the Papal Bull within a few months.[129]

Disastrously, Pope Boniface did not learn wisdom or humility from this state of affairs. Instead, he set out on another crusade to crush the political power of the Italian family of Colonna. They had often opposed the ambitious papal initiatives of past pontiffs. With his eventual victory over the Colonna family in 1298, he pompously assumed he had the influence to take more control. Afterwards, he was buoyed by the attendance of well over two million pilgrims who flocked to Rome for the jubilee of the year 1300. The success of this jubilee added to Boniface's extreme wealth and also gave him an exaggerated confidence that he could take on royal opponents with renewed vigor. He set his sights this time on Philip IV of France. The King of France had charged the Bishop of Pamiers in Languedoc with treason and other serious crimes against the state. He had ample evidence to convict this bishop. Again, Pope Boniface VIII issued a Papal Bull called the Unam Sanctum in 1302 that forbade the King of France from taking such actions and again stated the Roman Pontiff had all supremacy over all secular rulers. He demanded complete submission in order that kings could have salvation. He then threatened to excommunicate Philip.

The subsequent fallout was overwhelming as King Philip called an assembly of all his barons and higher clergy to charge the Pope with simony, heresy, and crimes of treason against France. This meeting led to an arrest warrant against the Pope that was carried by soldiers to the summer mountain town of Anagni to take into custody Pope Boniface and bring him to trial in France. Fortunately, he was able to escape with the help of the townspeople, but Pope Boniface would never recover his power or prestige. The aging Pontiff died within a month (1303) of shock and chagrin to realize he was now an outlaw himself. In fact, the French boldly declared the papacy vacant. They elected their own Pope named Clement V. While the French Pope Clement reigned almost 9 years like Boniface did, the papacy was later reunited but would never hold such enormous temporal power over kings or rulers again.[130]

I can't find the original source of the quote, but as the popular cliché goes, "Those who forget history are doomed to repeat it." The lessons learned from Boniface are pertinent and personal. If bishops become kings, so what? This is more than a hyperbole question. No other spectrum of life has been tempted like bishops, popes, pastors, overseers, chancellors, and evangelists. Tempted by demonic or fleshly tendencies, the sacred realm offers a cauldron of teaming seductresses that beckon to those who enter this realm of spiritual elevation. Lurid temptations of power and money not only strike the secular world, but even the religious bastions of authority. Through the years, many of us have watched the superpowers of clergy rise to the top of their ministries, denominations, and churches. We have also observed scores of them usurp too great a power, strive for too much wealth, expand their positional influence, be desensitized to sexual entrapments, and/or be caught up by the popularity of their own image. It leads over and over to ministers, educators, or politicians that superciliously develop a dictatorial spirit, carelessness, greed, immorality, self-sufficiency, isolation, aloofness, and a refusal to be accountable. Yet corporate CEOs, politicians, and teachers have fallen down this same slippery slope!

What causes the human creation of God that holds such promise and exaltation to fall for the Temper's delight called "power." The creature Lucifer used this scandalous technique in the beginning of time with the first couple as he seduced Eve with these enticing words:

> Now the serpent was more subtle than any beast of the field which the LORD God had made. And he said unto the woman, Yea, hath God said, "Ye shall not eat of every tree of the garden?" And the woman said unto the serpent, 'We may eat of the fruit of the trees of the garden: But of the fruit of the tree which is in the midst of the garden, God hath said, Ye shall not eat of it, neither shall ye touch it, lest ye die.' And the serpent said unto the woman, *"Ye shall not surely die: For God doth know that in the day ye eat thereof, then your eyes shall be opened, and ye shall be as gods, knowing good and evil."* And when the woman saw that the tree was good for food, and that it was pleasant to the eyes, and a tree to be desired to make one wise, she took of the fruit thereof, and did eat, and gave also unto her husband with her; and he did eat (Genesis 3:1–6, italics added for emphasis).

We see this enticement of control appearing in all walks of life today. Like Adam and Eve who were lured by the persuasion that they could be "like gods," this influence over the centuries has struck down rulers, clerics, administrators, and politicians. The phenomenal district attorney turned politician, Eliot Spitzer, took office as New York's governor on the first day of 2007. He won with a record margin of victory and a profound sense of promise. He resigned on March 12, 2008, in a scandal over his involvement in a sex ring, bringing to an abrupt close his stormy tenure as the major kingpin of New York. His administration was marked by an almost unbroken string of stumbles and frustrations. But how could he fall so swiftly and completely? His popularity began to dissipate almost immediately after he took the high office, as Mr. Spitzer repeatedly and belligerently challenged legislative leaders and lost. Mr. Spitzer's difficulties were a stark contrast to his long and steady rise. Over the previous eight years as attorney general, Mr. Spitzer, a Democrat, gained national recognition as the 'Sheriff of Wall Street' for his pursuit of corporate corruption and his self-styled role as the defender of the American investor. During his campaign, his signature promise was to change state politics "on day one" of his new administration, with ethics reform high in his sights.[131]

After doing some background reading on Eliot Spitzer, it was astounding that there were so many archived documents that under girded his reputation as a zealot of morality and a campaigner for integrity. If there was ever someone who could have taken the express elevator from bishop to king, Spitzer was the perfect candidate. But the ostentatious position of king can turn a once ennobled prosecutor of righteousness into a shadowy character few of his friends could recognize or envision. How many others would also wilt under such a spotlight?

The purpose of this section is to honestly ask some hard questions of leaders who are reading this book. I have served for more than thirty-eight years in leadership, and my experience has given me a heavy dose of modesty and reverent fear of holding offices or positions. Perhaps the sternest admonition was offered by an English clergyman in the nineteenth century named Caleb Colton: "Power will intoxicate the best heart, as wine the strongest heads. No man is wise enough, not good enough, to be trusted with unlimited power. Power, like the diamond, and also the wearer; it dignifies meanness; it magnifies littleness; to what is contemptible, it gives authority; to what is low, exaltation."[132] I am impacted deeply by such warnings, as well as by the many observations of my peers over the years gone by.

Every day as I pray and meditate upon my duties, roles, and expectations, like many of you, I wrestle to keep my ambitions and convictions from overwhelming me with a spirit that my way is always best or that my rule can be justified by the task to be done. We must wear the mantle of bishop, pastor, president, or whatever the title, with care that it does not mesmerize the bearer and quickly seduce us to think we carry a scepter of invincibility or infallibility. These are great attributes of God, but they are like quicksand to a mortal selected to serve other men!

Let me step back for the next couple of pages and speak about a favorite hobby of mine called chess. Picking it up while still in junior high (what most call "middle school" these days), I continued to learn and play in chess club in high school and college. After competing in several tournaments and winning some, it also gave me a realization that I would never be a grand master of the game. Therefore, my late brother Felton and I loved to challenge one another as siblings often do. It was my distinct honor to teach my oldest grandson who has also been in a tournament or two. Since this hobby is my favorite after reading, I have made it a pleasure to acquire chess sets from such places as the Ukraine, Russia, Hungary, Greece, Belgium, and Columbia. There are no two alike, but each is uniquely decorated and made of finely crafted granite, pewter or wood. Unlike many hobbies, chess is both intellectual and recreational. What I have learned about this game is that it often mirrors life and helps a contestant to learn to explore new moves, changing situations, determined opponents, incredible patience, resiliency, and a willingness to look ahead for many variables that you may have to face. No wonder chess masters in many world cultures are looked upon with such awe.

Having studied various strategies of chess through the years, there are some basic principles that apply to this ancient game from China that developed in the fifth century.[133] Allow me to list five chess tips; they have a strong applicable nature to those who serve as leaders of industry, education, religion, or smaller groups. If you were to teach a young student about chess or even leadership, these valuable tips would serve well for those who also serve in a role of sacred trust for the benefit of others:

The Turning Point That Changed Everything

1. A good chess strategy is to avoid moving a chess piece twice during the opening of the game. Overuse of one chess piece or overexposure of a leader is risky. Any pastor or bishop who assumes that they alone must tackle every problem or challenge that comes along is mistaken.

2. It is better chess strategy to develop the knights before their respective counterparts, the bishops. The earlier a leader can learn this key lesson the better. Discipling, training, and inclusion of other key workers in the strategy and operation of an organization is wise; it also saves the bishops to move later when their movements are less hindered. For instance, the king may move very little, but he is irreplaceable. A bishop's role is likewise indispensable to the king, and he needs to keep himself available to protect and to advance when called upon by the king. Remember, we are the pieces; God is the player!

3. A good chess strategy is to avoid exchanging bishops for knights early in the game. It is foolish to assume that you have "bettered yourself" simply by taking out others you feel have equal value or opportunity as yourself. Attacking a rival in leadership can backfire and simply liquidate both of you. When one realizes that the bishop's stature only grows more vital in the latter stages of the contest, he will be reluctant to push his piece into the forefront of the stage and expose fatal ambitions.

4. A good chess strategy is to develop both of your knights before the queen's bishop. Because a queen has the strategic ability to move more ways and distance across all color squares than any other piece, retaining the Queen's Bishop will serve as her protection until the time is right to bring her into the fray. Too many leaders expose their most valuable assets by feeling they must be the center of all the action when it really requires them to have more patience to serve more and be the "star" less.

5. A good chess strategy is to avoid pinning the opponent's king's knight before he has castled or moved his castle into the game. For those who do not play chess, this analogy may seem difficult to understand. But many bishops have such a desire to topple a knight or become the king that they try overzealously to put them into situations where they will lose their position early on in the contest. Unfortunately, this often backfires, and you have placed them into a position they cannot move from and it ends

up causing the game to end in a draw. In that case, the king loses, but so does the bishop![134]

Why do I apply these unique chess examples to the office of a bishop or anyone who serves as a leader? The reason is that during a major turning point of an organization or church, some leaders are enticed into opportunism or jockeying for a higher position. The result is usually catastrophic to the player trying to move up the corporate ladder or the ecclesiastical hierarchy.

The temptation of leadership has a common thread that weaves through both history and various groups. Not even the small but growing band of Jesus' disciples was spared the reptilian deception that often blinds people to the devil's dark shadowy figure that creeps through the ranks of leadership. James and John were among the most intimate three that Jesus allowed into close proximity to some of his greatest miracles and personal moments with God (i.e. the mount of transfiguration, the raising of Jairus' daughter from the dead, and the prayer of Gethsemane). Could such men of God be tested to rise from bishops to kings? Take a look for yourself at this embarrassing event:

"Then the wife of Zebedee came to Jesus. *Her sons were with her.* The mother bowed before Jesus and asked him to do something for her. Jesus asked, 'What do you want?' She said, 'Promise that one of my sons will sit at your right side in your kingdom. And promise that the other son will sit at your left side.' But Jesus said, 'You don't understand what you are asking. Can you accept the kind of suffering that I must suffer?' *The sons answered, 'Yes, we can!'* Jesus said to them, 'Truly you will suffer the same things that I will suffer. But I cannot choose who will sit at my right side or my left side. Those places belong to those for whom my Father has prepared them.' The other ten followers heard this and were angry with the two brothers. Jesus called all the followers together. He said, 'You know that the rulers of the non-Jewish people love to show their power over the people. And their important leaders love to use all their authority. But it should not be that way among you. If one of you wants to become great, then he must serve the rest of you like a servant. If one of you wants to become first, then he must serve the rest of you like a slave. So it is with the Son of Man. The Son of Man did not come for other people to serve him. He came to serve others. The Son of Man came to give his life to save many people'" (italics added for emphasis).[135]

The Turning Point That Changed Everything

What has happened in modern times is no different than in those ancient days! Wherever a peripeteia awakens a people who have been "sleep walking" down a path of destruction or decay, there is an innate seed that is waiting to be germinated by fresh ambition and selfish opportunity. At this juncture, you need to understand something about the nature and subtle forces that are also birthed in a genuine peripeteia. Where do these "bishops who become kings" originate? How do these secondary players, these understudies, get projected into the lead roles of the drama that is unfolding?

First, we must discard the presupposition that those who become "power grasping" individuals during this reversal of circumstances are opposed to the change or that they do not understand the sphere of the transition that is occurring. Second, we must also dismiss the notion that these "emerging leaders" were inherently corrupt and like wolves were waiting to devour others (Acts 20:29). Third, understanding a peripeteia requires us to become conscious that this emergence of those who would be kings is not always due to men or women of ambition taking advantage of a new plot. More than not, the most pervasive cause will be the vacuum of old leadership that is being swept away and the lack of preparation for the sudden reversal that has been thrust into the organization. Into this void, gifted individuals are often mistakenly led to believe that strong leadership is needed and they are the best suited to fulfill that role. Logic says, "I have remained after the peripeteia and, therefore, it is obvious I was left or introduced into this moment because it is my right or opportunity to be the star. With fewer actors on the stage, the spotlight illuminates players who stood on the side of the stage for many performances. With such reasoning, new stars are born and the crown is prepared for coronation even when there is no intentionality by the newly born star. Ridiculous! Well, not to the player who has served in the shadows.

The dynamics that come to the forefront of a peripeteia are varied and complicated. In the area of poetics and theater, no one understood this circumstance any better than Aristotle. He wrote extensively about the characteristics of this kind of drama. He identified key factors that dominate this kind of change and the emerging actors who become elevated:

- Some characters act consciously and with knowledge that the situation affords them opportunity. They may do this with mischief intent or by pure desire to use the potential for good.

- Many will act in ignorance that is discovered afterward; when they realize their deeds were in actuality evil, they will withdraw.
- Still others will act or move in ignorance and when they discover their apparent misguided deeds, they will refuse to turn back from the evil deeds they are doing because they desire their new status.
- Finally, he describes the actor who has knowledge and opportunity to take advantage of the peripeteia but consciously chooses not to use this misfortune or opportunity for his self-promotion.[136]

Could it be that we have been neglectful in various institutions or organizations to comprehend and manage where possible the dynamics of such dramatic turnarounds? How heartbreaking is it to continue without seriously examining our historical and present changes so we might avoid where possible in the future the same identical mistakes. In retrospect, we see those in the secular community sometimes adapting to this pattern of managing change better than ecclesiastical groups. Certainly, since Jesus knew human behavior more than anyone, He validates this omniscience so keenly in the following excerpt from one of his parables: "And the lord commended the unjust steward, because he had done wisely: for the children of this world are in their generation wiser than the children of light" (Luke 16:8).

Indeed, it is painful when people are caught up in this kind of phenomena either through their ignorance or by prior knowledge. What is more catastrophic is that they could have been approached by the right person or group in a spirit of love and humility which would have helped them realize the inherent danger of these moments in a peripeteia. I believe the counsel of the aged apostle Paul is applicable to such unusual times: "Brethren, if a man be overtaken in a fault, ye which are spiritual, restore such a one in the spirit of meekness; considering thyself, lest thou also be tempted. Bear ye one another's burdens, and so fulfill the law of Christ. For if a man thinks himself to be something, when he is nothing, he deceiveth himself" (Galatians 6:1–3).

I cannot remember where I read it, where I heard it, or if I just stumbled on it, but there is axiom that says, "He embraced the concept of laws higher than kings, and rights higher than laws, and finally relationships higher than rights." Over the last year, since I wrote that proverb down and taped it up near my desktop computer, I have reflected on it almost every week. It almost always begs a question like, "How can I live this truism out in my own life?" As a bishop of many years, what is it that sneaks up on me and attempts to enthrall me about this honor bestowed upon me. Actually, I became a bishop at too young of age, but my state bishop thought me ready and solicited me to accept this great honor. I was a novice to think I was ready for it. Yes, my State Supervisor had decided to approve me for this lofty office because I was a good pastor (he said), and he was going to appoint me to be a District Supervisor over six other pastors in the Cajun region of Louisiana. My supervisor was a strong, compassionate and gifted leader, but reality be told, I was too young at twenty-seven years to be given this privilege. Since our church organization views a bishop higher than a pastor (even though the terms are synonymous in the Greek), the ordination to bishop among us is more ceremonial prestige than authoritative in scope. Either way, lifting up a young man to such an honor was mind numbing. I was blessed to have tender-hearted men and women who addressed my young ambitions and inexperience to keep me grounded in such a world of grand superlatives.

This brings me to the grand deception that enters into even a divinely designed peripeteia. Those who already have stature and recognition as gifted bishops or leaders almost always get thrust into the spotlight in these awkward moments as the stage transitions to a new scene with a fresh cast of key players. In the rush to appear ready and groomed for this rare opportunity, an actor(s) will sometimes be disillusioned by the grandeur of it all, and there arouses a pride that is pitifully observed by discerning observers in the audience. When a keen observer points out to others this ambition and pride among the cast players or to audience members, the reaction can lead to an attitude that borders on animosity by the audience or another cast member toward the new star on the platform. Any of you who have ever attended such an occasion know that I speak graphic truth. The entire run of the production can be tainted for months or even years, and it can "curse" the new play with mediocrity or failure. While the bishop, who has become king, is damaged by this development, so are the observers who react harshly without ever grasping they may have effected a great drama that could have become a masterpiece of the creator. If you think I grieve, you are astute. But your perceptive reading does not lessen my pain or dry my tears. Why do leaders allow such ill-fated coronations? And why do the subjects of the kingdom so unmercifully slaughter their own princes? We must all contemplate such neglected opportunities and weep for such cruelties that deplete our ranks of so many promising protégés.

Before I move forward, Jeff Kinley, in his heartwarming book, coauthored with the singing group called MercyMe, awakens us to this fragile action that can result in disobedience. No person ever desires kingship to fail miserably, but often when we go somewhere not intended by God, it results in a far greater cost than perceived. Jeff writes, "Though it's an old maxim, it still rings true: Sin will take you farther than you want to go, force you to stay longer than you want to stay, and make you pay more than you want to pay. For Adam and Eve, they maxed out their credit card and the bill arrived at their doorstep just seconds after swiping the card. They had pushed the button that set in motion a long-lasting avalanche of negative and damaging consequences. What they now began experiencing were things they had never known before—things like shame, guilt, grief, pain, sadness, loneliness, loss, and confusion."[137]

Harsh realities and discarded opportunities live in my memory. Watching political or religious theater can be a daunting task. People step to the platform at a pivotal turning point in history. They have all the potential of famished people wanting to see real change that will produce something of substance to satisfy their hunger. Promises are made, visions are launched, programs are created, and new faces appear with fresh ideas and potent energy. But within a few passing scenes, the audience has grasped the plot and realizes they are not watching a messiah or deliverer, but a tragedy with another king that falls in the final scene. Jesus described it by rehearsing a child's song often heard in the streets of Jerusalem: "We played the flute for you, and you did not dance; we mourned to you, and you did not lament" (Matthew 11:17).

Even Jesus realized the expectations of people, who are easily disappointed when they realize that things will not happen as they thought they would be played out. If I dare, this brings me to some annotations about those who rise up to a leading position of influence. Let me share six of these observations with you:

1. Too often, when a person is thrust into a position of great influence because of a sudden reversal of circumstances, they may have many good ideas or inspiration, but they limit those who assist them in the transformation to a few trusted friends or highly positioned people. By limiting their sphere of leaders' privy to the change, they doom themselves for lack of clear

information, ground support, and pivotal points of two-way communication. This decision is dramatically seen in the biblical king Rehoboam (1 Kings 12:1–15).
2. Frequently, they are more concerned about their image of being "in charge" or "confident-in-command," and they quickly remove or repel those who they fear to be more gifted or influential in the nation, institution, or organization.
3. Sometimes, they concentrate too much on details of implementing change and direction so that they become encumbered with menial tasks that others could easily and better perform.
4. Overexposure to the stage is tempting and seems merited to "sell yourself" to the other players in the group or invested observers who you feel you need to solicit or get their approval. After awhile, the emerging leader is beginning to appear more like a king than the bishop who once served so humbly. This is applicable to pastors, overseers, managers, teachers, principals, and supervisors of every rank or position.
5. "Haste makes waste" is the old adage. Nothing is more verifiable in times of a major turnabout in a group. After the first observation we listed, this is the next frequent cause of unfavorable reaction by those in the second or third levels of influence in an organization. Many a king has fulfilled the ironic saying, "Fools rush in where angels fear to tread" (author unknown). Even in a turnaround divinely ordained or practically required, too much change too quickly is a recipe for failure.
6. Although there are perhaps smaller concerns, the emerging leader must have honest evaluations of his performance. Without accountability for how he plays his new role or examining the perceptions others have of his leadership, he is as naked as the king in the Hans Christian Anderson's fairy tale called "The Emperor's New Clothes," who parades his frailties before his subjects without realizing his shame. Above all else, the leader must choose his evaluators carefully from among those who do not fear his power or who seek to advance their own positions. Even a peripeteia requires this accountability to be successful.

While recently reading from various media sources, I came across William Shakespeare's great play about the noble kings of England. There is a series of

The Turning Point That Changed Everything

four plays about four kings, but it was *The Tragedy of King Richard II* that captivated my attention. The registry says it was first recorded as originally written on August 29, 1597. If this is the case, Shakespeare was not only a brilliant playwright, but a bold and brave man in an age when kings ruled with an iron fist over most of the world. No other play exposes so much of the travesty of people caught up in their own illusion of venerable authority. A summary of the play is necessary for us to fully realize the unsuspecting grip of power that overtakes even the most common man when a sudden reversal of events can sweep him off the stage. Look long and acutely into this king's parlay into power.

Richard II is the main character of the play. The first Act begins with King Richard sitting majestically on his throne in full grander. We learn that Henry Bolingbroke, Richard's cousin, is having a dispute with Thomas Mowbray, and they both want the king to act as the neutral judge. The subject of the quarrel is Bolingbroke's accusation that Mowbray killed Richard's uncle the Duke of Gloucester. What is more, Mowbray is further accused of having stolen money that would have been used for military purposes. Richard cannot pass judgment because it is later revealed that he ordered Mowbray to kill the Duke of Gloucester. Bolingbroke and Mowbray challenge each other to a duel, over the objections of both Richard and John of Gaunt, Bolingbroke's father. But Richard interrupts the duel at the start. He condemns both men and as punishment, banishes them from England. Bolingbroke has to leave for six years, whereas Mowbray is banished forever. King Richard's decision can be satirized as the first mistake in a series that will lead eventually to his overthrow and death. Indeed, Mowbray predicts that the king will fall sooner or later. After that, Bolingbroke's father John of Gaunt dies and Richard II seizes all of his land and money. The king's tyranny grows bolder.

Nothing is shocking about a king taking this course, but this compounds his other arrogant mistakes and a peripeteia is birthed of tragic proportion. This angers the nobility, who accuse Richard of wasting England's money, of taking Gaunt's wealth to fund a war with Ireland, of overtaxing the commoners, and of fining the nobles for crimes their ancestors committed. Next, they help Bolingbroke secretly return to England and hatch a plan to usurp Richard II. However, there remains some subjects faithful to Richard, among them Bushy, Bagot, Green, and the Duke of Aumerle. King Richard leaves England to administer the war in Ireland, and Bolingbroke takes the opportunity to assemble an army and invade the north coast of England. When Richard returns, Bolingbroke first claims his land back but eventually claims the throne. He crowns himself King Henry IV and Richard is taken to prison at the castle of Pomfret. After interpreting King Henry's "living fear" as a reference to the still-living Richard, an ambitious nobleman goes to the prison and murders the former king. King Henry repudiates the murder and vows to journey to Jerusalem to cleanse himself of his part in Richard's death.[138]

The above illustration is more than just a drama on stage played by some theater guild; it is a reality of power thought harnessed by those who do not realize they are simply players in a tragedy they think is a pageant of glory. When we leaders, whether spiritual or secular, forget these kinds of "twists of fate," then we take liberties with our titles and positions that rapidly take us down a fork in the river where we do not want to drift.

About sixteen years ago, I was in the process of helping my congregation through a major shift in the history of our local church. We were moving from a pastor-oriented, one man approach, to a team leadership philosophy. During my early days in that church, I intentionally scheduled meetings on Saturday nights in our home to discuss with all the leaders where my vision was taking us, how the vision must be "our vision," and, therefore, they would need to contribute to further shaping that mission. Subsequently, we agreed to put everything on the table for negotiation, adjustment, or replacement. We added the necessary ingredient of prayer, as well as time to incrementally make changes and do analysis of the results. Things began to grow and advances made swiftly. Then it happened, like with so many pastors or administrators, problems cropped up by the bushels. One day, it occurred to me that we were dealing with an age-old problem that would hinder our team leadership as much as it had hindered the old centralized pastoral system. You see, in every institution there is an "undeclared but clearly known" player or group that controls the direction and health of the organization. They have through years in that group or body become the hidden system that truly determines the success or failure of churches and pastors.[139] In reality, time and circumstances have given them "kingship."

Having both eye witnessed and studied such complicated systems over the last several years, it has become very apparent that many churches and organizations are governed by many variations of these unofficial groups that eventually take hostage of groups. In fact, back during those foundational years with my leadership team, I realized that these would-be kings must be dethroned if we were to move forward. A peripeteia was occurring in my church, but forces were gathering above and around me that sought to hinder this transition. One day, I bought an insightful book whose subtitle pulled me in like a giant magnet. Transfixed the first time I began to read it, the Lord revealed to me what I had either been ignorant of or ignored for fear it would be too impossible to face. In so doing, I contributed to my own defeat. This remarkable truth spoke loudly and persistently to my heart. Unless I first identified the underlying systemic group in my church and mustered the courage to deal with it, then I could be little more than a "puppet leader." Here are the three most prominent and common groups that dictate the power structure or base of almost every church, school, or organization:

1. Church Family Structure—This kind of systemic group develops with a clearly understood role of a prominent church parent(s) and their "not necessarily related offspring" who operate as a subsystem in the church or organization. Their influence is not dependent on title or position, but has been obtained through a period of years as they exuded tremendous pressure on others through their overbearing personalities or reputation of not being someone you would want to challenge. Because they predate most pastors or other administrators, they have either gained the respect, loyalty, or fear of others who differ to them in any given power decision. Nothing of significance happens or gets the "OK" without their unofficial approval. Furthermore, not everyone will agree with them or enjoy their parental influence, but the deference they receive will not be challenged. More than half of all existing churches and organizations have these unofficial parental leaders.[140]
2. Unofficial Elder Structure—This "behind the scene" systemic group or persons are an actual blood family that helped in establishing the church or organization. It may deposit all its final authority in one patriarchal or matriarchal person, but often is exercised through the entire family to a greater or lesser degree. Sometimes, this group has become the elders or deacons, the organizational board, or individuals who hold key leadership positions. Often, they have been retained as the corporate or church treasurer. Regardless the underlying place of influence they hold, other members of the larger body are subservient and submissive to their will in the operation and basic direction of the church or organization. Sometimes,

these "controlling powers" do not like each other and will try to undermine each other's influence. But a new administrator or pastor would want to be cautious of misunderstanding their animosity or uncooperative nature with each other. The old adage is good to remember with these systemic, power brokers, "Politics and war make strange bedfellows." If they do not get their way, their dislike for one another can quickly turn to a tenacious loyalty if the old power structure or balance is threatened.[141]

3. Pastoral Independent Structure—While this third prominent form of systemic group has developed more in the last three decades, it has become a rapidly rising and deadly influence over churches. With the rapid rise of what is called "non-denominational churches," there has emerged a sense of a dictatorial spirit among pastors who start their own independent church. In a backlash to these systemic systems that lie behind most internal church problems, which have paralyzed many denominational churches, there has emerged a new spirit of kingship. This egotistical system occurs where a founding pastor or his heir has developed a warped theological explanation for his "totalitarian" approach to running a church. Consequently, it leads to a body where he solely determines the doctrinal, financial, and administrative leadership. While the pastor or leader will have a board of directors (ministry team), it is little more than a figurehead to cover their absolute control. Wherever rules of strict accountability by outside authority and examination are not followed, abuse is always there to some degree. As this kind of arrangement has grown, so has the disenfranchisement of honest seekers who desire biblical churches and leadership. Both Western and Eastern countries have been victimized by it.[142]

As this last example of negative systems has emerged in organizations at an alarming rate, it calls upon leaders today to take the lead in expecting and praying for true integrity in those who lead others. No source has more succinctly spoken to this need for leaders to break this silent code that fosters the kingmaker attitude than Gilbert Rendle of The Alban Institute. This institute studies and consults local churches in how they can escape this perilous resistance to change and find healthy solutions. Gilbert writes about one church coalition of leaders that came to them with a willingness to deal with past hindrances brought on by repeated conflicts: "The leaders of the coalition broke the collusive cycle of leading by doing and used the force field analysis to identify what needed to be learned, not done. In times of great change a critical responsibility of leaders is to identify and to respond to what needs to be learned. Often this means identifying what the leaders themselves must learn."[143]

Throughout the political nations of the world, economic and military fear, as well as self-serving ideological interests, has created a schizophrenic nationalism. This kind of political passivism has opened the way for nations like Venezuela in South America, North Korea in East Asia, and Iran in the Middle East to plunge their areas into terrorist havens. While such rouge nations are not loved nor embraced by their neighbors as role models, other nations around them want to pattern after them in their own quest for economic and political stabilization. Therefore, they tolerate such dangerous attitudes and ambitions of their neighbor and even publicly endorse them. In reality, the nations around such rouge nations fear them and behind the scenes confess privately that the condition is unacceptable. I mention this kind of political example because the church and its clergy have in many ways operated with the same ambivalence toward ministerial counterparts who are pastors, supervisors, religious broadcasters, and evangelists. Likewise, the same schizophrenic position taken by many Christian groups has also been prevalent among corporate European, Asiatic, and North American business leaders. When nations, corporations, and churches do not speak out to condemn and deal with such abuses as kingship, then you can believe that it will reproduce and multiply even more. To speak out about the tyrannical political leadership of men like Hugo Chavez of Venezuela, Mahmoud Ahmadinejad of Iran, or Kim Yong-nam of North Korea is hypocritical when we remain silent about the abusive power of fellow clergyman or corporate presidents who do horrible things to those they are to serve. Wall Street and banks have become the epitome of this wholesale toleration of unethical behavior.

I am particularly concerned about my own profession and the resistance or reluctance within the ranks of the ministry to discipline our own colleagues when they are damaging the glory of the gospel of Christ that we are to be presenting to the world. Furthermore, when ministers encounter those who are independent pastors or from another denomination, they must not stand silently by as these abusers fleece their flocks or use oppressive power to control people. While we may not have any disciplinarian rights or entrance to their congregations to defend their people, we must speak clearly and directly to them with straightforward admonition and prayerful love that such action opposes the spirit of Jesus Christ.

The early apostle Peter wrote expressly about such leaders and their ungodly mind-set or nefarious activity in his first general epistle to the church: "Now I have something to say to the elders in your group. I am also an elder. I myself have seen Christ's sufferings. And I will share in the glory that will be shown to us. I beg you to take care of God's flock, his people, that you are responsible for. Watch over it because you want to, not because you are forced to do it. That is how God wants it. Do it because you are happy to serve, not because you want money. Do not be like a ruler over people you are responsible for. Be good examples to them. Then when Christ, the Head Shepherd, comes, you will get a crown. This crown will be glorious, and it will never lose its beauty."[144]

This brings up the point of how such clergymen, corporate CEOs and managers, as well as educational supervisors rise from the lower ranks into the position where they emerge as kings. Addressing this is essential to understanding and taking action to prevent such exaltation to kingship. As a business major from Monona Grove High School in Madison, Wisconsin, I had the opportunity to travel to Chicago with fellow members of the Future Business Leaders of America. While touring the infamous International Mercantile Center, a large skyscraper that serves as a year-around exhibit for businesses, I was able, in the spring of 1968, to meet personally a writer named Laurence J. Peter. He later coauthored a controversial book entitled The Peter Principle. In this publication, he had unnerved the business community by propounding the theory called the "salutary science of hierarchiology."[145] In a nutshell, the introduction summarizes his principle that in many hierarchy systems, members are promoted so long as they work competently. Sooner or later, they are promoted to a position at which they are no longer competent (their "level of incompetence"), and there they remain. Peter's corollary states that "in time, every post tends to be occupied by an employee who is incompetent to carry out his duties" and adds that "work is accomplished by those employees who have not yet reached their level of incompetence."[146] Having met him personally, his persona and beliefs were memorable.

As time has passed, my fascination with Dr. Peter has subsided, but his theory is still viable and accepted as having great merit by many sociologist and corporate critics. As we review the grievances charged against executives and leaders both in secular and religious positions, it is abundantly evident that this situation

The Turning Point That Changed Everything

has changed very little, if any. The media hounds continue to turn up ample proof of this principle in action. The cover-up by Catholic hierarchy of the sexual abuse by priests throughout the United States and other nations around the globe has only aided in legitimizing the degree to which "The Peter Principle" has infiltrated the ranks of the ministry. The same proof is found in the corporate buyout of CEO's who have literally guided their companies into the largest financial losses or bankruptcies in history, while these corporations are giving huge retirement or severance pay to have them quietly exit their positions. Overall, we are no better than in 1969 when "The Peter Principle" was first advocated and warnings to corporations were given.

Accountability and maintaining focus can best address the temptation to become kings. With all his multiplicity of faults, King David had one endearing quality that helped him retain integrity as a leader. He was willing to be submissive to accountability and able to refocus on the necessary priorities. When David was tempted into an adulterous relationship with Bathsheba and arranged the subsequent murder of her husband, Uriah, he was confronted by Nathan, the prophet. In today's world, it makes you wonder how many CEO's or bishops would be willing to submit to be accountable to a mere itinerant prophet that many scorned anyway. But, I love the simple words of submission and accountability given by King David at this turning point in the nation of Israel. The historical record of the incident in 2 Samuel 12:13 contains the simple words of David to Nathan: "I have sinned against the Lord." But to fully grasp the submission and accountability demonstrated by the king, the complete confession that he prayed to God must be read. Forgive the inclusion of the older King James Version at this point, but the literary beauty of it is too much to abandon for a newer adaptation. Here is King David's prayer to the Lord in Psalm 51:

> Have mercy upon me, O God, according to thy lovingkindness: according unto the multitude of thy tender mercies blot out my transgressions.
> Wash me thoroughly from mine iniquity, and cleanse me from my sin.
> For I acknowledge my transgressions: and my sin is ever before me.
> Against thee, thee only, have I sinned, and done this evil in thy sight: that thou mightest be justified when thou speakest, and be clear when thou judgest.

> Behold, I was shapen in iniquity; and in sin did my mother conceive me.
> Behold, thou desirest truth in the inward parts: and in the hidden part thou shalt make me to know wisdom.
>
> Purge me with hyssop, and I shall be clean: wash me, and I shall be whiter than snow.
> Make me to hear joy and gladness; that the bones which thou hast broken may rejoice.
> Hide thy face from my sins, and blot out all mine iniquities.
> Create in me a clean heart, O God; and renew a right spirit within me.
> Cast me not away from thy presence; and take not thy holy spirit from me.
> Restore unto me the joy of thy salvation; and uphold me with thy free spirit.
> Then will I teach transgressors thy ways; and sinners shall be converted unto thee.
> Deliver me from bloodguiltiness, O God, thou God of my salvation: and my tongue shall sing aloud of thy righteousness.
> O Lord, open thou my lips; and my mouth shall show forth thy praise.
> For thou desirest not sacrifice; else would I give it: thou delightest not in burnt offering.
> The sacrifices of God are a broken spirit: a broken and a contrite heart, O God, thou wilt not despise.
> Do good in thy good pleasure unto Zion: build thou the walls of Jerusalem.
> Then shalt thou be pleased with the sacrifices of righteousness, with burnt offering and whole burnt offering: then shall they offer bullocks upon thine altar.

Strolling through many major airports, you can find a small paperback entitled *The Man in the Mirror* by Patrick Morley. Although I've seen his books in various airport bookstores, I admit that it was my youngest daughter Melissa who gave me a copy as a Christmas stocking stuffer. My girls know I love to read, and this one she felt would speak to me. She was correct. Under a chapter heading

The Turning Point That Changed Everything

named "Solving Our Time Problems," I came across a list of four priorities that can help us as leaders be more accountable to others and also keep our focus on why we serve in positions of trust. Patrick gives us four questions that we need to be conscious of and ask ourselves on a regular basis:

- What does God want me to be and to do?
- How does God want me to use my time and my money?
- What character and conduct traits does God desire in me?
- What relationships and tasks does God want me to emphasize?[147]

If Bishops become kings, So What? This is more than an overstatement. Rather, it is a question of every person's integrity. It lies at the heart of leadership. It is also the underlying temptation of every peripeteia. Until we recognize this element growing and spreading behind every major reversal of circumstances, we endanger ourselves to its developing tendrils that take root in the fertile soil of the new emerging administration. Through the years, I've watched with trepidation this seduction from CEO's to pastors. Therefore, we must be willing to ask ourselves those aforementioned questions and make sure to allow others to hold us accountable to each one of them. Anything less is catastrophic for the institution and its players.

This past year, I read with a grateful heart an article that had appeared in a monthly publication that I subscribe to with my church. This piece of writing was so transparent and humbling that it caused me to admire the writer even more than I had in previous years. Bishop J. E. Brisson warmed my heart when he spoke of his retirement. He viewed it with such forthrightness. He had no desire to become bitter, critical, or negative about the future. He concluded his words of encouragement with a great example by Benjamin Franklin who stood before the Constitutional Convention and pointed to a picture of either a sunrise or a sunset behind the President's chair. He remarked, "I have often and often in the course of these sessions, and in the vicissitude (ups and downs) of my hopes and fears, as to the issues, looked at the painting behind the President without being able to tell whether it was a rising or setting sun. But now, at length, I have the happiness to know that it is a rising and not a setting sun."[148] Bishop Brisson observed that these remarks were made about our troubled nation. He is correct. Beyond this application, these words speak to this bishop's outlook on life and his refusal to take a negative view of his successors that followed him. Bishop Brisson has brought dignity to his lofty ordination by his meek and dedicated spirit. Until each leader can take up a similar spirit of humility and cooperation with those who serve around him, the best of peripeteia's can be sidetracked, brought to a halt, or to catastrophic conclusion by those ushered into the glory of its center stage.

Chapter 7

The Improbable Degree of Reversal

"Shakespeare said we are creatures that look before and after; the more surprising that we do not look round a little, and see what is passing under our very eyes."
—Thomas Carlyle

In January 1959, more than one million people filled the main Havana Plaza in Cuba to attend the largest rally in that nation's history. They had come to celebrate the overthrow and recent execution of ousted dictator Fulgencio Batista and the members of his government. They had been summoned to demonstrate their faith and enthusiasm for their new Communist revolutionary leader, Fidel Castro. The country of Cuba was alive with hope, dreams, and excitement of a new nation of prosperity and a turnaround from the tyranny of the past. Noted historian Andrew St. George, a writer and photographer, was there to record the incredible reversal of circumstances that had given rise to Fidel Castro, Camilo Cienfuegos, and Ernesto (Che) Guevara. Born Andras Szentgyorgyi, Andrew belonged to the Hungarian resistance that had been instrumental in helping opponents of the Nazis escape Budapest. Later, he also went to Austria when the Soviets occupied Hungary after World War II. But now Andrew St. George was a renowned photographer and amateur historian. He initially supported and wanted to capture this remarkable peripeteia taking place in Cuba.[149]

Sadly, this reversal of circumstances was going to end up careening much farther to the left and to an oppressive future than anyone in the Plaza that day realized, including Andrew St. George. He had joyfully chronicled with expectation the progress of Fidel Castro's revolution, beginning in 1957. Thousands upon thousands of Cubans celebrated this incredible mid-January spectacle only a month after Castro's rebels had overthrown the past dictator. This massive event brought a hope of a new openness that many poor and oppressed Cubans had longed to see for many years. They were mistaken. The reversal of the state of affairs went far beyond what was expected. Within a few years, all the lieutenants around Fidel Castro would subsequently be replaced or murdered. His brother would become his chief enforcer who would direct the secret police. Hard-lined communism copied after Russia was put into place, conflicts with the U.S. grew tense, and relationships came to a halt between the two nations. Financial mismanagement and an end to free-market trading stymied the once robust economy and deepened poverty. Representative government and electoral voting was replaced with an oppressive police state. Disillusioned, Andrew left Cuba a year later and was accused by Castro's lieutenant Ernest Guevara of being a FBI informant. Of course, he was not, but when a peripeteia takes place, no one quite notices how far or sometimes where it is going. Besides, among the main cast of this drama, who would care about one freelance journalist or a very good historical photographer?[150]

Few observers or players on the great stage of events ever realized the improbable degree to which this peripeteia will be played out. Like the events in Cuba in the 1950s and 1960s, The Improbable Degree of Reversal could not be ascertained, even by Castro's regime or the U.S. State Department. Even in a transformation that seemed destined to bring good, there can be deeper actions or results than known. Having witnessed various changes in people, institutions, or circumstances that have veered around to the opposite, I can attest that some went further than I would have believed and others to a lesser degree than I desired or sought. Irrespective of how far the change has gone in a positive or negative sense, the extent to which it goes is the greatest mystery of all.

As I researched and browsed through abundant resources, the answers continue to baffle writers and so-called experts of change. For that matter, when does a good peripeteia develop too much and become a negative on the horizon? Perplexing questions multiply as the scale of the transformation grows. More often than not, those who helped foster or birth the peripeteia abruptly realize that it cannot be stopped where they would like. I am not speaking of "unmanageable change" or a "bad change" as we examined in Chapter 5. Quite to the contrary, sometimes the positive and reoccurring benefits of the change continue beyond what was anticipated, planned, or hoped for. Time and experience has taught me that trying to predict or determine this kind reversal is unwise. As a friend of mine that surfs on the beaches of California told me, "You can anticipate the big waves, but you cannot know with certainty how far they will take you." He was right, and this has given me some personal consolation as I have ridden the waves of some of those sudden reversals in life.

The paradoxical question frequently comes up in my various readings on change. Does life imitate what we have been shown in art? Moreover, does art simply mirror what has occurred or is now happening in life? Shakespeare loved to inject into his dramas, especially the tragedies, the plot that thickens beyond the expected perception of his audience. His mastery of taking the action beyond what would be probable is typical of his works. To Aristotle, the greater degree to which the characters were changed could not be irrational, yet he insisted it could reveal a greater intent to expose good or evil than otherwise known. Therefore, in plays like the *Odyssey*, *Iphigenia*, *Cyprians*, or the *Oedipus*, Aristotle's analysis praised the action that causes the observer to discover far more than expected from the early characters or plot within the play itself. The actor in the drama did not matter to this lover of peripeteia, but the depth to which the action will turn. He considered the plot subservient to the poet. He wanted very much for his readers and audience to discover more than they recognized was coming from the earlier action.[151]

Here I am, watching the plot thicken in my own life and family, yet curious how far this conversion will take me. What about the direction of your own life?

The Turning Point That Changed Everything

I have a favorite verse of Scripture that many of my friends have heard me refer to in Proverbs 37:23: "The steps of a good man are ordered by the LORD: and he delighteth in his way." I love the way it reads in the older King James Version. It is the assurance of this promise that helps me when the plot thickens and scenes transition on the stage of my life. Indeed, the improbable degree of a sudden reversal in my life has time and again turned more than I expected before or during the modification or complete transition to the opposite. No doubt, I try more to enjoy what God may be authoring for my life.

Before I met my wife, I had been engaged to a wonderful Christian girl. We had planned so many things together. We had shared hopes, expectations, and values. Our relationship blossomed during our second year of college together, suddenly and completely, we were so right for one another. But the transformation this brought in our thinking and openness to the voice of God was setting the stage for a radical departure from what either of us envisioned. One month prior to our special day, invitations were sent, family pictures made, showers completed, and many gifts had already been received. Then, out of the blue, there came a hiccup in the perfect drama. In conversations and events leading up to the wedding, we opened our hearts to God's calling and designs for each of our lives and found ourselves unable to walk together into the dawning sun. In a brisk forty-eight hours, events and untested feelings were shared that would send us spinning in opposite directions to the dismay or disapproval of some of our friends and family. Confidently, we knew the plot was turning, and we simply followed the new lines being written by the playwright. To this day, I am glad there were no lingering regrets.

Since I cannot from this point on speak for the other dedicated young lady, I can examine my own situation. Without denial, I heard the order of the Lord and knew that my path would be turned far more drastically than expected a few months earlier. God would first break me, love me, heal me, and restore me to the undiscovered path he had designed for me. Although in itself, there was a peripeteia taking place, it was not a new one. Shocked, after extensive self-examination and counsel with trusted parents, it occurred to me many seasons later that it was part of a larger peripeteia that had been developing for about two years. Unimaginable before or during the transformation was the colossal degree to which this road was turning. It was during this transition that I met my gentle wife named Judy (a woman with a calm presence and godly character). In a few months we were married—the whole plot had been revealed. Unlike the modern "rebound theories" of irrational love, this involved a complicated and intriguing plot that required obedience to the voice of my Heavenly Director. Not only did the final scene that unfolded surprise the audience, but as the lead actor in the drama, I was amazed at the intent of the Divine. This is how turnarounds happen—the reversal often surpasses what is imagined. Instead of fighting the move to a place we do not plan or instinctively desire, finishing the turnaround becomes a welcomed new scene.

While reading, back in 1996, for a course entitled "Understanding and Learning to Live with Change," I came to discover a necessary truth about transformations. In one of my textbooks, there was an imperative insight that stood out above many others for me:

> Many, many adults cannot conceptualize tomorrow until after they have experienced it. Similar comments are made by a liberated widow several years after her husband's unexpected death, by an individual who lives for years with a severe handicap but surprisingly can walk comfortably after a surgery for replacement of a hip joint, by some empty nest parents, and by teenagers who mourned the departure of the former youth minister and later become enthusiastic supporters of the successor. Who can conceptualize tomorrow?[152]

Even the great Aristotle realized that a peripeteia goes far beyond the expectations of the audience.[153] What is true of theater only mimics life itself!

There is one particular area where change is occurring so drastically, completely, and suddenly that both churches and schools are ill prepared for the revolution occurring before their eyes. For almost two decades, this turnaround within the American, Canadian, and European cultures has been overwhelmingly evident yet severely resisted by many churches and some educational institutions. The massive influx of immigration and other ethnic religions has diluted the typical Christian culture of both Western Europe and North America. Even the exposure of people, both young and old, to divergent thinking and belief systems has swept into living rooms of these nations through the constant barrage supplied by the Internet and Cable (or Satellite) Television. In a recent video circulated by "YouTube" on Muslim demographics, experts on population movements and birthrates warned about this peripeteia reversing the entire religious makeup of Europe and eventually America. The conclusion propounded that Islam will overwhelm Christendom unless Christians recognize the demographic realities, begin biologically reproducing again, as well as sharing the gospel with Muslims.[154]

This diminishing Christian orientation is pushing a turnaround in the approach schools and churches are taking. Confession being good for the soul, churches must be honest in their recognition that we have prepared less for this reversal of circumstances than the corporate world. Both public and private education has failed to some degree in making the proper transformations to deal with this phenomenal growth of other religious beliefs such as Islamic, Hindu, and Buddhist immigrant values inundating the historically Christian nations. Right now, spiritual interest among Millennials, as well as the growing Post-Millennials, remains extremely high. Instead of engaging in this peak interest in spiritual things, churches as a whole remain committed to a few minor changes and the "big-box" church movement. Frankly, this astronomical loss of Christian principles and church influence in North America is following the pattern of Western Europe. Here is the news that many Christian leaders and even many secular educators do not want to hear. Church denominations and other church associations will continue to decline sharply in North America, so will their loss of a financial base of support, their doctrinal exclusiveness will be diluted, and the way they have functioned structurally will have to be trimmed down or consolidated.[155] As this phenomenon continues, the Western world's education will lose the very Christian culture and beliefs that underpinned the foundation of traditional education. While the humanistic educational institutions will welcome this departure from faith in Jesus Christ, the turnaround will go further than they anticipate and usher in severe philosophies that will bring them where they did not intend to go. Furthermore, it will be a much more dangerous, radical, and new religious belief system.

Few could have predicted the speed, size, and type of reversal we are seeing in Western societies. During the last fourteen years, I have had the rare privilege and responsibility of serving on the International Doctrine and Polity Committee of my organization. During these past years, the group has seen many issues brought to us for consideration, study, and recommendation. The task has been daunting and nearly overwhelming. The societal norms and practices of our people are changing constantly, yet we make recommendations every two years.

We are simply playing a game of "catch-up," and we will never overtake the swift reversal of circumstances occurring in the United States, much less globally. We work with presbyters from around the world who have their own unique, quasi support group.

In the last few years, I realized we were involved in a futile effort to overtake a "diminishing Christian orientation." In truth, every church or educational institution must in four ways address their crisis of relevance to the modern dilemma. I am convinced that few, if any, corporate bodies can make this change because of the built-in weaknesses of their present structures that require long-term and "snail-like" corrections. Frankly, we do not have the time for these old structures to deal with these challenges. Bluntly, their inherent systems were designed to control. The financial pressures that threaten their own existence have tempted them into "personal turf wars" between invested parties who still want their piece of the pie. This is not meant as criticism, nor does it come with any bitterness attached; it is simply a reality check or matter-of-factness. I will not credit one lone source since this has come from observation and collective readings. It is my belief that the churches and schools must address these four things to bring them into a relevance to the modern dilemma:

1. There will be more increased difficulty with finances and time restraints for Christians, especially leaders, to gather in a single place for training. Local churches and schools will have to decentralize training to make it more flexible and affordable. There will be new "academies" to allow people to use technology and other non-traditional ways as conventional ministerial and on-campus academic degrees will decline.
2. A large number of existing churches will have to merge to have better and more eye-catching property to attract this newer generation. Sharing of facilities will become more and more essential to utilize property and be able to reach diverse ethnic groups that are growing. Many will have to do so to meet new religious educational needs since public schools will become even more secularized.
3. House churches will become the new wave of future ministry. This has already begun to occur in Western Europe, and others will need to follow. Rising real estate costs and changing views on taxation will force some of this change. The old traditional role of dividing church ministries by

ages, such as youth and children, may need to change as people feel the need to get back to family emphasis. House churches and family ministries will become the rave. Sunday worship will change to other days or times because of the expediency of families to have some quantity time of sharing together.
4. Denominational churches or major church organizations will have to streamline their operations, or they will become irrelevant. The power base of the body of Christ will move from the Northern Hemisphere to the Southern Hemisphere. While the North's financial mission giving will continue to dominate for awhile, the spiritual epicenter will go south. Programs offered by these organizations will become more social and less invested in serving the affluent people or the old church power people. Educational and leadership training will also liquidate old models and spawn new contemporary methods.

The Improbable Degree of Reversal, as related to the aforementioned example, was seen forthcoming for more than three generations. One of the first Christian educators to observe this phenomenon and warn about it was Dr. Francis Schaeffer. I had the wonderful opportunity to hear him speak posthumously through a series of videos during my years of attending Colorado Christian University in Lakewood, Colorado. His sense of anointing, candor, and prophetic voice was undeniable. Little did I realize back then what a vision he had of the future! During the twelve video lectures on theology that he gave to our class, he punctuated his presentations with warnings about what was about to happen in the coming years to Western Christianity. My theology professor liked Schaeffer but disagreed with his ominous declarations. We ministerial students should have given more heed, but confined within my church limits, my vision was at that point neither sharp nor fully open enough to some of his prophecies. During my reading of his five-volume set on *The Christian Worldview*, there emerged a pattern of truth and revelation that was undeniable.[156] Something was changing, and he knew it right well. Amazingly, he also was one of the few who comprehended the degree of the reversal that had already begun and would continue for the next three decades. Let me summarize some of what he saw happening in 1982 and what he adamantly declared was yet coming.

The Turning Point That Changed Everything

Mr. Schaeffer could foresee the church near the end of the twentieth century and at the beginning of the twenty-first century. He predicted that the "Big Lie" would overtake Christianity with a majority of Christians becoming converts of relativism and evolution. But he went further than Christian belief; he understood the patterns that would emerge in churches that survived the onslaught of secularism coming in like a flood. Schaeffer also warned that Islam would become the greatest danger to the Christian Culture in America and Western Europe. He believed that the rescued churches would become "hot-beds," intellectually and spiritually. They would prepare themselves to knowledgeably "contend for the faith" as mentioned in Jude 3. He also saw these churches practicing "Compassionate Christianity" toward the poor, the undesirables, as well as minorities and ethnic groups pushed to the outer parameters of society. He further declared the "Home" would become the new community to rise up to take the place of new ministries or new churches. He encouraged Christians to "Open Your Home for Community." He dared to write in 1982 that the "Home" would emerge as the place where Jesus would be lived out as we welcomed people there to serve them, worship with them, learn about Jesus, and to make it a place where everyone could dwell without the hindrance of church laws, traditions, and power groups that historically closed the church to sinners. Dr. Schaffer went even further to declare that "Homes" would become the place where the outcast of society would find the love and compassion of Jesus. Remember, this was in 1982, yet he was saying that churches would have to move away from traditional times and days of worship.[157]

But Francis Schaeffer was not done. He condemned the "meaningless meetings" as churches that do nothing to minister to people's needs. He charged that the "structure of churches" would undergo radical change if they remained relevant and involved in their community. He mentioned that family settings are what kids and teens need if they are going to escape the tribes they have joined at school or in their neighborhood. Finally, this powerful theologian who became a prophet to the modern church in Western Europe and North America, advocated that the only way for us to survive the new Millennium was to practice and teach purity of doctrine, yet be willing to change church polity and practice where it needed to be corrected. To do this, churches would be required to become more outspoken on the major issues of the faith and stop dwelling on traditional positions about polity that had been so divisive in the last two centuries of the church.[158]

The Turning Point That Changed Everything

When Christian educators, church leaders, and evangelists entered the twentieth century, they could not have imagined how far the change would take their institutions and churches. As we approach the second decade of the twenty-first century, we must now grasp new approaches that first-century Christians were willing to embrace in their age. It was the Croatian voice of Miroslav Volf who challenged so brilliantly the theology that blinds men to the truth of complete reversals. When I realize how far my own mindset has turned around, I sympathize with someone who was born and raised in a culture of violence, hatred, and division. It also makes me cringe and cry at the increased racism, hatred, and exclusion going on in America today. Americans and Europeans are more prejudice and separated than they have been in my entire life. A few years back, no one could imagine Europe being splintered as national boundaries and political loyalties have been transformed since 1989. The writer Volf challenged the misguided presuppositions that guide Western mindsets. Generally, people in the West, including Christians, have a propensity to point out the abuses of "ethnic cleansing" that have gone on in places like the Balkans, Macedonia, Iraq, Republic of Congo, Sudan, India, China, Laos, or Guatemala. But in the United States, we have seen similar forms of abuse and denial of humane treatment to the Irish, Germans, Japanese, Chinese, Afro-Americans and now Hispanics. In the name of political expediency, self-preservation, border security, gay rights and economic globalization, we have witnessed the denial of moral law to the elevation of frequently ungodly civil law. Remember, that moral law is based on biblical principles and civil law often relies on a dominant ethnic group who has the "bully club" of governmental power.[159]

What causes some peripeteia's to turn so completely opposite of their beginning? It is clear from reading numerous social, political, and religious accounts about dramatic turnarounds that the deeper the injustice, the more entrenched the tradition or the longer the denial of human dignities, the greater will be the likelihood of an Improbable Degree of Reversal. Where people have been denied the opportunity that all mankind yearns to have, where individuals have been so oppressively lorded over, or where years of mistreatment have been measured out through leaders or a privileged caste of people, the greater the reversal of circumstances will eventually become. For example, the Bolshevik Revolution that produced Communism in the beginning of the twentieth century is proof of this kind of radical revolution.

Historically, as resistance grows to the turnaround, so also will be the bitterness and risk people will take to make the change complete.[160] For example, we have witnessed again this potent change in Eastern Europe, as well as in South Africa, Peru, and Vietnam. You see this revolution in the Roman Catholic Church as they deal with the massive exodus of church members in the Latin American nations to Pentecostalism and the fallout of the Priestly sexual abuse scandal in the United States. A Papal visit may pacify some in their ranks, but the departure of thousands has quickly escalated into perhaps as many as two million who have left for some other form of liberation hope.[161]

Any institution or nation that attempts to fight the inevitable reversal of the status quo may be able to do so for decades, but the size, type, and degree of the change only heightens the tensions that can thrust the circumstances into such a radical opposite that anyone remotely connected to the past history or status quo is left both displaced and ostracized. China's Emperor family was able to push this change aside for hundreds of years beyond what other historical governments had been able to do because of their isolation and worship of hierarchal leadership. But when the change came it was fierce in the form of Communism that could not be prevented regardless how brutal it became. Sadly, this will happen again as China has tried to reinvent itself into a brand of Capitalistic Communism, which in itself is holding off further change that may not be stopped as forces for revolution secretly weave discontent.

Today's Pentecostal Revolution in Africa is directly related to the intense and elongated struggle against the old colonial nations, and the ethnic dictators that took their place as the rulers of the Dark Continent. In fact, the rise and resistance of great bishops like Archbishop Luwum and Archbishop Christophe Munzihirwa are proof that even martyrdom will not prevent the eventual overthrow of these political forces. As in Africa and South America, even America will soon begin to witness the affects of institutions and churches that refuse to make substantial alterations in how they have done business and handled the delegation of authority.[162] I have watched with particular interest within the ranks of the American church the refusal to make some essential changes while advocating transformation in other areas we want to see altered. I call this type of change "Selective Transformation." In effect, it simply covers up someone's invested desire to make a few adjustments in hopes of appeasing other people to obtain a present or future benefit for themselves. In stark contrast, there is no real consequential change for the people

The Turning Point That Changed Everything

who need something remarkably different. Enough said on this entrapment, let me illustrate with a stark example this improbable degree of reversal.

To any historian, the French Revolution and the eventual French Republic led by Napoleon is a classic study in how something so loathsome can be removed yet become another government so vile. Not every peripeteia is good or lasting. In 1789, France erupted with ideological ideas of change, and then violent revolution initiated by mobs of discontent citizenry. By 1792, the nation was embroiled in internal battles of political wills and external war with old German landlords. By 1793, the French Revolution had become the bloodiest in European history. Austrians and Prussians were amassing troops for an onslaught of Paris. King Louis XVI had been guillotined to the outrage of most European nations, and the government of France was in chaos.

Indeed, no one could deny the outrageous, arrogant, and violent tyranny of King Louis or his wife Marie Antoinette. This Monarchy had pampered itself on wasteful luxuries and wantonness while the ordinary peasants lived pathetic lives of destitution and hunger. Then a savior appeared on the horizon of France's political vacuum. By 1794, this national peripeteia had taken place in only five years. Conversely, the American Revolution had taken some forty years to evolve and produce a steady nation. The French were encouraged by the rise of two new powerful forces called the speculators and the regicides. By 1795, they had composed a group of five leaders to lead the government called "The Directory." Tragically underestimated, most of these men and the new legislature could not stop the rising power or influence of the French army that had benevolently under girded the French Revolution and, therefore, were highly trusted by the common people. Among this group, a young Corsican officer of the artillery was becoming a popular hero after putting down the revolt of the Vendémiaire 13 (a radical group wanting to restore the old ways). This cunning officer named Napoleon Bonaparte was to become the most renowned figure in Europe.[163]

Remembering the beginning scene of the French Revolution helps any observer understand the significant need for a peripeteia. But when this turnaround began, no one among the French populace or even the aristocrats who hated Louis XVI could have envisioned the reversal of circumstances that would sweep an entire nation up into its whirlwind. A young second lieutenant had been promoted to general of the brigade by 1794 and received appointment to command the Army of Italy by 1797. Before long, this improvising, bold, and resourceful young man of

27 was the most decorated general in Europe. By 1799, he had deviously become the dictator of the French Republic; he was a man to be both loved and feared. The Italian, Swiss, Dutch, Germans, and the people of Belgium fearfully and reluctantly gave him full allegiance. In 1804, Napoleon Bonaparte was crowned by Pope Pius VII as the Emperor of the French Republic. The hope and light of the bloody French Revolution had not only brought a complete reversal of fortunes on France, but the improbable nature of this turnaround swirled around to another ruler who would be more dangerous. King Louis XVI had ruled his monarchy with the tyranny of his own ignorance, slow-action, irresoluteness, mismanagement, and inability to control his wife's extravagance. Emperor Napoleon ruled the republic with swiftness, brilliance, resolve, charisma, and nepotism. They were remarkably different men, but the same catastrophic result played out in a defeated France.[164] France never regained its past stature or glory among nations.

While editing this book recently, I found myself compelled to add a paragraph about the economic and political drama that is taking place globally. It is alarming to observe how the media, big business, and world leaders are being held under the spellbinding charm of an individual with unusual charisma unparalleled in the last twenty years. His unexpected rise without the use of an army, religion, or significant family clout in his repertoire makes this person's "bigger than life" presence parallel that of an emperor or a Caesar. And, yet, he is rewriting the entire political and financial structure of his nation for generations to come. Such drastic transformations are rarely detected by the masses until like the Third Reich they have achieved power beyond what anyone intended to give them. Who will have the courage to impede such progress that appears to be so essential to the common man who is ready for anything or anyone disguised as a savior that will deliver him from his present suffering? Yet the warning by Jesus speaks of such perilous times, "... and upon the earth distress of nations, with perplexity: the sea and the waves roaring: Men's hearts failing them for fear, and for looking after those things which are coming on the earth: for the powers of heaven shall be shaken" (Luke 21:25, 26).

Even so, peripeteias are not always simple, quick, and understood. Neither is the degree of the turnaround a scientific equation. In fact, sometimes like in the French Revolution, we find the finish goes to a scale or measure unintended. This finished product can be better than expected or far less desirable than we anticipated or advocated. I watched recently an event that some parties were using

The Turning Point That Changed Everything

to oust a pastor from his pulpit. The whole situation backfired on them. During their manipulation of events and jockeying for the people to support their plans, the pastor simply rose up one Sunday and announced his resignation. This development was certainly not expected and revealed the fragile state of this body of believers to really care for a future pastor. As the next few months went by, some of the congregation left and others joined nearby churches. This left the already too small congregation unable to support the church and sustain any viable future. All of this resulted in the breakup of the church and the transfer of its property to the general denominational trustees. Later on, one of these parties that had tried to manipulate the ouster of the pastor confessed that none of them had anticipated the unintended and eventual outcome.

As I viewed this development, I was reminded that often one event or action escalates to influence another unanticipated reaction. The English poet and minister, George Herbert, realized this truism years before when he wrote: "Be not too presumptuously sure in any business; for things of this world depend on such a train of unseen chances that if it were in man's hands to set the tables, still he would not be certain to win the game."[165] I love the God-designed peripeteia, but I also respect and realize the uncertainty of life that can spin out a web in a direction no one could have known. We must all be alert to the seducing spirit of creating a turnaround that we suppose someone can organize or supervise. This is reckless dreaming.

When I ponder back over my life, basketball looms high on the things I've enjoyed. I never really was great, but I sure loved playing in school, college, and in many pick-up games around the neighborhood or the church. As a teenager, I really enjoyed a player in college named Lew Alcindor. He was phenomenal. Recently, I was able to read an article written by him about his professional career. It was fun and brought back a lot of fond memories. He would later change his name to Kareem Abdul-Jabbar. As a Christian, I never liked his new name or the ideology it symbolized, but I still loved his game. Kareem won his first Most Valuable Player Award in 1971, his second year with the Milwaukee Bucks' professional basketball club. He certainly enjoyed the honor since it went along with his team winning the world championship. Besides, he had the privilege to play with the legendary Oscar Robertson. During that season, he had to play several games against Wilt Chamberlain, who was the standard prior to Kareem for excellence in pivot play. Kareem was able to outplay him with 40.2 PPG in five games,

The Turning Point That Changed Everything

including a 50-point game. There was no doubt as I watched those games that basketball fans around the world were watching a legend in the making. During the 1975–76 basketball campaign, Kareem was traded to the Los Angeles Lakers. He was very fortunate to win his fourth "Most Valuable Player Award" that year because the team didn't do well. They finished 40–42 and missed the playoffs. But he had such a great year statistically, that's why he won MVP.

In 1980, Kareem Abdul-Jabbar won his last regular-season MVP, but it was also the year that the greatest peripeteia in professional basketball occurred with the Lakers. Fortunately, the team was able to draft that prior year of 1979 a rookie named Earvin Johnson from Michigan State. Called "Magic" because of his playmaking ability, Johnson burst onto the professional basketball scene like an exploding volcano of energy and laughter. Kareem said that "when we got Earvin, we had somebody that could run the team's offense. He was a genius of making everyone he played with better and doing things no one could imagine possible with a basketball."[166] Prior to 1980, the Lakers had dropped to the status of mediocrity that keeps so many teams from success. But a fantastic turnaround had begun in Los Angeles with the joining of Kareem and "Magic" Johnson on the basketball court at the LA Forum. The team became the favored team to win the National Basketball Association Championship each year. No one could have expected this team to go on to win five NBA Championships, but they were the team of the 1980's before it was over.

Just how great a basketball player was Johnson? He was what Bob Cousy was to the 1950s, what Oscar Robertson was to the 1960s, what Julius Erving was to the 1970s. Still, Earvin Johnson was even more than a revolutionary player, who, at 6' 9", was the tallest point guard in league history. His sublime talent elicited wonder and admiration from even the most casual basketball fan. Whether it was a behind-the-back pass to a streaking teammate, a half-court swish at the buzzer or a smile that illuminated an arena, everyone who saw Johnson play took with them an indelible memory of what they had witnessed. From the moment he stepped onto the court, people pondered: How could a man so big do so many things with the ball and with his body? It was Magic. Johnson accomplished virtually everything a player could dream of during his 13-year NBA career, all of which was spent with the Los Angeles Lakers. He was a member of five championship teams. He won the Most Valuable Player Award and the Finals MVP Award three times each. He was a 12-time All-Star and a nine-time member of the All-NBA First

Team.[167] It was tragic when his dalliance with a "call-girl" caused him to become infected with the HIV-Virus that prematurely ended a stupendous career.

Without question, the pairing of Kareem and "Magic" turned their team into a perennial power that made history beyond what any sportscaster could have forecast. Such turnarounds do not happen by chance, indeed much planning, strategy, and coaching were required, but how far this team went must be accredited to more than these factors. The degree to which this team succeeded required that someone keep their trust in those recruited to run this exceptional program. I wonder how many great things fall short because leadership does not make the right decisions, fails to get the right players in the action or begins to tinker too much with the critical chemistry of a group.

This brings me to a subject that is mistakenly overlooked by advocates of change and even by some talented playwrights. In the next chapter, I will take up the subject of anagnorisis, "a distinctive literary device by Aristotle that deals with character." Sufficient for now, there is one vital characteristic that often determines the scope and distance whereby a turnaround occurs. It is the issue of trust. Generally, when a party witnesses a change that has unlimited influence for good on an individual, group, or institution, it is directly proportionate to the trust that the key "change agent" has earned or received from the parties involved in the transition. While the media loves to preach the doctrine of trust, it is usually not verifiable or objective trust they advocate, but only trust that sounds more like "blind faith" to accept what the status quo wants or pursues. This is pragmatic trust. Too much of this kind of trust is simply seeking leaders who will serve our own interests, leaders who simply act as conduits for our personal agendas, or who tantalize us with their flamboyance and charisma. This kind of blind trust usually works better in fostering negative change, but it does not bode well for those wanting something more positive and long-lasting for the overall good of a group, institution, or nation.[168]

So I speak not of a surface-type trust quickly built on something in search of content. I refer to the traditional understanding of trust that was common in the 1950s home or workplace. Faith based on works as the writer James would say in the Bible (James 2:14–26). This kind of trust is distinguished by honesty, integrity, reliability, and consistency. These attributes assist a group or institution to navigate through unchartered and troublesome times of change. We desperately need this revival of character to lead us these days. With a majority of the Baby

Busters, Generation X, and the Millennials bankrupt of any examples of this kind of trust, they have turned toward the "live for today" mindset at the expense of the "prepare for tomorrow" lifestyle. This "trust of convenience" is deadly if it is the primary belief used during a major peripeteia when genuine trust is needed.

There is a fitting example of this trust in the Bible where a king named Josiah wants to bring reform to the nation of Judah. He has heard from childhood about the reckless reforms of Rehoboam and other kings who turned their back on God. He had heard how people's trust in them was placed in the wrong criteria that eventually resulted in those kings reverting back to evil practices and abusing the people they were to serve. Names like Abijam, Asa, Jehoram, Athaliah, and Jehoash were kings that relied on illegitimate trust that brought no lasting turn of Judah to God. Although extremely young, King Josiah relied on leaders who had long been known for their steadfast trust in God and for their integrity before the people. Furthermore, he placed his confidence in something so trustworthy (the Word of the Lord—2 Kings 23:2) that it gave people the same desire to rely on his judgment and leadership. Second Kings, Chapter 23, gives the full account of his actions to bring a turnaround to Judah. Of these many verses, two stand out as a lasting tribute to one man's trust in God that eventually brought the greatest revival ever to the House of Judah: "Josiah destroyed the mediums, fortune-tellers, house gods and idols. He destroyed all the hated gods seen in the land of Judah and Jerusalem. He did this to obey the words of the teachings. They were written in the book Hilkiah the priest had found in the Temple of the Lord. There was no king like Josiah before or after him. He obeyed the Lord with all his heart, soul and strength. He followed all the Teachings of Moses."[169]

There is another factor to consider when anyone becomes convinced of the need to intervene in the structure, political dynamic and operational principles of an organization, church, or even a nation. Whenever or wherever there is a religious interest mixed in the ingredients that will be affected by the change within a group, it is like adding ammonia to chlorine. Years ago I was working at a shoe store near my high school. My boss asked me one day to clean the windows of the store, and I was thrilled because it sounded like fun to be outside for a while. I went to the utility sink to mix up the solutions needed to clean the windows. Maybe you have guessed it already; in my hurry to get started, I forgot what solutions to mix, so I put ammonia and chlorine in the same bucket and proceeded to fill it with water. A few minutes later, my boss and a fireman are standing over me trying to revive me. I wasn't really in a lot of danger, but if the door had not been opened at the time, and if I had been alone, it literally could have been a lot more serious. Religious and political conflicts have a way of becoming much more deadly than any other mixture you can throw into a bucket.

This is illustrated graphically during the 1990s in the old nation of Yugoslavia where Christian Serbs were in an all-out war with ethnic Bosnia's and Croatians, which were Muslim. Most certainly, the old nation of Yugoslavia was going to be transformed peacefully or violently into two or three nations. Although all parties were guilty of violence, partisan politics, and genocide, the Western powers supported the predominantly Muslim states of Croatia and Bosnia. NATO used its military might and peacekeepers to occupy territory to ensure new boundaries and even supplied enormous monetary, medical, and food aid to these new regions. At the same time as this was going on, the Muslim nation of Sudan was emerging as a much more diabolical breeder of violence, slavery, and genocide against the predominately Christian population of Darfur. None of the Western powers took up arms against the Islamic extremist of Sudan, who were wiping out an entire region of people, because they were Christians. In fact, to this day, there has been no military intervention, no massive NATO support for a new Darfur independent region, and only token humanitarian effort that came years too late. Today the radical divisions of Serbia, Bosnia, and Croatia have produced three nations. Darfur continues to be an impoverished, drought-stricken region of innocent Christians and some Muslims caught in the religious crossfire. Many Christians who survived were forced to flee to Ethiopia, Uganda, and the Republic of the Congo.[170] As you can see, religion and politics is a dangerous mixture.

Why is this pivotal to understanding the brewing pot of religion when it comes to a peripeteia? When one looks at Iran, Iraq, Turkey, Pakistan, India, China, and Southeast Asia, there is already a turning point destined on their horizon. Religion either helps or hurts a group, an ethnic people, or a nation when they are faced with a major change required by years of denial of basic human dignities and rights. We cannot ignore this multiplier as we enter into change as a church or institution. To ignore such explosive factors will make the Improbable Degree of Reversal greater than anyone involved can imagine or possibly control. Every nation on the earth, every religion of the world, and every denomination or particular doctrinal group is being challenged by a global shift in people's loyalties and old presuppositions. This change is rupturing groups from Muslim sects to Pentecostal organizations. Yet many church leaders, institutional boards, mullahs, and pastors are blindly hoping they can just weather the storm. Until we realize that no synagogue, temple, mosque, or church will be excluded from this challenge, many will continue plummeting toward the next coming peripeteia with no awareness or understanding of this slippery slope. When I read of current beliefs and challenges being published daily about the force and extent of societal changes on churches, schools, and even corporations, it alerts me to be a voice crying out to others to pay heed to these impending circumstances. Let me just give one such example that belies the power of this change.

The Church of Jesus Christ of Latter Day Saints was founded in 1830 at Palmyra, New York, by a religious seeker named Joseph Smith. Believing that other Christian churches had strayed from the God's Will, Smith preached that the LDS Church would restore the faith as conceived by Jesus Christ, whose return was imminent. The next year, Smith moved with about seventy-five congregants to Ohio and sent an advance party to Missouri to establish what they believed would be a new Zion. In the agrarian democracy that Americans were building, both land and votes were important in determining future growth. Traditional Christians felt threatened by the Mormons' practices of settling in concentrated numbers, voting as a block, and in their belief in polygamy. Although Joseph Smith was to a great degree a pacifist, the Missouri Mormons were forced to relocate twice in the mid-1830s. In Ohio, an anti-Mormon mob "tarred and feathered" Smith in 1832, an experience he narrowly survived.

Joseph Smith left the state in 1838 after several lawsuits and a subsequent charge of bank fraud from the failure of a bank he had started. By the time he arrived in Missouri that January, non-Mormons were assaulting Mormons and raiding their settlements; a secret Mormon group called the "Sons of Dan" responded in like manner. That August, Missouri Governor Lilburn Boggs issued an order to his state militia directing that the Mormons "be exterminated or driven from the State for the public peace." Two months later, seventeen Mormons were killed in a vigilante action at a settlement called Haun's Mill. Smith and his questionable integrity caused enormous suspicion of the Mormons. But consistent to his nature, he moved his Mormon adherents to Illinois, founding the town of Nauvoo there in 1840 under a charter that gave the city council (which Smith directed) authority over local courts and police. This settlement grew to about 15,000 people, making it the biggest population center in the state. But in 1844, authorities jailed Smith in

The Turning Point That Changed Everything

the town of Carthage after he burned a Nauvoo newspaper that had alleged he was mismanaging the town and that he had more than one wife. At that point, Smith's polygamy was acknowledged only to the LDS Church's senior leaders. In a raid on the jail, an anti-Mormon mob shot the church's founder to death when he was only 38 years old.[171]

Before Joseph Smith's death, no one could have imagined or planned the militancy of the post-Smith Mormons. Prior to the emergence of Brigham Young as the leader of the LDS, the early Mormon relationships with outsiders were characterized by "self-righteousness" and "unwillingness to mingle with the world." After Smith's death, the LDS Church's ruling council, the Quorum of the Twelve Apostles, temporarily took control of church affairs. The lead apostle, Brigham Young, a carpenter from Vermont and an early convert to Mormonism, was able eventually to secure control and succeed Smith.

Unlike Smith, who often would flee opposition or confrontation with non-Mormons where possible, Young began to take a much more offensive attitude. In February 1846, he led the beginnings of an exodus of some 12,000 Mormons from Illinois, determined to establish their faith beyond the reach of American laws and attitudes. Brigham Young and other church leaders knew about the Great Salt Lake Valley from trappers, explorers, and travelers familiar with this vast wild region. At the time, most of what would become the American Southwest belonged to Mexico, but Young believed that the nation's hold on its northern frontier was so tenuous that the Mormons could settle in Utah free from outside interference.

In the spring of 1847, he led an advance party of 147 from an encampment in Nebraska to the Great Salt Lake Valley, arriving in July. Over the next two decades, some 70,000 Mormons would follow; the grueling journey would be one of the defining experiences of the LDS Church but would also reveal the more ambitious nature of Brigham Young. Violence, massacres, aggressiveness, threats, and corporate politicizing of the LDS Church exposed the drastic turnaround from Smith's pacifist philosophy to the brilliant, political, and militant vision of Young.[172]

While reading various historical accounts about Joseph Smith and Brigham Young, it becomes very clear that the two men, while holding similar ideological backgrounds, had radically different goals. Joseph wanted to build a new faith, a separated people and a new church. On the other hand, Brigham wanted to build

The Turning Point That Changed Everything

a nation, a political power, and a new religious kingdom. To the average adherent to the faith in the early nineteenth century, most, if not all, would have never envisioned what the LDS became in the latter part of the same century. To preserve their self-rule and the land they had wrestled from the native Ute's of the Utah Territory, the Mormons had become the kind of people they had feared and fled in the East. The tormented had become the tormentor. In such cases, the result of this incredible turnaround forever transformed their religion, their families, and their ambitions. This is the way a peripeteia so often develops; The Improbable Degree of Reversal frequently takes those caught in the transition to alter the future and their own character.

I endorse the need for change in our lives, but we would do well to consider what we are becoming and how far this turnaround may take us. Remember the biblical prophet Jeremiah and the words God spoke through him to Israel when they became something He did not want them to be:

> Has a nation ever exchanged their old gods for new ones? (Of course, their gods are not really gods at all). But my people have exchanged their glorious God for idols worth nothing! Skies, be shocked at the things that have happened. Shake with great fear, says the Lord. My people have done two sins. They have turned away from me. And I am the spring of living water. And they have dug their own wells. But they are broken wells that cannot hold water."[173]

Chapter 8

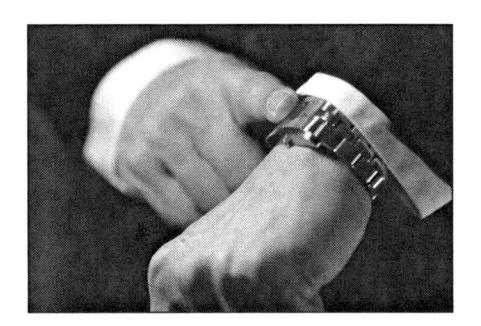

The Tyranny of the Urgent... God's Liberation

Be avaricious of time; do not give any moment without receiving it in value; only allow the hours to go from you with as much regret as you give to your gold; do not allow a single day to pass without increasing the treasure of your knowledge and virtue.
—Nicolas Le Tourneux

Europe was in the early stages of World War II. On June 2, 1939, a thirty-two year old German pastor stepped onto American soil as an internationally known theologian and leading minister of the German resistance. He was met by a high-ranking delegation of American clergyman and educators. Fired from the University of Berlin, banned from public speaking in Germany, Dictrich Bonhoeffer was under constant surveillance by the Gestapo in Germany and by spies in the United States. Christians and non-Christians alike celebrated his

The Turning Point That Changed Everything

escape from certain imprisonment, torture and, most assuredly, execution as an enemy of the Third Reich. Before summer was over, Bonhoeffer did the unthinkable. He got back on another airplane and flew back into Germany to face eventual arrest, incarceration, torture, and eventually death. He made this return with one fact plainly articulated to all his constituency and admirers in a letter to his closest friend Reinhold Niebuhr: "There was a decisive change coming. I have made a mistake in coming to America. . . . Christians in Germany will face the terrible alternative of either willing the defeat of their nation in order that Christian civilization may survive, or willing the victory of their nation and thereby destroying our civilization. I know which of these alternatives I must choose; but I cannot make that choice in security. . . . . Step by step it became clearer to me how far we must go."[174]

Bring up the name of Dietrich Bonhoeffer, and the reaction is varied. Some say he was a double-agent for the United States in World War II, many will call him a Christian martyr, and others will say he was simply a brilliant theologian. But none will call him a coward or an insignificant player in World War II. As you read the writings of Bonhoeffer, one characteristic stands out above all others. He recognized the urgency of time, but lived with a sense of calmness and resolute belief in Jesus Christ. Understanding the nature of God, he served Jesus Christ, who is beyond time and space, the source of all there is in life, and thereby the supreme ruler over every aspect of life. Bonhoeffer lived and wrote in prison with an assurance that even though things were not changing in Germany and the rest of Europe at the pace that he and others desired, it was still moving in the direction and will of God. He believed a man should live with a sense of urgency when it came to the Coming of Christ and to sharing the gospel, yet not live troubled or chaotically without direction because their work seems void of success. To Bonhoeffer, ruthless speed was necessary with the truth while patience was necessary with the grand idea that God wants to accomplish.[175]

Through the years, I've learned to read the Bible as God's personal message to me but also as His plan for all mankind. The agnostic and secular Christian will find this a morbid thought while I find it liberating and intoxicating with a smell of tranquility. As a student who has made a lifetime out of studies in theology and philosophy, the Word of God has come down to a simple formula—it has brought a vital change in me. Twenty years ago, I felt that change must come instantly before too many became discontented and fled the ranks of Christian churches and higher institutions of learning. Now, it has dawned on me that we do not have to live in constant fear of a ticking clock that many have coined as "the tyranny of the urgent."

Chuck Colson described the profound misjudgment this way: "Life's value doesn't depend upon where we are in time; whether we are young, middle-aged, or old. We see life; all of life and all of the time God has created for us, as a gift. The greatest time of our life, then, may occur at any point in our lives. Maybe the most important insight we'll ever have or the greatest contribution we'll ever make is in our dying words or in a youthful experience of learning. Maybe it will come during our productive years or in aging maturity. But the point is we are not restricted. Each moment of life is a gift open to the possibility of eternity, and so what we are now matters for eternity. The gift of time enables us to prepare ourselves for an everlasting relationship with God. This is what gives significance to every one of our actions."[176]

I read this statement in the early part of 2008, soon after the publication of Colson's book. I had been writing some of the original thoughts that would lead to this book and had to make notations about this statement. In essence, we view the dynamic peripeteia based on transitions, some move glacial and others like lightning. More than not, they change the future, and they frequently upset the bravest of participants. But this time equation referred to by Chuck Colson removes the simple factor of whether it is quick and drastic or snail-paced with methodical increments. There is a current advertisement slogan that emphasizes the truth of life itself, "Enjoy the Ride." I am convinced more and more that we do not anticipate, participate, or welcome the transformations made in our lives and institutions. One astounding example emerges in the closing hours of the life of Jesus. We see something that reminds me of a natural wonder I've seen a few times in my life—the dazzling appearance of a rainbow within a rainbow. If you've observed these natural phenomena, you will know of what I write. Being from the upper Midwest in Wisconsin, three or four times I have beheld the remarkable sight of triple rainbows—three rainbows, each slightly smaller within the other, but none less spectacular. This is the way a peripeteia sometimes appears. While one larger peripeteia is slowly making a turnaround effecting history, nations, and future events, there can be a lesser one developing and moving at a faster pace toward the opposite. And, yet still, there can be a smaller peripeteia within that larger one that will happen quicker and instantly secure a transformation in a soli-

The Turning Point That Changed Everything

tary person and their eternity. We witness this kind of change in the Bible where Jesus is being crucified; an event that will reshape monumentally the history of all mankind and all nations. Yet there is a smaller rainbow of change within this larger context.

The Twelve Disciples will be forever transformed by the events unfolding before their eyes. Their families, lives, occupation, character, and perspective will be accelerated on a stage that will move faster than the actions or results purchased for all time by the decisions and sufferings of Jesus. Within that picture, there is capsulated still a smaller and weighty peripeteia. It is the drama recorded in the Gospel according to Luke: "One of the criminals began to shout insults at Jesus: 'Aren't you the Christ? Then save yourself! And save us too!' But the other criminal stopped him. He said, 'You should fear God! You are getting the same punishment as he is. We are punished justly; we should die. But this man has done nothing wrong!' Then this criminal said to Jesus, 'Jesus, remember me when you come into your kingdom!' Then Jesus said to him, 'Listen! What I say is true: Today you will be with me in paradise!'"[177]

Without question, there are times we need the urgent peripeteia to occur. This was the scenario of the dying thief on the cross next to Jesus; he needed immediate change in his life, and Jesus granted his request instantly. As Chuck Colson points out, "Each moment of life is a gift open to the possibility of eternity, and so what we do now matters for eternity."[178] This moment of transformation counted eternally for one man who needed this to happen. On the contrary, many a peripeteia awakens painstakingly at a crawl, almost imperceptible in its infancy, but with the same resolve as the one described by the Gospel of Luke. Sadly, so many characters on the stage miss this unhurried and less pronounced transition. In fact, the greatest and most historic changes often begin with little fanfare and evolve over a span of time that sometimes disenchants those who have awaited it.

Years ago, Timothy George was invited by Prison Fellowship to speak at their annual board retreat where he spoke about time factors and subsequent tensions as they relate to institutions. He referred to how we live in time and how difficult it is for us to deal with this elusive factor. He also expressed how that we are so nostalgic for the past that we often live only in our memories. Even more taxing on our emotions is how swiftly the present disappears. Finally, he also observed that whatever the future may be, nothing could be assured that has not yet happened.

We humans are always trying to measure time from one point to another, and this habit causes us perpetual anxiety here on earth.[179]

How liberating would it be if we could free ourselves from the tyranny of the urgent? I've witnessed a lot of wonderful changes be stolen away by pastors, educators, and administrators pushing change too quickly, too hard, and expecting everyone to adapt as quickly as they perceive they should adjust. This insistence that scurries to make everything happen within a straight line contradicts the very Creator who tells us: "But, beloved, be not ignorant of this one thing, that one day is with the Lord as a thousand years, and a thousand years as one day" (2 Peter 3:8). If we believe this Scripture, and that our lives are not measured by forcing everything into a prescribed period of time, then we are free to allow God to do what He wants whether it takes a day or much more longer.

Our culture thinks of time as moving along a straight line; our clock is ticking off seconds as one day after another drops from the calendar. People are treating time like a product to be consumed. This scenario causes us to see part of our lives as used up; there's another sense where it is being consumed even now; then there's a part we look forward to using in the future. As we take this humanistic approach, it becomes a rat race, and we are pressured to get things done or accomplish it before the opportunity is gone. We are fighting traffic to get to the beach, pushing to get in another camping trip to the mountains before the weather turns cold, or getting another degree or another position that offers more prestige or salary. What's worse, we see the hourglass filling up at the bottom, and we start making nervous jokes about middle age or the "golden years."

Somehow we must see God as Sovereign over all events, situations, and even today's peripeteia. He is the source of all things and over every aspect of our life. Worrying about the start, the characters, the length, or the outcome of the transformation taking place will only produce anxiety and rarely benefit or hasten its eventual results.

Evaluating turnarounds, whether individual or corporate, and witnessing how they veer around to the opposite, exposes how leaders are often destroyed by their insistence on measuring goals and objectives without considering relationships. This entails more than just considering people in the midst of change, but even more the ever-increasing habit of our society to hurry everything along some kind of abbreviated timetable. More than 140 years ago, one of the most far-reaching peripeteia in America's history occurred during what we call the Civil

The Turning Point That Changed Everything

War between the States. While there are several historical changes that resulted from the Civil War, none had the far-reaching effect toward the unity of America than a private meeting held a few days before April 9, 1865. Some may not recognize this date—it was the day that Confederate General Robert E. Lee surrendered at Appomattox to Union General Ulysses S. Grant. This event, along with the surrender of Confederate General Joe Johnston to Union General Bill Sherman and the surrender of two other remaining top generals, culminated the end of the Civil War. But, a few days leading up to these monumental dates, plans and directions were given by President Abraham Lincoln, which would change forever the future of this nation. The President had extensive knowledge of how defeated armies and people had fared under victors of past civil wars in various nations, especially the fresh memory of the French Revolution, which had horrible consequences. He did not want the Confederate States to be punished or rendered puppet states perpetually ruled by the North. Neither did he desire that the captured prisoners or surrendering officers or troops to be shamed unnecessarily. The President felt that letting the Southerners retain their honor would help facilitate healing and bring the nation back together more swiftly.

Meeting with General Grant and General Sherman in the privacy of an unknown location on the last day or two of March 1865, Lincoln gave an executive order to the effect that specifically included: "When this war ends, there must be no bloody work, there must be no hangings . . . there must be none of that."[180] President Lincoln demonstrated an understanding of relationships and always spoke in such meetings of the South as brothers. History does not give him enough credit for thinking forward. He displayed mercy, benevolent peace, and unusual visionary ability under stress. He wanted no guerrilla warfare breaking out afterwards. Grant and Sherman left that private meeting and carried out his orders to every detail and allowed the generals who surrendered a few days later to keep their horses, side arms, and even gave back to them their land. Much of the same courtesy was extended to their officers.[181]

When a leader becomes a slave to time, possessed with a compulsion to squeeze every ounce from the day to force others to meet his goals, he or she can become a tyrant to themselves and to others. President Lincoln realized the danger of haste to make everything happen when, how, and where you want it.

As any avid student of Abraham Lincoln's legacy knows, his life reveals a man of intense personal relationships. He often cherished his relationships so

The Turning Point That Changed Everything

highly that many ambitious politicians and a few generals considered him too soft-bellied for war. Not so! In fact, history records that while hated by the masses in many of the Northern States, as he was in all the South, those around him that ran the war or plotted the course of the nation in that violent era acutely recognized his love of the nation and its leaders (even many who fought against the Union). The private meeting called by the President with Grant and Sherman forever transformed the future of individuals and a nation. But he was making a decision based on prayer and his conscious love of people. To Lincoln, relationships and welfare of people were more paramount than his agenda to defeat the Confederacy.

Even though it would take more time, he eloquently renounced in a speech on April 10, 1865, the policy of anger and rejection that would punish Confederates.[182] It may have been this one meeting with these generals that frames the entire time of this man on the stage of life. Explicably, as earlier quoted from Chuck Colson "the greatest time of our life, then, may occur at any point in our lives. Maybe the most important insight we'll ever have or the greatest contribution we'll ever make is in our dying words. . . ." As always, he was concerned about the nation of the United States above any personal ambition; therefore, he would not be hastened nor prevented in his pursuit for a people who could live together as true brothers. His belief is clearly articulated in his journal and other biographies written about this leader; he honestly confessed that whether he endured or not, the Union had reached a turning point that was more important than his own personage or survival.[183] John Wilkes Booth who had earlier stood in the crowd and listened to the President's speech would assassinate President Lincoln only four days after his passionate words for reconciliation. But in those private meetings with two war generals, only a little more than two weeks before, Lincoln had initiated the most profound peripeteia of all—a recovering nation united by his spirit of reconciliation and forgiveness.

Unquestionably, I have discovered in my mid-life years the amazing truth about time and change. Having come to realize that God exists, outside time or space, He reveals Himself for you and me as the "Eternal Present." Therefore, God's liberation from every circumstance, even the losses of time, acquires a rich new meaning to me. Like the Great Emancipator, I am learning to live in a new manner. You and I must learn to live in what Paul called "the glorious liberty of the children of God" (Romans 8:21). We need not be slaves of the moment.

The Turning Point That Changed Everything

When great turnarounds come, as they so often do in the lives of people and in the history of organizations and nations, we will not surrender to the temptation of the urgent. The success and completion of a peripeteia is not necessarily restricted to timetables or even to the lifetime of one person.

Of course, the timeless Word of God unwraps this understanding to the man or woman that is willing to observe the infinity of God: "I know that, whatsoever God doeth, it shall be forever: nothing can be put to it, nor any thing taken from it: and God doeth it, that men should fear him. That which hath been is now; and that which is to be hath already been; and God requireth that which is past." (Ecclesiastes 3:14, 15). With this prized revelation, I am less tempted to expect everything to change when it is convenient or wanted by me. I have also learned to be more patient as the Lord does something that seems to be returning to the past.

In my introduction to this book, I referred to a resourceful and insightful book called *The Human Side of Change*. Of the many volumes I've read in the last two decades about changes or transitions, none has so succinctly handled this subject with practical wisdom. Using what the author Timothy Galpin termed as a "Change Management Process Model," we are cautioned about the temptation to use one's power or position to manipulate turnarounds. In his nine-piece model, six require individuals or groups to incorporate relational applications. In these six essential areas that facilitate movement and growth, he includes such affirmative attributes as "creativity, team orientation, listening skills, coaching skills, accountability, and appreciativeness."[184] To enhance the return on any reversal within a group or institution, if we are naïve enough to believe it will be simple or quick to fix long-held beliefs and structures, the turning point becomes nothing more than a declaration of war. Someone wins, but everyone loses! Hard changes alter the landscape quickly, but soft changes enhance the success of the long-term positive effects. Galpin sums it up appropriately by saying, "Moreover, unlike equations, managing the soft side of change often does not yield immediate, observable results. Some people learn faster than others. People have varying likes and dislikes and hold diverse beliefs about the way an organization should operate and the way work should get done. All of these human differences must be taken into account and managed during a change initiative . . . organizations can successfully combine the technical and people aspects of change to create a more effective and lasting transformation."[185]

The Turning Point That Changed Everything

While enjoying the examination of the methodologies and dynamics of change, I want to delve deeper into the unexpected and improbability of a peripeteia as it relates to people. If we can reduce the expediency of time and free ourselves from the task-oriented leadership of the past, we may be able to better appreciate the "ride of a lifetime." Those who live through any peripeteia would do well to answer this one question. How many times in life do you get the opportunity to witness and be involved in a major turning point, a complete reversal of circumstances, or to learn something of which you had previously been ignorant? This will beg for a second question. Have you ever been part of a major peripeteia without enjoying the experience as it rotates to the opposite of your past thinking or knowledge? These two questions are legitimate and need to be explored if a person's character is to be influenced or improved.

Recently, my wife and I took a spectacular trip to Ashland, Oregon. Located in the foothills of the beautiful Siskiyou and Cascade mountain ranges near the Rogue Valley, it is the home of the internationally renowned Oregon Shakespeare Festival. It has been named "the best Shakespearean Festival outside London, England." Each year for ten months, this quaint town situated on Ashland Creek (only five miles off Interstate 5) becomes a haven for thousands who come to see the Elizabethan theater and three other venues where world-class Shakespearean plays take on life aided by world-class actors and actresses. Judy and I have loved live stage dramas for many years. The regional churches I serve gave us this wonderful trip as my birthday gift. The lady who coordinates such events and gifts for our family, once again, demonstrated her knowledge of what we enjoy. We decided that one play we would see that weekend would be the infamous drama entitled Othello. I shared briefly in the first chapter the plot of this story and the dramatic peripeteia that transpires in the leading character named Othello. While I've seen other Shakespeare plays over the years and even read Othello on two occasions before viewing it, nothing can prepare you for the climax that unfolds in this masterful tragedy. I left the theater that night sobered by the sight of what I'd been writing about these past months. To watch the disturbing images of the characters unfold as the villain of Othello named Iago weaves his ghastly web of lies and deceit is spellbinding. You want to yell out to Othello and his beautiful wife Desdemona not to be beguiled by Iago, but it's only a play that toys with your emotions.

The Turning Point That Changed Everything

Tragically, art imitates life and Shakespeare knew very well what he penned. Remarkably, the audience begins to realize in the third act the descending mental state of Othello that is leading him swiftly into a negative peripety. As I listened to the deteriorating language and the subtle imagery used by Othello, it was becoming clear that everything was being rushed to its inevitable climax because none of those who could have altered the outcome were willing to take time to test the veracity of Iago's words. His cleverness was deadly. After Othello and Desdemona are dead, the evil plot is discovered but the effects are irreversible. As my wife and I returned to our hotel room, we discussed the script and the unwillingness of other characters to question the occasional tongue-slips from Iago. Why could not the others detect Iago's devilish fantasy and intervene to slow down the action and prevent the evil plot? Alas, I've wondered about this as I've witnessed good and bad peripety unfolding on the stage of life. Whether it's in a church, an institution, or a nation, perhaps like me, you have wanted to yell from behind the curtains for the actors on the stage to take another action instead of the ones they have chosen. Sometimes, this peripeteia is not designed to be a tragedy as Shakespeare made famous. Instead, they have grand promise, but the key players need to move more slowly, skillfully, and with sensitivity to others who are affected by their words and movements.

Jesus Christ was the Master on the stage of life. From the outset of His public ministry, He was under constant pressure by His enemies, His family, and even His closest friends to make or not make changes as others warranted. On the other hand, many often tried to influence Him to alter, slow-down, or speed-up His plans. More than any other actor that had stood on the stage of life, He was constantly scrutinized, criticized, and second-guessed about His desire to fulfill His Father's Will concerning Salvation, the nation of Israel, and the Kingdom of God. Unwavering, unhurried, and unnerved, He set His sights toward bringing about the greatest peripeteia in history. We would do well as pastors and leaders to imitate His resolve. He would fulfill the definition given by Aristotle who appeared on the stage only briefly before our Lord's entrance. Aristotle emphasized "a change by which the action veers around to its opposite, subject always to the rule of probability and necessity."[186] Jesus had purposed to fulfill the will of the Father. While the greatest turnaround in history is continuing to reverse everything man has ever known or experienced, Jesus will not get too excited or intimidated to move the transformation along one day sooner, not even one hour before the action or the words need to be spoken (2 Peter 3:8, 9). Here are His responses to such temptations to accelerate or alter the grandest peripeteia:

Response to Family
- And it came to pass, that after three days they found him in the temple, sitting in the midst of the doctors, both hearing them, and asking them questions. And all that heard him were astonished at his understanding and answers. And when they saw him, they were amazed: and his mother said unto him, "Son, why hast thou thus dealt with us? Behold, thy father and I have sought thee sorrowing." And he said unto them, "How is it that ye sought me? Wist ye not that I must be about my Father's business?' And they understood not the saying which he spake unto them" (Luke 2:46–50).
- And when they wanted wine, the mother of Jesus saith unto him, "They have no wine." Jesus saith unto her, "Woman, what have I to do with thee? Mine hour is not yet come" (John 2:3, 4).
- Then one said unto him, "Behold, thy mother and thy brethren stand without, desiring to speak with thee." But he answered and said unto him that told him, "Who is my mother? And who are my brethren?" And he stretched forth his hand toward his disciples, and said, "Behold my mother and my brethren! For whosoever shall do the will of my Father which is in heaven, the same is my brother, and sister, and mother" (Matthew 12:47–50).

Response to Disciples
- From that time forth began Jesus to show unto his disciples, how that he must go unto Jerusalem, and suffer many things of the elders and chief priests and scribes, and be killed, and be raised again the third day. Then Peter took him, and began to rebuke him, saying, "Be it far from thee, Lord: this shall not be unto thee." But he turned, and said unto Peter, "Get thee behind me, satan: thou art an offence unto me: for thou savourest not the things that be of God, but those that be of men" (Matthew 16:21–23).
- Then said they unto him, "Who art thou?" And Jesus saith unto them, "Even the same that I said unto you from the beginning. I have many things to say and to judge of you: but he that sent me is true; and I speak to the world those things which I have heard of him." They understood not that he spake to them of the Father (John 8:25–27).

- Then Simon Peter having a sword drew it, and smote the high priest's servant, and cut off his right ear. The servant's name was Malchus. Then said Jesus unto Peter, "Put up thy sword into the sheath: the cup which my Father hath given me, shall I not drink it?" (John 18:10, 11).

Response to His Enemies
- And therefore did the Jews persecute Jesus, and sought to slay him, because he had done these things on the Sabbath day. But Jesus answered them, "My Father worketh hitherto, and I work." Therefore the Jews sought the more to kill him, because he not only had broken the Sabbath, but said also that God was his Father, making himself equal with God. Then answered Jesus and said unto them, "Verily, verily, I say unto you, The Son can do nothing of himself, but what he seeth the Father do: for what things so ever he doeth, these also doeth the Son likewise" (John 5:16–19).
- And he said also to the people, "When ye see a cloud rise out of the west, straightway ye say, There cometh a shower; and so it is. And when ye see the south wind blow, ye say, there will be heat; and it cometh to pass. Ye hypocrites, ye can discern the face of the sky and of the earth; but how is it that ye do not discern this time? Yea, and why even of yourselves judge ye not what is right?" (Luke 12:54–56).
- Then said Jesus, "Father, forgive them; for they know not what they do." And they parted his raiment, and cast lots. And the people stood beholding. And the rulers also with them derided him, saying, "He saved others; let him save himself, if he be Christ, the chosen of God." And the soldiers also mocked him, coming to him, and offering him vinegar, and saying, "If thou be the king of the Jews, save thyself." (Luke 23:34–37).

During the last two decades, I have fallen in love more than ever with studying the life and words of Jesus. I say more because in the 1970s, there was one book that influenced me beyond anything I had read previously. Admittedly, even now I can remember the lessons learned from it better than most volumes of material that later came into my library. Authored by A. B. Bruce, *The Training of the Twelve*[187] impacted my heart, my mind, and most certainly my ministry. Writing about the lessons taught to the Twelve Disciples by Jesus, Bruce shows us how the Master was trying to reproduce Himself and multiply His efforts beyond His brief appearance on earth. Let me digress just slightly at this point. I was fortunate that the revised edition came out in 1971; A. C. Armstrong edited even this from the prior edition of 1894. Originally, the author's full name was Alexander Balmain Bruce. He was a Scottish clergyman and theologian who wrote this collection of studies and called them, *Passages Out of the Gospels Exhibiting the Twelve Disciples of Jesus under Discipline for the Apostleship*. Well, I am glad that later reproductions shortened the title. Since I am also of Scottish descent from near Edinburgh as Bruce, there is a certain amount of delight in his contribution to understanding the journey of Jesus Christ. Coming back to the point of relevance, the one overwhelming passion of Jesus was to impart His example and life to these twelve ordinary men. But the Christ was not about to let the urgency of other distractions or peripheral agendas move Him from helping those Twelve prepare to handle the greatest peripeteia in the universe. To help keep them focused and trained on this reversal of history, we are given two examples that disclose His resoluteness not to be hurried or delayed in this turnaround:

1. And the apostles gathered themselves together unto Jesus, and told him all things, both what they had done, and what they had taught. And he said unto them, *"Come ye yourselves apart into a desert place*, and rest a while:" for there were many coming and going and they had no leisure so much as to eat. And they departed into a desert place by ship privately (Mark 6:30–32, italics added for emphasis).
2. And *Jesus going up to Jerusalem took the twelve disciples apart in the way*, and said unto them, "Behold, we go up to Jerusalem; and the Son of man shall be betrayed unto the chief priests and unto the scribes, and they shall condemn him to death, and shall deliver him to the Gentiles to mock, and to scourge, and to crucify him: and the third day he shall rise again." (Matthew 20:17–19, italics added for emphasis).

The model of Jesus is irrefutable evidence that we must resist the "tyranny of the urgent" that cries out from every quarter to manipulate what is often a providential transition. Certainly, some changes are divinely ordained. The urge to control the direction, size, and scope of a peripeteia is enticing, but it is filled with pitfalls. In the mid 1990s, there was another more contemporary writer who caught the desire to understand Jesus and His life. He had witnessed how churches and parachurch organizations had become obsessed with their programs and organizations while neglecting the most profound transition in modern Christianity.

The Latino, African, and former Soviet Union nations were experiencing Jesus in ways the Western nations were not. Philip Yancey wrote his intriguing small book named *The Jesus I Never Knew* with a desire to help people come to a new perspective on His life, His work, and His purpose. In the midst of his writings, Yancey contributes to our understanding of Jesus and the peripeteia that the Sovereign Father had initiated: "The temptation in the desert reveals a profound difference between God's power and Satan's power. Satan has the power to coerce, to dazzle, to tempt, to destroy and kill. Humans have learned much from that power, and governments draw deeply from its reservoir. Satan's power is external and coercive. God's power, in contrast, is internal and non-coercive. 'You would not enslave man by a miracle, and craved faith given freely, not based on miracle.' In its commitment to transform gently from the inside out and in its relentless dependence on human choice, God's power may resemble a kind of abdication. As every parent and every lover knows, love can be rendered powerless if the beloved chooses to spurn it. . . . God made himself weak for one purpose: to let human beings choose freely for themselves what to do with him."[188] Hopefully, we can learn from Jesus' heart and His pattern of dealing with pivotal events.

I believe that change can be managed if done timely and with an honest heart to consider people, but reality has shown that someone in a powerful position or an invested interest group can interfere with what was intended to be a true providential intervention in the past. Some will subtly attempt control of a reversal of circumstances to twist things in their desired direction. In contrast, there will be those who see no danger in remaining unchanged and glued to the past, regardless of the real catastrophe awaiting those who fail to recognize such shortsighted trappings. Nearly sixteen years ago, a visionary leader arose within the ranks of my church affiliation. I wrote briefly of this great man in Chapter 2. Bishop Billy Murray was a man who understood the necessity of transformation. But he was also cognizant that as our Pentecostal organization embarked on new waters that we had to be mindful not to return to the same mistakes that had ground our church to halt before. We were believers entrenched more in celebrations, traditional methodologies and doctrines, and arrogant exclusivity. In Bishop Murray's address to the leadership and membership of the Church of God of Prophecy in the General Assembly of 1992, he would speak these words: ". . . we must recognize and acknowledge that this is truly a work of the Spirit, a work which human strategies can never accomplish. Some of our plans and projections of the past, we are now able to see were evidently of our own thinking, rather than being the product of Holy Ghost direction—not all, but some. Misguided zeal without knowledge can take us away from the course that God's will dictates. Now, we are having to determine where we have followed God and where human wisdom may have been accepted as being divine."[189] Even as he spoke those words, anyone present (as I was) should have grasped not only his remorse of the past, but his caution about what needed to be adjusted and how those essential changes would be made. In retrospect, too many changes were made too quickly and much was lost in the transition that followed. This is not a condemnation or justification of Bishop Murray or anyone involved, for I also was part of those reversals.

Leaders in every spectrum of life must learn to a greater extent from such transformations. There are just as many snares in resisting changes as there are in rushing changes. Again, discernment and balance must be wedded to such turnarounds. While breezing one afternoon through an old "Turning to the Harvest" manual that was published in 1994, I came across an interesting analogy used by the editors. Its purpose was to guide pastors and churches in their great turnaround to becoming churches that harvested people again. This illustration referred to Leith Anderson, who tells of setting on an airplane next to a man who was reading an aeronautics magazine. Leith looked over his shoulder long enough to see a picture of a Boeing 777 and read the article headline: "Boeing Risks the Company—Again." Politeness and inadequate eyesight kept him from reading the rest of the article, but he could ascertain what it was saying. Boeing had moved commercial aviation from propeller aircraft to jets by introducing the Boeing 707 in 1958. It was a big risk that could have destroyed the company, but it didn't. Boeing risked itself again in 1970 with its Boeing 747, and the age of wide-bodied jet aircrafts was born. He realized that it must have been hard for the successful corporation to gamble stability and profitability with such a new venture. The risk taking by no means ended. Boeing Corporation would not be satisfied with yesterday's progress, and then they produced the 777 model. Another winner![190]

So, how do we balance the screaming urgency for change with sensitivity for people's abilities to make rapid transition and with discernment to move forward with a visionary plan? Reaching a turning point as an organization is even more daunting than making changes as an individual. The dynamics involved require groups to be more than static institutions. Frankly, if a group or even a corporation is not numerically growing there can be no measurable progress. Many years ago, I heard a radio interview with the late founder of Wal-Mart. He made a statement I shall never forget: "I never worry about how many stores we have or how much debt we have as a corporation. Instead, I am always focused on how many stores we are opening and how much revenue we have coming in each day." During his days as the CEO of Wal-Mart, Sam Walton instilled within his management and employees a relational approach to customers that endeared him not only to his sales associates, but to the strongest customer base in modern times. His philosophy was a splendid example of retailing success. Even more, it is a great illustration of how a group or organization can achieve success by establishing a dynamic relationship with its members, yet be innovative in crossing past boundaries or methods previously considered sacred to sound business principles. Such corporations like Microsoft, Nike, Boeing, and Wal-Mart have proved that finding the right balance between transitions and their employees were necessary to future advances.

In churches, schools, and governments, this balance or discernment has lacked the same success. Curious! You would expect "spiritual" organizations to excel in this area. Thankfully, there are those individuals and groups that are finding ways to transition their ministry for the global changes taking place in all cultures. I was reading one day a captivating article about Irish gospel singer Moya Brennan. She and her husband Tim Jarvis have had incredible influence and results from their ministry in Northern Ireland. Having suffered sectarian violence for more than thirty years, Northern Ireland seemed unchangeable from its endless cycle of hatred and violence. You could credit her influence on mystical Celtic music and her Irish heritage. But even this would not be the source of her unifying ministry. Others credit her vibrant Christian message and a heart of worship as her true contribution. But she told writer Clive Price that it was more than just revival rhetoric and singing concerts. She became a Goodwill Ambassador for the Christian Blind Mission and added her voice and musical skills to help composer Hans Zimmer on the film *King Arthur*. She has also offered her voice and music to the highly acclaimed motion-picture series called *The Chronicles of Narnia*. Everywhere she goes she lives out the faith by making her Christian walk more action than words. Building relationships with political and social leaders has allowed her to be a welcome friend and emissary of reconciliation in Europe and

The Turning Point That Changed Everything

Africa, as well as transforming her own nation where Catholics and Protestants now come to hear her voice and music in a melodious harmony.[191]

Moya Brennan is just one model of God's liberation from the tyranny of the urgent. She confesses, "God works in the most amazing ways. . . . It's really good to be involved. We encourage people to leave their Catholicism and Protestantism outside and come in to participate and inquire. There is a political process that is what you see on your TV screens every day, and there's a peace process, which is what's going on in everyday life—people building bridges and changing attitudes. The two sometimes run together, sometimes run on parallel lines, and sometimes don't go at the same pace. So long as we're going forward, we'll be OK."[192] Moya has a point to her mission and life. Throughout this splendid article, she illuminates the truth that gigantic and awesome turnarounds require patience and persistence. She has spiritually discerned the tide is turning, but she knows that the passing sunset is part of that transforming grandeur. Too many of us leaders get in such a hurry to get to our goals that we miss these sublime moments.

Last February, my wife and I were sitting on a beach in the Grand Cayman Island enjoying one of those earthly splendors of sunset on the ocean. I had been there on business for four days, and we were allowed to take just one day to enjoy our spectacular surroundings. Conflicting appointments and finances erased the opportunity for more relaxation. We watched for three hours as the sun slowly made its graceful movement to the western horizon. When I first sat down on a beach chair next to Judy, all I could think about was upcoming dates in my appointment book. After a few minutes, my wife invited me into those turquoise and light blue waters for a swim. As we floated around in those gentle waves, I forgot about time and work. Like Moya, I am learning that turnarounds and progress go slower than we often wish or pray for. But you and I must learn to discriminate between the urgent and the seasonal transitions.

Later, when we were on a flight the next day from Georgetown to Portland, I reflected on those Caribbean moments under the blue sky as essential to helping me to keep a better perspective on not only where I am going, but why and how I am going there. Instead of taking the nonstop elevator swiftly to the Penthouse, leaders should take the regular elevator with all its interruptions to pick up and allow other passengers who may contribute enjoyment to the journey. Could it be that someone who comes into our life from one of those pesky and frequent stops is the person we need to observe, hear, speak to, and befriend along the journey?

I have now assessed that we worship the ascension too much while ignoring or hurting the very people who make the crossing memorable and meaningful.

At this juncture, let me step aside to explore some annotations that have been made about growing congregations, successful parachurch organizations, and innovative schools or denominational churches. Without exception, they have a common ingredient that serves as a catalyst for healthy transitions. In referencing these healthy components, we perceive characteristics that produce ongoing essential transformations. Here are twelve distinctive observations:

1. They rarely give a high priority to institutional survival goals.
2. They are exceptionally open to new ideas and innovation.
3. They provide a high level of tolerance for and occasionally even affirm the maverick personality.
4. They usually respond enthusiastically to big challenges.
5. They welcome and enjoy surprises.
6. They display a strong and positive future orientation.
7. They support leaders who often color outside the lines.
8. They are comfortable with discontinuity with the past; the lines.
9. They display an above average sensitivity to needs of outsiders; they are able to offer meaningful responses to those needs.
10. They are as comfortable with the new as with the traditional.
11. They are able to give serious consideration to proposals for change without being threatened or feeling their past performance is being challenged.
12. They tend to be able to attract and keep paid staff members who are at or above the average level of professional competence.[193]

I have cited only one source for a list of common components found in groups that have properly discerned how to adapt and utilize change. There are many other superb pastoral and educational groups that have implemented similar principles worth your study. While all of the above key ingredients may not be present, we should expect that there would be a majority of them already existing and others beginning to develop within the organization. Granted, I have not written this book with the expectation that this would be a manual on organizational growth or change, yet it would be impossible to completely ignore some of these valuable principles.

Confronting the failure to be conscious and proactive in dealing with what has happened in the past half of the twentieth century, churches and other organizations have been flatly swamped by the changes in Western Culture. Many of these transformations have made radical inroads into Christianity. To say the least, it is embarrassing to witness in churches and parachurch groups the lackadaisical manner in which we have adjusted to these transitional decades. I am in a position of leadership that must rely on pastors to take more initiative, yet I quake in my own ability or influence to get these leaders to stop taking the easy road and hoping they can survive as their church's future "goes to hell in a hand basket." If you're offended by the phrase, you should be more enraged by the steady decline of attention to these deteriorating conditions in most local churches. How will we face the present crisis where a humongous peripeteia was ignored or slightly dealt with? Even more, how will we deal with the inevitable peripeteia that will face all of us in the next decade? Pay close heed to the warning issued in 2001 by the director of the Barna Research Group, a market research company that deals primarily with religion in America:

> God does not expect us to enter the spiritual battle on His behalf without adequate strategic intelligence or reasonable knowledge about what's coming; He wants us to be ready for the challenges we will face. In fact, if the role of the church is to influence all dimensions of culture rather than to be shaped by the culture, then we must be alert and assertive in representing God to the best of our ability in the world. That means serving Him with excellence, but we cannot achieve excellence without appropriate preparation. . . . Keep in mind that we are not asking you to like what seems about to unfold in our lives, but to understand it and deal with it. You have two options: 1) play the victim—someone who is bulldozed by the inexorable march of progress and change; 2) or to be an innovator—someone who helps to shape his/her reality and make the most of the possibilities that emerge. Your choice of which role to play will influence both your joy in life and your value to the kingdom."[194]

I am convinced empirically that we cannot enjoy or reap the full benefits of most peripeteias until we are also liberated by God from the pressure to force transitions. This does not imply that changes must be drug out for years for fear of others who want to keep the same old methods and ways. Quite the opposite because freeing yourself from the urgent also means not permitting present opposition or support to unduly influence the course of the turnaround. Any leader or administrator can reach the place of God's liberation. What is this kind of liberation? It is a calming confidence that you are moving in the right direction regardless of the opposition, distractions, and doubts of those around you. This presence of assurance can inspire a pastor, educator, and even a leadership team. We are in dire need today for "Leaders of Leaders" who can rise above criticism and pressure to operate undistracted in a cocoon spun by their confidence in the vision that God has bestowed upon them.

Again, I emphasize that "the tyranny of the urgent" can arise from both those with you in a turnaround or those against the reversal of circumstances. Slavery to the bully pushers or to the feet draggers will ensnare you in bondage. Conversely, real liberation comes when you follow your vision without becoming entrapped by time, which cries out for an urgent response. In the Bible, there is this recognition of those perceptive enough to read the times and respond in an appropriate fashion. This group was called the "sons of Issachar." They are accredited in King David's reign as wise men—men who "had understanding of the times, to know what Israel ought to do; the heads of them were two hundred; and all their brethren were at their commandment" (1 Chronicles 12:32).

In one of the most performed plays in American theater, *Our Town*, written by Thornton Wilder,[195] the audience is able to observe both the correlation of time and a peripeteia. For any reader not having seen or read this sentimental drama, it is a brutal and honest view of humanity. Basically, the story is about George Gibbs and Emily Webb who grow up as children in Grover's Corner. It is in simple terms a drama about growing from fun-loving dreamers into indifferent citizens, falling in and out of love, losing friends and family to death, and watching people find and lose things. But as you view it in a live production or take time to read its storyline, you find that it offers rich insights into life itself. It presses you to see life in its most common occurrences, to appreciate each moment and relationship, to be mindful of the painful consequences of conformity and confining people to boxes. Finally, it celebrates the three interludes of life, love, and death. Containing three acts, the stage manager is in the key role as he helps lay out the story through narration and occasional appearances in the play itself. Indeed, it is a classic irony as anyone who loves theater could appreciate.

The Turning Point That Changed Everything

The drama begins in Act I with two central characters. George and Emily are children who spend endless hours playing together and attending their community Congregational Church. From the beginning, it is obvious that Emily will have great influence over the future of George. The entire first act is short but stereotypical of the "American Family."[196]

In Act Two, love and marriage becomes the focus of the play. George and Emily announce their intentions to wed. Emily's father, Mr. Webb, meets with George and gives him some strange advice to treat his daughter like property and never respect her needs. He then encourages him to do the opposite of his advice; he had learned this from his wife's father and had been happy ever since. The influence and pressure of family is examined. But there is something wrong with their relationship that has hung over the scenes from their adolescence. Emily must help George with his schoolwork, and there emerges a codependency that forebodes trouble ahead. The most drastic thing in this part of the play is that both George and Emily talk to their parents since they have doubts about their relationship that depends heavily on the strength and thinking of Emily. Fittingly, George tells his mother he is not ready for marriage, but she convinces him that this is just nerves. Emily also tells her father of her anxiety about marriage, but he assures her this feeling will pass by very quickly. Inexplicably, after several minutes of dialogue that awakens the audience to the apparent tension in their relationship, the decision to go ahead with the wedding represents a major peripeteia. The "die is cast" for a troublesome future, etched into their nuptials, and the action here will drift into a life of misery soon after the wedding. The scene moves to the church as they regain their composure and happiness as they stand before the preacher to swear their vows. It is raining on the day of their marriage, and this is an ominous sign of what is to come.[197]

In Act III, the opening shows a graveyard on top of a hill. Emily has died in childbirth. This is the most compelling and mysterious Act of the play—the dead people set around in their graves and talk about the living. Emily is granted by them an opportunity to view one day in her life that is past, but she is advised to choose an insignificant day. Ignoring them, she chooses her twelfth birthday and it turns out to be a disappointing decision. It starts out with joyful feelings but spirals into misery and tears when she realizes how life passes by too quickly. Interestingly, it is the lines repeated by the dead in their conversations with her that remind us that changes in life come all too quickly, and we do not take time

The Turning Point That Changed Everything

to think about what we are doing, where we are going, and what we want to be. Even so, it is Emily's words that bring the climatic end: "We don't even have time to look at one another? Doesn't anyone ever realize life while they live it? My, wasn't life awful—and wonderful! Why don't the living understand and treasure each minute by minute? Maybe saints and poets understand some."[198]

A turning point in life comes around like the planet Pluto, rarely and sometimes unheralded—perhaps, because we have become familiar with the constancy and glow of the planet Venus. Created as beautiful vessels to travel through time and space, we seldom realize that it would be so liberating if we could only see the life and opportunity in every moment or event. I am learning to appreciate the reversal of circumstances and to make those changes with less timidity and urgency, wisely to take pleasure in an unexpected opportunity to do differently. Realize the weather vane is shifting. Turn your face to catch the gentle and fleeting breeze. Any peripeteia appears very daunting, but we should welcome them as a relieving sigh that makes the body relax and the mind to be refreshed.

Chapter 9

The Arrival of Anagnorisis

It is with nations as with individuals, those who know the least of others think the highest of themselves; for the whole family of pride and ignorance are incestuous, and mutually beget each other.
—Caleb Colton

Jonas Salk's parents came to the United States from Russia as Jewish immigrants at the beginning of the 1900s. Encouraging their children to get a higher education, their eldest son Jonas started as a law student at the City College of New York. His interest though quickly turned to medical science. He later graduated from the University of New York Medical School. While attending medical school, he was given the opportunity to work on the influenza virus that had swept the United States and other nations. His work with the influenza virus and other viruses that caused the flu had only recently been discovered, and the young Salk was eager to learn if the virus could be deprived of its ability to infect while

The Turning Point That Changed Everything

still giving immunity to the illness. Salk succeeded and was heralded in this attempt. But the best was yet to come. The polio epidemic struck before WWII, and it remained a great mystery for almost two decades. Out of his research on flu viruses, Dr. Salk completed his medical degree and also discovered the key components that he used for his later work on polio.[199]

In 1947, Salk accepted an appointment to the University of Pittsburgh Medical School. While working there with the National Foundation for Infantile Paralysis, Dr. Salk saw an opportunity to develop a vaccine against polio, and devoted himself to this work for the next eight years. In 1955, Salk's years of research paid off. He discovered through human trials of the vaccine that it effectively protected the subject from the polio virus. When news of the discovery was made public on April 12, 1955, Salk was hailed as a miracle worker. He further endeared himself to the public by refusing to patent the vaccine so it could be massed produced inexpensively and without laborious red tape. Dr. Salk had no desire to profit personally from the discovery, but merely wished to see the vaccine turn around the devastating effects on children and young people. Salk's vaccine was composed of a "killed" polio virus, which retained the ability to immunize without running the risk of infecting the patient. Salk became world-famous overnight, but his discovery was the result of many years of painstaking experimentation and happenstance (by his own admission). Even until his death in 1996, he continued to pursue a new vaccine to defeat the dreaded HIV epidemic.[200]

More than twenty-two hundred years before Jonas Salk was born in New York of immigrant parents, Aristotle describes this breakthrough that leads to a peripeteia. He labeled the event or breakthrough as a special cause that leads to a reversal of circumstances. He coined this definitive turning point as an anagnorisis or discovery. In fact, Aristotle considered it the greatest change of them all and postulated that it required both intellect and logic. In some rare cases, something divine could infuse the person and bring about life-changing drama.[201] At this point, I want to invite you into a personal chapter of this book. It doesn't deal with churches, institutions, or corporations although they could be peripherally affected by the influence of an anagnorisis. This change occurs in an individual and becomes intensely personal and life altering. As you read this chapter, have the courage to resist applying it to any group or organization. You are embarking on a personal journey to understand yourself and to face a world that is perhaps beyond your present knowledge or empirical reasoning. Without any fear of contradiction, only God understands or foresees the significance of this transformation.

Anagnorisis has been defined in both literary and philosophical circles as the following: "When a character learns something he had been previously ignorant of, this is normally distinguished from peripeteia as the actual discovery. Aristotle himself regarded anagnorisis as the mark of a superior drama."[202] Based on Aristotle's definition, *peripeteia* is "the dramatic change or transition" while *anagnorisis* is "the discovery that initiates or leads to the reversal of circumstances." It is obvious that this kind of discovery is understood and referred to in the New Testament Scriptures that were being composed only three hundred years after Aristotle's introduction of this term. Indulge a slight delineation to explore some of these expressions.

Several derivative Greek words have their origin in the Greek term γινώσκω (*Ginosko*), whose primary meaning is "to come to know, taking in knowledge, to recognize or understand completely; it frequently means to know in the sense of realizing something not previously understood completely."[203] While there is a unique Greek word αναγνωρίζίς (*anagnorisis*) that "refers to this discovery," the specific term does not appear in the Bible. Yet there are several key passages in the Greek New Testament that use similar terms, yet they still point to this kind of discovery. One such reference is found in Luke 24:31 when two disciples on the way to Emmaus realized that their traveling companion was really Jesus. In this case, the Greek term ἐπιγινώσκω (*epiginosko*) is defined in lexicons as 1) "to become thoroughly acquainted with, to know thoroughly"; 2) "to recognize, by signs, hearing, or revelation; to perceive who a person is, to know, find out, or to understand."[204]

We see the transforming illustration of this in two powerful passages of the New Testament. Luke 2:15–17 reveals this kind of remarkable understanding: "And it came to pass, as the angels were gone away from them into heaven, the shepherds said one to another, Let us now go even unto Bethlehem, and see this thing which is come to pass, *which the Lord hath made known unto us*. And they came with haste, and found Mary, and Joseph, and the babe lying in a manger. And when they had seen it, *they made known abroad* the saying which was told them concerning this child" (italics added). There is a similar discovery in John 15:15 where the author records the words of Jesus: "Henceforth I call you not servants; for the servant knoweth not what his lord doeth: but I have called you friends; for all things that I have heard of my Father *I have made known unto you*" (italics added). The inference is clear in both passages that there is a true anagnorisis taking place, first in the lowly shepherds and later with the ignorant disciples that will revolutionize forever what they had known. Even more, that which is being learned is beyond just simple human cognitive reasoning, empirical observation, or academic pursuit. It is a remarkable life-changing revelation or radical experience that ushers one forward into new horizons of knowledge and understanding.

I wince slightly because I fear some may read the above and simply want to debate subjects like revelation or Greek lexicons. Read on and allow yourself a spiritual oasis to consider something remarkably different from your past experiences or understanding. There comes a point in time when every person's life and thinking must move from the known or the understood into a discovery that will require unearthing truths they had not perceived before. Call it revelation, call it conversion, call it a vision, you can even call it anagnorisis; but there comes a summit in your journey when reaching the maturity or completeness that life can give you will demand more than what you have understood, presently know, or what you have striven in the past to achieve. So, if you're a pastor, educator, administrator, or serve in another leadership position, I challenge you to take off the mantel for a while and realize one critical relational verse from the Bible. "But as it is written: 'Eye has not seen, nor ear heard, nor have entered into the heart of man, the things which God has prepared for those who love Him.' But God hath revealed them unto us by his Spirit: for the Spirit searcheth all things, yea, the deep things of God" (1 Corinthians 2:9, 10).

Before we speak more intimately about this amazing anagnorisis or personal transformation in your life, let me share with you the amazing story of Aimee. Born in Canada and raised in the Salvation Army, Aimee was converted to Jesus Christ at the age of eighteen. She was "born again" in a storefront meeting being held by the evangelist Robert Semple. She engaged herself completely in this Pentecostal, oriented faith and became a minister in the Full Gospel Assembly. She later married Robert Semple and traveled with him to China on an extended mission trip. While abroad, her husband fell gravely ill and passed away. By her own admission, something happened to Aimee through this heartrending event, a discovery of her true relationship to Christ and an awakening of His Great Commission on her life. She returned to the United States with an evangelistic zeal that even caught the attention of the media in America. Making nine transcontinental preaching campaigns that included hundreds of meetings, she became one of the most renowned Christian speakers for the next two decades. She would lay the foundation for the International Church of the Foursquare Gospel and their four tenets of the life and work of Jesus (Savior, Baptizer, Healer, and Returning King). By the time of her death in 1944, Aimee Semple McPherson was considered one of the greatest evangelists in America.[205]

In her remarkable autobiography, Sister Aimee shares her dramatic conversion and, even more, the discovery that led her to become so addicted with evangelistic fervor. She talks about how God revealed to her the knowledge of sin, the understanding of the Holy Spirit, and the conviction that she must take the gospel of Christ to the world. As you read her extensive testimony, you realize that she had passed through an anagnorisis that would change her immediately and turn her life around in the years to follow.[206] Yet Aimee is not alone. As you read the history of people who have shaped both secular and religious history, there is frequently an anagnorisis that reroutes their life and intensely leads them into a life-altering decision. Such discoveries shake them to the core and become a revelatory experience. They can no longer remain the same person, nor even live as they once lived. Aimee's experience may be accredited to spiritual conversion or divine empowerment, some critics might even add "psychological delusion," but no one can deny that she discovered something that extremely increased her level of enthusiasm and effectiveness in the lives of thousands of people.

In 1994, I was settling in very comfortably in the church I pastored in Phoenix, Arizona. After the normal "honeymoon" experienced by many pastors in the first couple of years of a new pastorate, I was excited about where God was taking our growing church. Then it came out of nowhere. While reading a new book by an author I liked very much named Gordon MacDonald, there appeared a Chapter that I was not expecting. The chapter was entitled, "What kind of old man do you want to be?" Those words were like a clarion call, awakening a warrior within me. Rereading some of the pages was required; prayer and meditation gripped my heart like a surgeon's clamp. Yet it was not the book that changed me; it was the conviction of the Holy Spirit on my heart. Kneeling in my office to pray, the question haunted me and stirred unrest within me. These were the words that resonated through my mind and heart: ". . . the senior years are not commonly considered to be the most attractive ones for most people. If my observations

The Turning Point That Changed Everything

are correct, I shouldn't expect to be invited out to a lot of ball games by younger people when I'm old. That unpleasant possibility bothered me. Because I realized that, barring a premature life-ending event, I would be joining the ranks of the old in the not-so-distant future, and younger men would be saying the same thing about men of my generation. I just might be included in their comments. But men like Abraham, Moses, Joshua, and Paul would be exceptions . . . one gets the feeling that they would have been good men to know. And one also has the perception that their last years were among their best."[207] I lay on the floor in the office praying and asking God to help me be one of those exceptions. Something began to happen that impacted me.

That event in my pastor's office that day was an anagnorisis for me. I had made this discovery that challenged me to get up and examine my attitude, my treatment of others, and the way I would live out my life. It was not like my life had been lived cheaply or carelessly, but there was room to improve. Indeed, all I could do was repent and ask God to forgive me for not understanding earlier my mortality and weakness. I wanted to be a person others enjoyed being around—a Christian of the highest character and a minister doing his very best work for God even near the end. Such times in prayer often bring deep conversations with God, but this was one of those times when groaning and weeping seemed the only way to communicate feelings to the Father (Romans 8:26).

During the next few months, the realization of my humanity and impending future were never very far from me. As the months slipped by, the force of what I had been previously ignorant of or oblivious to was causing me to realign many priorities. Then, the unexpected event occurred that brought my anagnorisis into sharper focus. At approximately 1:00 a.m. on Thursday, November 16, 1995, my sister-in-law Helen called to tell me that my brother Felton Pratt had passed away while sleeping. His heart had been failing from a lifetime struggle with juvenile diabetes that had finally taken its heavy toll. I drove as quickly and safely as I could from Phoenix to Tucson. Had God been preparing me for this event? My childhood hero was dead at only 48 years old. He too had been a minister of the gospel and had pastored for 28 years. Wondrous is the only word to describe God's thoughts and plans for us! "For I know the thoughts that I think toward you, says the Lord, thoughts of peace and not of evil, to give you a future and a hope. Then you will call upon me and go and pray to me, and I will listen to you. And you will seek me and find me, when you search for me with all your heart."[208]

The Turning Point That Changed Everything

In the weeks and months that followed, I would ask God to help me to live as brave and faithful as my brother had lived. The Lord would take me back to my anagnorisis a year before, and He would remind me of His revelation to me. That book by Gordon MacDonald had steadied me and gave me resolve. He wrote about Caleb who at the age of 85 had the rare qualities that only a few old men have these days:

- Whatever he had done, he had done it wholeheartedly, nothing held back.
- He was always a man who had strong convictions and lived by them.
- He was a man who continued to love challenges and preferred the toughest of them all.
- He was a man who had unlimited faith that the God of his youth was the God of his old age.
- He refused to live in yesterday's victories, but sought out new ones.
- If others were fearful, he wasn't: if you will stand back, he will swing into motion.[209]

During the last fifteen years, the Lord has reiterated to me the call of passion and excellence, faith and courage, thankfulness and virtue, but most of all, He whispers to me that cruise control is an unacceptable way of living as an old man in my future years. Whether you speak about Dr. Salk or Aimee, they each came through a remarkable discovery (anagnorisis) that would begin a life-changing turnaround (peripeteia). If there is one thing that you learn from reading the journals of legendary and noble men and women, it would be that you usually take note of something that happens to "jump start" the process or the dramatic reversal of circumstances in their life. I've read the journals of John Wesley, D. L. Moody, Charles Finney, A. J. Tomlinson, and Dietrich Bonhoeffer; they all demonstrate this rare commonality.

Years ago while pastoring in a small town in the bayous of southern Louisiana, I had a dear sister who attended church with her grandchildren. It was obvious she had a very hard life. While her Cajun husband was a good provider, he was also an alcoholic, heavy smoker, and was addicted to filthy language. To protect his family, I will simply call him Louie. He and his brother had a notorious reputation of violent behavior, which ended in tragedy for many who encountered them. Louie hated game wardens, churches, Christians, and most of all, preachers.

The Turning Point That Changed Everything

Every time I came to his house, he left out the back door or made a point to intentionally badger me to have a beer. This frustrating and awkward relationship lasted for months.

Realizing that I now knew his reputation and belligerent attitude, he intentionally baited me one day to go down the bayou with him and his brother to trap and kill alligators. Then, it occurred to me that as frightful as this invitation was, it might be my only opportunity to become his friend. Well, I survived that day with Louie and his brother although seeing a live twelve-foot alligator come into your boat was not one of my fondest memories. Frankly, I was scared to death that entire long, mosquito-infested, hot and humid day. They laughed at me, they mocked me, and they taunted me. When I got home, I never wanted to be around those dangerous and ungodly men again.

Two weeks later, Louie called me again and asks me to go deer hunting with him and a bunch of his sordid relatives. Now, I confess right up front that I'm no hunter or fisherman. Before I knew what I was doing, I had accepted. What was I thinking? Scared and reluctant, I went with them hunting deer with dogs and boats flying at high speed. Talking about a preacher who felt like a "fish out of water!" As the weeks rolled into months, we crawled for shrimp, hunted, fished, boated, trapped, and shelled a lot of crayfish. None of which are my favorite activities. Then one day while we were rabbit hunting (which became an enjoyable sport), we were sitting on the side of his boat eating and talking. Before I knew it, my mouth opened, and the words escaped quickly, "Louie, would you go with me to a men's retreat up north?" He looked at me blistering hard and said, "Preacher, expletive, don't go there!" His eyes frightened me. But it was done, and God was helping me. I responded, "Louie, haven't I always gone wherever you invited me to go?" Now, he simply looked at the bottom of the boat. This emboldened my attempt. "Louie, you're not afraid, are you?" That shot into his male ego. ""No, expletive you! I'm not expletive afraid of anywhere you would go." My confidence was rising, and I said, "It's next Friday, and I will come pick you up at 4:00 p.m." He stared in bewilderment and slowly mumbled, "OK!" Needless to say, I wasn't sure that even those Cajun Christians were ready for Louie.

I picked Louie up the next Friday, and we drove to the campsite in Northern Louisiana where the men's retreat was being held. He was very quiet and pouting the whole three hours to the camp. Thankfully, the men there were Cajuns, and he liked how they talked about hunting, fishing, and LSU football. On the way home

The Turning Point That Changed Everything

two days later, he was no longer quiet. He talked constantly, asking questions and listening intently to my answers. I was driving, but when I got home, I could not remember driving any of those snake-like roads that crawled along those bayous. The last ninety miles along those twisting roads was a total blur. The anointing came over me as I shared about my friend Jesus and what a difference he had made in my life. Before long, Louie was quietly crying. Before we pulled in his driveway, he was asking Jesus to come into his fifty-two year old heart. Story ended?

No, that last hour on that treacherous road had brought an anagnorisis. An extraordinary discovery had been made during those sixty minutes. Louie had learned something he had previously been ignorant of; it had impacted his life to interrupt everything he once knew or understood. The peripeteia that followed was unbelievable in human terms. The next day, his wife told me that Louie got up very early and crept out of the house before dawn. She thought he had gone hunting or fishing as usual, but he had not. When he came home, he was dressed in his one suit reserved for funerals. He asked her if she and the grandchildren (who lived with them) were going to church. She was shocked; even more as they hurried around the house preparing for church, she discovered that his tobacco, beer and liquor, as well as his dirty magazines were all gone. They came to church that morning to the amazement of everyone. It was Louie's first time ever in a church service. By the next week, she realized that he was catching his bad words and asking forgiveness when he swore. Within two weeks, the swearing and profanity had stopped. But the turn for the opposite went even further. Within a month, word was spreading along the bayous and within his portside town. Louie was changing and transforming quickly. He was down making restitution to game wardens, returning stolen items, and witnessing to his evil brother who tried now to avoid him. Even the mayor of the town praised his reversal. Louie became the most generous and kindhearted man I've ever been around in my lifetime. His wife told me over and over, "it was better than their honeymoon; it was like living with a resurrected man."

If crisis describes an event we cannot control, and if wonderment is a word attached to an event we cannot explain, anagnorisis is an event that opens the way for us to experience a lifetime turnaround. As I write this chapter, there is an upheaval on Wall Street and in the mortgage broker business of America. Businesses are filing bankruptcies, and banks are closing; CEO's are running scared, politicians are promising they can solve it with our money, the economic layoffs are epidemic, and investment counselors are perplexed. What is happening in business and government is appalling. High student dropouts, inferior education, woefully tenured teachers—they all testify of the need of radical change in America's education. On the other hand, there is a steady decline in church attendance; too many pastors or leaders are treading along in comfortable sameness and religious ambiguity. What is happening in churches and schools is also pathetic. Yes, so many are in need of an awakening—a spiritual anagnorisis. Families are also in disarray as television, the Internet, recreation, entertainment, and pleasure are evaporating morals from the average home. Wall Street, Corporate America, Boards of Education, Teacher Unions, presbyters, pastors, churches, even parents are in dire need for a reversal of circumstances. There is a need for an urgent anagnorisis to awaken the shuffling herd caught in the mind-numbing cadence of sameness.

But it is the individual I speak to in this chapter. Every "Leader of Leaders" must realize the situation facing us! A few years ago, I came across a short and poignant statement that reminds me of the human predicament. The missionary George Young, while apprenticing under the dedicated George Hunter said, "He taught me . . . that the man who will keep right to the end of the chapter is the man whose gaze is fixed on God, whose joy is in God's company and whose heart is pure in its devotion to the will of God."[210] Maybe you are browsing through this book while sitting in your comfortable den, perhaps you are reading it on an airplane, or possibly having analyzed every chapter, you are asking this question, "Why did he write on this subject?" Because we do not examine our personal hearts enough, because we do not realize how imperative it is to make changes, and/or because so much of what we come to know is to get a job or to get ahead. But when do you seek more understanding about your own path in life. There comes a time when you must stop avoiding the deep questions and begin learning more about your own heart. Have you ever asked yourself one of these questions: "Could I become someone different than I am today?" "Is there more to understand about my life than I already know?" "How long can I ignore what God has planned for me?" And, finally, "When will I stop asking why and begin to discover the way to change things in my family, school, church, or where I work?"

In 2002, there was a compelling film made that was entitled, *The Magdalene Sisters*. The movie was about the sad chronicles of the "maggies" of Ireland. They got that nickname from Mary Magdalene in the Bible. The primary reference of this character in the New Testament begins with Jesus driving out the seven demons that possessed her [See also Matthew 27:56, 61; 28:1; Mark 15:40, 41, 47; Luke 8:2; John 19:25; 20:11–18]. Centuries later, a church authority said that Mary Magdalene must have been the prostitute that washed Jesus' feet with her hair. Henceforth, when a strict order of nuns agreed to take in young women who had got pregnant out-of-wedlock, they labeled the fallen girls as "maggies." Tragically, the plight for the girls was anything but merciful and kind. The nuns treated them like prisoners and slaves. Up until the 1980s, more than 30,000 Irish and some English girls who got pregnant out of wedlock were incarcerated at the Magdalene Asylum. In many cases, it was simply teenage girls considered to have conducted themselves in a loose and unbecoming manner who were placed there by their parents or church authorities.[211]

The "maggies" came to public attention in the 1990s when the religious order sold their convent. Those who purchased it found the graves of 161 women inside the walls—women who had spent their lives working as virtual slaves in the convent laundry. Singer and songwriter Joni Mitchell was inspired to write a song about the "maggies," which caused a public outcry. Her song led to a campaign that not only disclosed all the ugly details of abuse, but launched a drive to build a memorial in a downtown park in Dublin. The subsequent investigations and journalistic scrutiny led to confessions by church authorities of the grievous injustice done against these "maggies." Joni was one singer who wrote one song, but her courage that could have easily cost her popularity in Ireland helped bring to light this travesty. It was a beginning of a healing in the hearts of these innocent girls and forgotten women.[212]

Whether from watching the movie or reading the full story, I found myself in awe of the bravery of Joni Mitchell to write her song in an Irish Catholic nation. When the discovery removed Joni's past ignorance of the horrifying injustices done to these girls, she began to bravely take action and heighten the conscience of a nation. In societies like North America or Western Europe, we so rarely see young people who deny their own pleasure and success to come out openly to condemn immoral actions. This begs a question: Can an individual experience a true anagnorisis unless it changes their character? Aristotle believed not! To him, it was the distinctive nature of a real anagnorisis.[213] Joni discovered knowledge of people and places she had never known; she could never remain the same again.

The Turning Point That Changed Everything

I propose that what is needed in any great leader today is a personal discovery so overwhelming that his or her life will be completely reversed—that it will begin a revolution in his or her family, school, church, or the corporation he or she serves.

In the great labyrinth of books written on change, there is a severe famine of any mention made about the individual's need for transformation. Some books will list characteristics of good leaders, others will describe the heart of integrity, a few of the books will even describe how leaders must develop certain coveted attributes, but a miniscule few actually address the dire need for anagnorisis. Describing a picture of excellence to the devil will not alter his innate propensity for self-serving thinking or behavior. Sadly, in our relativistic age, many people, even Christians, have lost the ethical categories of right and wrong.

During a recent discussion about the savings and loan debacle crushing Wall Street and the financial institutions in America, I listened as a television news journalist reported how that England, Belgium, France, and other Far East nations were beginning to experience the same deplorable dilemma. On another newscast, a University of Harvard professor was being interviewed about a course he was teaching on business ethics. At the close of the interview, he was asked for the one piece of closing advice he would offer executives today. His response eerily sounded like more hallow wisdom when he replied, "Don't do anything that will get you in the newspapers. It's hard for business. The critical point these days is stay out of the attention of the media." Remember, this is a professor teaching business ethics. A leader today does not need another leadership seminar or another book on character; he or she needs an anagnorisis.

During my lifetime, I can mark out three dates that stand out above all others. These demarcations are more than signposts in my life; they are turning points that were each birthed out of a discovery. They propelled me literally by altering three key components of who I am:

> 1. The first demarcation occurred when I was sixteen. Since I desired to be a lawyer and had designed my high school studies accordingly, God had to literally give me a revelation of my calling to be a minister of the gospel. The setting was a youth campground in Wisconsin, and while there, I discovered something so enthralling and mind-altering that it made me come home and initiate changes that before were unthinkable. My parents

The Turning Point That Changed Everything

tell me I went through a metamorphosis in my behavior, speech, ambition, and the preoccupation of my mind. To this day, I can point back to that year of 1966, to that place, and to the supernatural empowerment that came over me. Call it what you will, doubt it if you dare, but I had an anointing. Up to this time, I had never understood nor had real knowledge of what it meant to be called by God, but from this moment forward, it was undeniable and powerful.

2. My second demarcation occurred in 1985 when I was thirty-five years old. A demarcation is often seen as a division of something so that its divided parts are separate and identifiable. This was no doubt, to this day, my greatest personal anagnorisis. This time, God would reveal something so deep, so hidden, and so painful that it figuratively resurrected my heart. Hurt, disappointed, angry, and bitter, the Lord had to catch me on the run to awaken me to my deplorable condition. As a young pastor, I had disguised my injury with deliberate hard work and a driven attitude (although these attributes in themselves are not bad). While reading a book for a college class one day, the Lord spoke straight into my heart. I discovered my hurt, my self-imposed resentment, and my critical need for healing. That day, I sat in my car reading those words and realizing I had just uncovered something no one else knew but God. The writer Ed Wheat was speaking about our "family of origin," and how it can affect our present relationships, even to our spouse. Throughout those key pages I was reading, it spoke about relationships in the past that hindered or twisted our perceptions and actions, which even poisoned our ability to function properly in present relationships.[214] This was me, and the Lord was using those words to help me discover understanding of my past and give me insight into changes I had to make. The anagnorisis gave me the knowledge I needed to begin a healing of my heart toward my father. I am thankful that this bitterness was soon resolved.

3. The third demarcation that can be identified in my life came in 1995; I had mentioned this earlier in this chapter. At the age of 45, I was jettisoned to take my ministry and service to God to a new level of commitment and passion. This anagnorisis so completely changed the way I lived and worked that even my wife observed that it seemed to possess my mind and heart. Yet it was more than obsession or becoming a workaholic; it

The Turning Point That Changed Everything

was like the burden of the prophet when he cried unto the Lord, ". . . His word was like a fire shut up in my bones" (Jeremiah 20:9). Such discoveries set in motion many events and alterations to one's life. With such powerful knowledge, you realize like the great prophet Jeremiah that it has "jump started" a turning point that, at times, will make you both afraid and emboldened. No man or woman is going to change events, people, or the world around them without this kind of monumental disclosure of the hidden truth about themselves.

Recently I was reading a true-life story of Heath and Pam Cloutier, who soon after they were married, encountered their own awakening moment. Settling into their comfortable lifestyle and enjoying their new marriage was keeping their days filled with anticipation of their first child. Then, it began with a simple dream one night in October 2005. Heath dreamed he was teaching English and standing before foreigners teaching the gospel. After rising the next morning, he recounted the story to his wife Pam. As soon as he finished rehearsing the dream, they both began to laugh. He told his wife that there was only one word in the dream he could hear over and over in his mind—the word was WASI. A few minutes of laughter turned into curiosity, so they went on the Internet to see if there was such a word. It turned out to be the term from Quechua, a South American language that meant "house or home." Learning this made them both feel a strange sensation of chills running over them. But Pam immediately objected and resisted such an idea. A few days later, she came to her husband with some shocking news. She told him to read the paper where she had marked something unusual. It was a job offer for someone to teach English in a town in Japan. Heath remembered the word from Quechua and wondered how this might coincide with this, but it seemed right that they should apply for the position that could lead to at least a three-year commitment. Heath would later admit that the unusual word (Quechua) WASI was just God's way of getting them to begin looking beyond their beloved home and their comfortable lifestyle. Nine months later, they were on a jet flying to Japan where Heath now teaches English, and they are helping plant a new church. Pam is also about to give birth to their first child. For this couple, they confess that this began a series of events that completely reversed the future of their life into an opposite direction.[215]

The Turning Point That Changed Everything

Astonishing what one new bit of knowledge can open up to those willing to learn something they have never known before. Whether you believe that the Bible is the infallible and inerrant Word of God (as I do), the fact that it is the most historical document in the history of mankind would make it an exceptional resource from which to learn.

One particular story is documented in three world cultures (Judaism, Christianity, and Zoroastrianism), which is the historical event of Moses receiving a discovery at Mt. Sinai. The event was so radically inspiring that it drove him to return to Egypt from where he fled to save his life. In fact, this one single anagnorisis was so vividly secure that he entrusted his life, his family, and his entire race of people to its validity. The best manner in which to judge an anagnorisis is to see its profound effect on the individual and others who are affected by the experience. Read carefully this breathtaking event:

> Now Moses kept the flock of Jethro his father in law, the priest of Midian: and he led the flock to the backside of the desert, and came to the mountain of God, even to Horeb. And the angel of the LORD appeared unto him in a flame of fire out of the midst of a bush: and he looked, and, behold, the bush burned with fire, and the bush was not consumed. And Moses said, I will now turn aside, and see this great sight, why the bush is not burnt. And when the LORD saw that he turned aside to see, God called unto him out of the midst of the bush, and said, Moses, Moses. And he said, Here am I. And he said, Draw not nigh hither: put off thy shoes from off thy feet, for the place whereon thou standest is holy ground. Moreover he said, I am the God of thy father, the God of Abraham, the God of Isaac, and the God of Jacob. And Moses hid his face; for he was afraid to look upon God. And the LORD said, I have surely seen the affliction of my people which are in Egypt, and have heard their cry by reason of their taskmasters; for I know their sorrows; And I am come down to deliver them out of the hand of the Egyptians, and to bring them up out of that land unto a good land and a large, unto a land flowing with milk and honey; unto the place of the Canaanites, and the Hittites, and the Amorites, and the Perizzites, and the Hivites, and the Jebusites. Now therefore, behold, the cry of the children of Israel is come unto me: and I have also seen the oppression wherewith the Egyptians oppress them.

The Turning Point That Changed Everything

Come now therefore, and I will send thee unto Pharaoh, that thou mayest bring forth my people the children of Israel out of Egypt.

And Moses said unto God, Who am I, that I should go unto Pharaoh, and that I should bring forth the children of Israel out of Egypt? And he said, Certainly I will be with thee; and this shall be a token unto thee, that I have sent thee: When thou hast brought forth the people out of Egypt, ye shall serve God upon this mountain. And Moses said unto God, Behold, when I come unto the children of Israel, and shall say unto them, The God of your fathers hath sent me unto you; and they shall say to me, What is his name? What shall I say unto them? And God said unto Moses, I AM THAT I AM: and he said, Thus shalt thou say unto the children of Israel, I AM hath sent me unto you.

And God said moreover unto Moses, Thus shalt thou say unto the children of Israel, the LORD God of your fathers, the God of Abraham, the God of Isaac, and the God of Jacob, hath sent me unto you: this is my name for ever, and this is my memorial unto all generations. Go, and gather the elders of Israel together, and say unto them, The LORD God of your fathers, the God of Abraham, of Isaac, and of Jacob, appeared unto me, saying, I have surely visited you, and seen that which is done to you in Egypt: And I have said, I will bring you up out of the affliction of Egypt unto the land of the Canaanites, and the Hittites, and the Amorites, and the Perizzites, and the Hivites, and the Jebusites, unto a land flowing with milk and honey. And they shall hearken to thy voice: and thou shalt come, thou and the elders of Israel, unto the king of Egypt, and ye shall say unto him, The LORD God of the Hebrews hath met with us: and now let us go, we beseech thee, three days' journey into the wilderness, that we may sacrifice to the LORD our God.

And I am sure that the king of Egypt will not let you go, no, not by a mighty hand. And I will stretch out my hand, and smite Egypt with all my wonders which I will do in the midst thereof: and after that he will let you go. And I will give this people favour in the sight of the Egyptians: and it shall come to pass, that, when ye go, ye shall not go empty. But every woman shall borrow of her neighbour, and of her that sojourneth in her house, jewels of silver, and jewels of gold, and raiment: and ye shall put them upon your sons, and upon your daughters; and ye shall spoil the Egyptians (Exodus 3).

Since some readers may not be familiar with the Bible or may not have one close to where they are reading, I have included purposefully the passage of scripture above. This one incident preserved in the Bible is so monumental to believers in Jehovah/Jesus Christ that it would be impossible to have a comprehension on the change that occurred in the leader, Moses, without reading and understanding this anagnorisis. So it is with any great discovery, no one can grasp its importance to the degree of the person transformed by it. I truly hope you, as a reader, will seek such wonderful insights into those things you do not understand about life. To do so will liberate more than your physical body, but your mind, heart and soul. Subsequently, it may even impact your church, school, or business.

I want to digress for a moment to make sure you understand what I mean by an anagnorisis. Under no circumstance, do I want you to confuse this with just finding a new or revised purpose for your life. Neither do I always mean accepting Jesus Christ as your personal Savior. Rather, both leaders and people, in general, today, need a genuine and radical transformation that will begin with a spiritual metamorphosis. In saying this, let me caution you about a false movement that arose in the early years of this decade that mislead people into thinking it is just a change of mind about their life, attitude, or their actions.

During the last seven years, much has been written about man's purpose. Beginning with Rick Warren's popular bestseller book, *The Purpose Driven Life*,[216] there has been a subsequent explosion of both Christian and secular publications exploring or postulating new thoughts about this successful theme. I have asked myself quite often since the emergence of Rick's book if anyone really questioned the contents thoroughly or unearthed a subtle exclusion. Somehow, this became a pop culture phenomenon or Christian philosophy without any real examination of those truths missing in this gifted work. Many writers and pastors automatically assumed or believed the "purpose driven philosophy theory" to be true and used it as the basis for argument and theories about how to turn a person's life around. But there were some critics among evangelicals who saw it as nothing more than new age humanism. In fact, the majority of those who oppose Rick Warren's philosophies have been Christian leaders such as John MacArthur and Richard Albanes. While I see some good that came out of this purpose philosophy craze, I will speak about my own deep concerns later. The best way to understand this surprising tiff is to read some of the objections noted by Tony Capoccia:

> It is a take-off and sequel to his book, *The Purpose Driven Church*,[217] which is not the right direction for any church—a very unbiblical approach. When one looks at the book, *The Purpose Driven Life*, one has to be concerned when any book makes a claim, which it does— "This book will change your life!" There is only one book that will change your life and that's the Bible. Also, while the book is not heretical in content, it does lay fast and loose with the scriptures, using 15 different Bible translations to ensure that his points are supported. Rick Warren has stated that you can best understand scripture by reading as many different translations as possible—this approach uses many different "opinions" to define the meaning of God's Word rather than a thorough exegetical study of the verse(s). In addition, the book presents an abbreviated, inaccurate definition of the gospel—there is no requirement for "repentance" in his Gospel. But I will say this about the book—it has a great marketing plan."[218]

But these kinds of reviews by Christian pastors, scholars, and writers went deeper into the problems with the current purpose philosophy. Mark Ratzlaff states, "This book misrepresents and distorts the gospel. It overlooks the fact that an unbeliever does have an identity, as well as a purpose in his life, outside of a relationship with Christ. That, in fact, man's purpose, nature, and identity is hostile to God, fallen, and totally depraved apart from salvation. It may not have a godly purpose, but it does have a definitive purpose. The book glosses over, minimizes, or ignores realities such as: the seriousness of sin before a holy God, the need for salvation, that God is righteous, just, holy, etc. The back cover of this book states that it is a 'groundbreaking manifesto on the meaning of life.' The introduction states that 'this is more than a book . . . it is a guide to a 40-day spiritual journey that will enable you to discover the answer to life's most important question.' This book did not live up to such promise. A major problem with this book is in proof-texting, selecting verses out of context to support a given proposition. The author goes beyond proof-texting, however, by relying upon excerpts from unusual paraphrases to make his points. The back of the book contains an extensive list of scripture references, but once you start looking them up in reliable translations, you will be sorely disappointed."[219]

Mark Ratzlaff went even further in his analysis of this philosophy. "Another major problem is a 'soft,' almost 'gospel-lite' emphasis. Infrequent mention is made of the holiness of God, sin, our human flesh nature, the cross, absolute truth, commands of God, His sovereignty, and other concepts which are emphasized in the Bible but which might interfere with a good self-image. There is an emphasis on family, on relationships, and even a section on how to be a global Christian. This is a warm, fuzzy, feel-good message, emphasizing what God can do for you. An entire chapter tells you why you should attend a church without once mentioning Hebrews 10:25. Another chapter discusses unity in the church as a primary goal, but there is no mention of standing for doctrinal purity or truth. There are parts of the book, which appear to contradict each other (e.g., pp. 146, 161). In other places, doctrines, which vanished from the paraphrased scripture, pop up later in the book where they are given lesser emphasis (e.g., 'it's all for God's glory' gets short shifted on page 310). The book is visually appealing, and endorsed by the right parachurch leaders, but exemplifies what is wrong with contemporary evangelicalism. The book could be used as an example of how not to use the scriptures to support a presupposition. I could not recommend this book to any serious student of the Word."[220]

I stated earlier that I wanted to share my own difficulties with this entire purpose philosophy movement. As you pay particular attention to the stories of great men throughout history, both biblical and extra-biblical, you become convinced that there must be a dynamic discovery or sudden turnaround that generates the conviction and will to change. My most extreme objection is the failure of the purpose philosophy is that it mentions nothing about the conviction of an individual's depravity, rebellion, ignorance, or disobedience to God. There are no calls for repentance, confession, and restitution. It lacks the spiritual transformation required to catch a person's heart and mind to thrust it into a place he or she has never been before.

Dear Reader, you absolutely need an encounter with God that leaves you with no alternative but to bow before Him and understand that your future has no promise outside His power to transform you (Romans 12:2). We witness this kind of encounter in the life of Abraham who must undergo the greatest test of sacrificing his beloved son Isaac in obedience to the Lord (Genesis 22:1–19).

The Turning Point That Changed Everything

His tearful and painful act of faith in God launches his entire life and family into another spectrum and destiny. No amount of rationalization, counseling, logic, or determination could have produced the stand Abraham took on that mountain. It took an experience and a discovery of who God was and a divine understanding of God's purpose. This kind of transformation necessitates a revelation and intervention in one's life by his or her Creator.

If you read the many volumes written on God's purpose for you and me, there is a common thread that ties them all. It is a preoccupation that dwells on your visible or seen life. Such writings generally muse over your occupation, career, happiness, and "being all you can be." What they often neglect or intentionally ignore is the unseen purposes of God in your life. If they mention righteousness, it is simply to create a more becoming you for others to see. Few delve into the individual's quest to come into the knowledge and understanding of our personal relationship with the Father through His Son Jesus Christ. Instead of our attention being given to our success and accomplishments, real change affects our thinking so that we can know we are here to seek God in His unseen kingdom.[221]

Could there be more to our existence than simply the earthly roles and identities we fill to please others or ourselves? I believe so! Therefore, I find myself waiting for another change to come soon in my life; an anagnorisis perhaps that will transform me on yet a deeper level with God (2 Corinthians 3:18). Besides, I get excited thinking about what He will do to help me know Him better and how He will entrust me with the strength to give him more glory that I presently do. Are you ready for the "Arrival of Anagnorisis?"

Chapter 10

The Plan of God in the Church Age

> *Even while she waits for the last day, the Church, as the bearer of a historical inheritance, is bound by an obligation to the historical future. Her vision of the end of all things must not hinder her in the fulfillment of her historical responsibility. She must leave not only the end to God's decision, but also the possibility of the continuance of history. She must set her mind on both.*[222]

On Wednesday morning, November 5, 2008, I watched the morning news with the solemn reality that radical liberalism is celebrating its firm control on American politics, government, education, and the media. Without God's calming grace, what is more frightful is that this persuasion has even captivated the church. In the church, I do not mean a particular denomination but the church as a whole—both professing adherents to Christianity and all true believers in

Christ Jesus. The first century apostle Paul cautioned us: "This persuasion cometh not of Him that calleth you" (Galatians 5:8).

In the last General Election in the United States of America, a stark contrast between moderation and radical liberalism was the choice. The great bastion of Christianity, called America, surrendered with joy and celebration to the reign of radical liberalism, which embraces homosexuality, abortion, and big government. Why? The Economy. Men and women swept along with the tide of promises that they would live financially better and more equally. Pushed off the radar were moral and ethical issues that were central to the founding fathers of America. Most believers who cast their ballots for this new order did so with the perceived justifiable excuse that "you can't legislate morality" anyway. In reality, most citizens now celebrate the illusion that we are independent or free people more than they do why the early settlers of this nation wanted to be independent or free! With this sobering chill in the autumn air, I realized that we must leave this decision to God who works everything according to His plan.

Covenant and Dispensationalist theologians are generally agreed that the period of time in between the Incarnation of Jesus Christ until His Return is called the Last Days. Also, many of them will concur that it is also referred to as The Church Age.[223] Be that as it may, there are many within the secular scientific community who believe that the existing world is in the last five minutes before an eventual cataclysmic upheaval that may destroy the earth. As I've pondered recently these things in relationship to a peripeteia that could alter life as we know it on the earth, it occurs to me that the church must be ready for whatever comes in the present and future. This was brought home personally as I was reading some notes on the Paul's letter to Philippians by Robert Wolgemuth: "It's not what happens to you that matters, it's what happens to what happens to you that truly counts. We can't control most of our circumstances, but we can usually control our reactions when circumstances change. The great challenge is not to try to squirm away from inevitable changes and tough times because we can't. Our challenge is to learn how to live peaceably with them, just like Paul."[224]

Certainly, the greatest weakness of mankind is two-fold: For many, they hope their present efforts to retain a prosperous life will succeed. On the opposite are those who live without, they hope their desire to obtain the good life like others will be rewarded sometime soon. This illusion that prosperity is ultimately hooked to democracy or America is misguided at best. Beginning with C. S. Lewis and later on with prophetic voices like Chuck Colson, many writers have documented the little publicized truth about the time clock running on earth's existence. The scientific community has confirmed what the Scriptures teach that history will have a catastrophic end, as we have known it on the earth.

As early as 1929, the renowned astronomer Edwin Powell Hubble warned that the universe was expanding based on his observations of the "red shift," the increase in wavelengths of light that returned to us from the various distant galaxies. He declared that the universe and the earth were not eternal; it had a beginning and that it would end. Wow! Were the atheists and agnostics asleep at this warning? He went on to explain that entropy was taking place and that the universe was winding down just as it had wound up. His conclusion rattled his scientific peers, but in the last two decades many reputable astronomers have echoed his same prediction. Sadly, many have also marginalized this caution with hopes we can "green" the earth back from the brink.[225] This false aspiration is supported officially while debate is muffled through the censoring of legitimate scientists and educators who might disagree.

Although sociologists and educators talked about a utopian society being reached in the 1990s, history will not end when we reach a "perfect union" in the United States, or when the European Union can control the politics and economies of the world, nor when the United Nations can bring all rouge nations under their submission. Instead, we will reach the ultimate deliverance and perfection when the Author of history, like the producer of a successful play, steps out on the stage to bring the curtain down. Within the religious bastions of education and on the televangelism networks, conservative evangelicals and liberal theologians disagree on how this world will end. But there is one actuality that they and many notable scientists agree on, this world will end but no one knows exactly when or how. Unequivocally, this world is facing many changes in the hours or years that may wait this cataclysmic day. If you have ever survived and prospered during a major peripeteia in your life, then you know there are always steps or reactions we can take to make the most of such dramatic turning points. Before we examine this exciting news, let's venture a little further into what God's plan is for Christians in this "Church Age." Furthermore, how will the so-called denominations, preachers, and Christian believers react as the world spins so speedily toward this uncertain future, which frightens God not at all?

The Turning Point That Changed Everything

I have a confession: Whenever I get concerned about the church and for that matter the destiny of my nation or the world, I find my mind traveling to a solitary cell in a concentration camp called Flossenburg, Germany. There, I sit down by a young but courageous and brilliant man named Dietrich Bonhoeffer. Although often tortured and moved from prison to various concentration camps, Flossenburg will be his final Gethsemane. I see the bespectacled gentleman writing in a little notebook these words: "When a man really gives up trying to make something out of himself—a saint, or a converted sinner, or a churchman (a so-called clerical somebody), a righteous or unrighteous man— when in the fullness of tasks, questions, success or ill-hap, experiences and perplexities, a man throws himself into the arms of God—then he wakes with Christ in Gethsemane. That is faith, that is metanoia, and it is thus that he becomes a man and Christian. How can a man wax arrogant if in a this-sided life he shares the suffering of God?"[226]

Like Aristotle declared before the Savior came to this earth as an infant, the best peripeteia is a tragedy, for such events produce the deepest and most profound "sudden reversal of circumstances" that can shape or change a man.[227] While such a peripeteia was believed by Aristotle to almost always be bad, he could not envision in his defense how God would turn the tragedy of a crucifixion and burial into a glorious empty tomb because of the Resurrection. I realize more each year in my life how the Lord takes an event that may seem at the turning point to be a defeat and uses it to work a far greater glory.

Many years ago I encountered the lowest point in my ministry when a supervisor over me decided to remove me from a church that I loved and who loved me also. We were, after several years of struggle, beginning to see victories, many new, young couples were being saved; a rapid increase of finances in my parish was finally allowing me the opportunity to do so many things denied to me before. Beyond these things, my family was enjoying our friends, our schools, and our beautiful house. It was not fair; it was not wholesome, and it wounded my family's spirits. But the disappointment and anger brought me to my knees. As I prayed and talked with my wife, it began to dawn on me that God was working in the "bitter cup." With hours and days of meditation, my heart and mind began to comprehend the opportunity God was opening to me. This did not justify what the supervisor had done, but I chose to live in the sunshine of Sunday's resurrection rather than in Friday's darkness. I was better for the change. With so many clouds on the horizon for the church, we could be tempted to forget the great harvest that awaits those who carry the gospel.

During this past year, I was tired after traveling for twenty-five days through three nations and sat back on a flight from Atlanta to Portland to read awhile. In my weariness, the young man sitting next to me interrupted to ask me about the book I was reading. A conversation developed that surprised me. He was returning to Portland, and like me he lived in Salem, Oregon. He began to energetically share with me his vision for the youth generation in the face of numerous problems awaiting them on the horizon in our nation. He told me how that the challenges facing today's confused adolescents and college kids were overwhelming, but he exuded a positive confidence that it was giving him and his leadership team an opportunity to reach young people where they were hurting. As I listened to his faith and enthusiasm, it was precisely the remedy I needed before returning to visit several of our dying congregations that are aging.

Two days later, I received a letter from one of our high school teens telling me what an inspiration I had been in her life during the past five years. Absolutely, the task is daunting before the church in our world, but the scars of today's battle do not negate the certainty of the victory God has prepared for the church. These two "children of the faith" were sent like ravens to the dejected prophet (I Kings 17:4–6). Forgive me, Father, in my times of hardness that I forget your love and care for me!

What about God's plan in the Church Age? Of course, the cynic and the atheist stand together to scoff at such declarations of a Divine Plan. They do not believe God has a plan since they believe there is no God. Subsequently, these skeptics refute any notion of a Church Age. Neither of these negations by them can disqualify the question. You and I, who know that God has a Plan and that we are no doubt in the Church Age, must continually strive to help them see such by the "good works" that can cause men to glorify the Father (Matthew 5:16).

Actually, I believe it is time for Christians to fight for the faith we declare that we embrace. I'm not advocating riots, protests, or court battles to stake out our beliefs. On the contrary, we must begin to live lives that have such boldness and power, such sacrifice and service, such clarity and witness, such winsomeness and love that it overwhelms those who oppose the truth. We must care more for the spreading of the gospel than we do for building our own comfortable houses. In an age where both believers and unbelievers are bemoaning the burdensome mortgages or the rising unemployment, what does the church need to be doing to let others know that we have a confidence in the future that attracts them to us? Everyone is crying out for "my space," today, but where is that space for the church? Dietrich Bonhoeffer understood and articulated this dilemma:

> The church is the place where testimony and serious thought are given to God's reconciliation of the world with Himself through Christ, to His having so loved the world that He gave His Son for its sake. The space of the church is not there in order to try to deprive the world that it is still the world, the world which is loved by God and reconciled with Him. The church has neither the wish nor the obligation to extend her space to cover the space of the world. She asks for no more space than she needs for the purpose of serving the world by bearing witness to Jesus Christ and to the reconciliation of the world with God through Him. The only way in which the church can defend her own territory is by fighting not for it but for the salvation of the world. Otherwise the church becomes a "religious society," which fights in its own interest and thereby ceases at once to be the Church of God of the world. And so the first demand which is made of those who belong to God's church is not that they should be something in themselves, not that they should, for example, set up some religious organization or that they should lead lives of piety, but that they shall be witnesses to Jesus Christ before the world."[228]

The admonition of Dietrich Bonhoeffer is both challenging and explosive in light of modern evangelical or Pentecostal thinking. On the one hand, the mainline churches of the Western world have done an admirable ministry in serving the social needs of society such as helping the impoverished or building schools, hospitals, medical clinics, and other various community shelters. Conversely, it has been the Pentecostals who have led the campaign to evangelize communities and nations with the radical gospel. Both sectors of Christianity have indeed promoted and fostered governmental change and even revolution to bring alterations in the political structures. Certainly, some of this has increased the opportunity for people to have religious liberty. But in light of the present secularization of America and other religious failed attempts around the world to have political clout against evil forces, we are only now beginning to realize the observations of

Bonhoeffer about the church. If Christians or church organizations think they can casually or half-heartedly partake in the secular politics of their nation, they are going to be in for a rude awakening.

A few years back, while pastoring in Phoenix, I had my consciousness awakened to this while I was engaging in the local government of that city. I had become a friend with city council members, school administrators, police officials, and even the Mayor through my community leadership and involvement in several civic programs. The more I became engaged in the campaigns or fights for people in our neighborhood and the greater City of Phoenix, I found Christians unprepared for serious confrontations with the powers of our age. This led to a quick exodus of the support of some parishioners when they realized that opposition would be harsh and plentiful. The challenge was being a Pentecostal willing to enter a secular society and help turn their attitudes around without finding myself distanced from the very Christians I thought would join me in making a difference in our community. For me, this development was a personal insight and most disturbing. Frankly, I do not think enough pastors take the tremendous opportunity they have open to them to participate in their community and bring the Kingdom of God into the public arena.

At this decisive juncture of community involvement, I was reading some warnings given by George Barna about the dilemma facing Christians and church institutions. He highlighted three factors why most Christians are poised for an ignominious defeat in this Church Age:

1. A majority of Christians do not take Satan seriously and do not believe that there is any type of specific spiritual warfare taking place today for which they need to be alerted and prepared.
2. Most believers are so overwhelmed by the pressures of the world and their only daily wants that they have lost touch with God's grand plan and His expectations for their life.
3. Denominational institutions and local churches have had little or no effect on the perspectives and pursuits of believers, rendering the average church defenseless in the contest for people's undivided allegiance.[229]

In light of this perspective, the modern church has done too little to engraft the words of Jesus into the hearts of converts. The prayer of Jesus to the Father

The Turning Point That Changed Everything

on the night of His betrayal was an ominous forewarning to the disciples that followed Him: "I have given them thy word; and the world hath hated them, because they are not of the world. I pray not that thou shouldest take them out of the world, but that thou shouldest keep them from the evil. They are not of the world, even as I am not of the world. Sanctify them through thy truth; thy word is truth" (John 17:14–17). If this impending declaration were not enough, Paul gave a likeminded clarion call to the church: "For we wrestle not against flesh and blood, but against principalities, against powers, against the rulers of the darkness of this world, against spiritual wickedness in high places" (Ephesians 6:12).

In this postmodern world, many in the church are not making decisions in life that reflect a biblical worldview. God's plan can only expedite the work of the gospel when believers are fully informed by their faith so that it impacts their daily decisions.

In the movie entitled, *Kingdom of Heaven*,[230] the main character Balian of Ibelin, is a French blacksmith who has doubted his faith ever since his wife committed suicide, thereby, condemning herself to eternal punishment through the eyes of the church. Into this upheaval of his life, a knight appears named Godfrey proclaiming to be his father, who had deserted Balian and his mother long ago. He invites his son to follow him back to the Holy Land to defend Jerusalem against the infidels led by a Kurdish Muslim named Saladin. Of course, a bitter son and recent widower, he refuses Godfrey's invitation. A short time later Balian encounters the priest who had proclaimed his wife damnation because she had committed suicide. He finds the priest wearing her gold crucifix that he stole off her body when it was being buried in a sinner's plot. Balian, in his rage, impulsively rises up and kills the dishonorable priest and eventually ends up trying to catch up to his father while fleeing from a murder charge. Ironically, his father (the knight) is mortally wounded defending him against the soldiers who come to arrest his son for the murder of the priest. But before Godfrey dies, he anoints Balian as a knight. To make atonement for the murder of the priest and his wife's sin, he takes his father's place by going to serve in the battle for Jerusalem.

What happens in this epic movie that is both historical and neutral in its treatment of Christianity and Islam is a testimony to the honesty of writer Ridley Scott. It also shows what can happen in this Church Age when we attempt to make our plan God's plan. Once the young knight Balian reaches his destiny of Jerusalem, he does not sense the divine forgiveness he had hoped to find. Soon,

The Turning Point That Changed Everything

he discovers the situation is much more political than he imagined. There is a tenuous truce existing between the powerful infidel King Saladin and Jerusalem's King Baldwin IV, a leper whose face and body must be covered by robes, gloves, armor, and a mask. This shaky ceasefire allows both Muslims and Christians to practice their religions openly. Paradoxically, the Christians are divided between two ideologies—the more zealot forces serve under a fanatical leader called the Knights Templar, but the majority serves under the noble King Baldwin. Balian tries to find his identity in this religious and political circus, only to be swept up in the upheaval that follows the death of King Baldwin to his leprous disease. Balian becomes the chief military officer that ends up defending the Holy City after the defeat of the Knights Templar. The movie concludes with his negotiation to leave the city with all the inhabitants given safe passage by King Saladin that had besieged the city of Jerusalem.[231]

I spent a couple of hours recently reading reviews by movie critics of this blockbuster epic. Unlike a fantasy novel or fictional tale, most were impressed by the straightforward and balanced truth exposed by both the writer and director. Honest observers are profoundly impressed when someone can objectively show both sides of a story. *The Kingdom of Heaven* lays naked before us one insightful revelation about the Church Age; God's plan is beyond our predictions, prophecies, and expectations. Leaders who we surmise to be good or evil may not turn out as we want or expect them to be. It seems inevitable that the greatest peripeteia (whether the Rapture, the Antichrist or the Great Tribulation) will occur on the horizon in a manner that does not fit so precisely or easily into our political ideologies or ecclesiastical interpretations. Before all of this occurs, the faith of every believer will be tested like Balian. Many of us will find that the religious institutions that we have trusted will be changed, political parties or loyalties will be swept away, and national boundaries erased. Consequently, even the political and military power of nations could be altered in months, not years.

The **faith** in Jesus Christ will become more important than ever in history. With ongoing debate, the end times might look more like the first century than the twentieth century. As Balian dealt with the religiosity, the morality and politics of Jerusalem, he discovered that both priests and kings had forgotten what the **faith** really entailed. Their agendas, ambitions, and prejudices negated the Faith they had once followed so happily. Gone was the power and hope of the **faith**. Like all spiritual and effective changes, the **faith** we have in Jesus Christ is the mechanism that fuels the individual's future travel with the Creator:

- "Because of your faith, it will happen" (Matthew 9:29).
- "Your faith has made you well" (Mark 5:34).
- "Your faith has saved you" (Luke 7:50).
- "We are made right with God by placing faith in Jesus Christ" (Romans 3:22).
- "My righteous ones will live by faith" (Hebrews 10:38).
- "We do this by keeping our eyes on Jesus, the champion who initiates and perfects our faith" (Hebrews 12:2).[232]

Observing what is happening in almost all cultures, with the church around the world, and with the progressive globalization of governments and businesses, we Christians must develop a tactical response that coincides with God's plan for this Age. There must be an aggressive and unified effort that will place the church in a position to bring the Faith back into focus. If we can do this in Christianity, we can once again challenge the worldly system for minds, hearts, and souls of earth's inhabitants. George Barna called for such a competition for postmodern people by offering three strategic pursuits:

1. We must motivate people to pursue, embrace, and live according to a biblical worldview. He argues that before believers can act like Christians, they must learn to think like Christians. We must help Christians understand and live their basic core beliefs. This means that in this highly competitive culture, believers must stand out because of the positive influence their Faith has upon their lives.
2. We must allow the church to be led by people whom God has called and anointed for the task—that is, anointed leaders. Too many ecclesiastical organizations, local churches, and other ministries are being led by teachers, nepotism, control groups, and influential persons who are not gifted with vision, energy, and impact on the church. We need leaders who can LEAD!
3. We must develop new formats, forums, and activities through which people will experience and serve God. New models of the church must

be allowed to rise up, including new expressions of the local church that meet the diversity of needs, give opportunity for all to be more involved, and allows different perspectives that define our culture. This means the Christian Faith must be more accessible and relevant to those who would otherwise be shut out of traditional churches.[233]

At this point, I will take a dangerous plunge into the greatest controversy of the twenty-first century. Unequivocally, the future tension of the world will reside in the seething caldron of debate between Christianity and Islam. If anyone dares to discuss *The Plan of God in the Church Age*, he or she will be forced to examine the influence and on-going struggle of these two belief systems. Since the storming of the American Embassy in Tehran, Iran, on November 4, 1979, the two world religions of Christianity and Islam have collided numerous times with increasing animosity. Not since the time of the Crusades in the eleventh through the thirteen centuries has mankind witnessed the clash of these two religious titans.

Anyone who has been following closely the rising tide of the Islamic adherents and the rapid infusion of terrorists among the nations cannot help but realize the disastrous conflict started long ago between Isaac and Ishmael that is swiftly coming to a dramatic conclusion (Genesis 21, 22). Subtly, there has been an outright attack on Christianity in the Western world where it once prospered. Most public universities and colleges allow and almost encourage biased attacks on Jesus Christ and Christianity. At the same time, few religious studies departments on public campuses provide any courses on the historical Christ or Christian beliefs. On the contrary, almost all universities and colleges promote courses on Islam and Mohammed. They also do it enthusiastically and with great emphasis on its best virtues. While this is done, very few places of academia present anything factual concerning Pentecostalism and conservative Christian values of the Bible. Quite to the contrary, American and European academia welcomes or demonstrates open ridicule and animosity toward Christianity. The Koran is encouraged as excellent philosophy while the Bible is viewed as intolerant "hate material" or as ignorant fables. Today the average American and European is woefully illiterate concerning the basic facts of Christianity.[234]

Throughout the global society, Christianity is the fastest growing major religion, but listening to the media and intellectuals, you would hardly envision this reality. For instance, in the strategic 10/40 Window that incorporates most of the population of the world, Christianity is far outdistancing Islam or any other religion. The gospel is spreading rapidly in Asia, India, Africa, and South America. Contrary to popular myth, the typical Christian throughout the global community is not a white, rich, or an affluent person in the United States, but the majority is poor people who are almost any color other than white. On the other hand, the media still doggedly portray Christians as mostly poor, old and uneducated, while demographics consistently refute this in places like South Africa, Belarus, Ukraine, China, and Russia, as well as in North America. Most of the millions of new converts are young and highly educated.[235]

I have just returned from a fourth visit to the nation of Belarus where I meet regularly with many Christians and church leaders who are overwhelmingly young and highly educated. In fact, I have visited with more than a hundred pastors who were all under the age of thirty-five and who are college or seminary graduates. In places like Hungary and the Ukraine, the same equation can be stated about their leaders. Many of them are in their twenties. Yet in the face of the rising influence of the Crescent throughout the world, Moslem converts and their Islamic extremist are not the greatest threat to Christianity.

There is ample evidence that a peripeteia of unprecedented historical comparison is taking place in Christendom and in the church. Many of the older congregations in Europe and North America will die. Christian leaders in various denominations loathe this prognostication, but it will happen anyway. Such congregations have resisted change for so long that spiritual resuscitation will only avail for a while or not at all. Candidly, this demise will happen in most denominations. When I speak to some churches and leadership groups, there is often a general denial or fear of this kind of transparency. These churches will not retool, rebirth, or humbly allow a makeover of their convenient and comfortable menial existence. They have no power in the Spirit and no influence in their communities. If they dry up and blow away tomorrow, no one will even realize they are gone! The light has gone out on the candlestick years gone by, and no one was willing to pay the price for new fire. Sadly, they revere the candlesticks (buildings) like precious gold. It is this tragic condition that will necessitate a peripeteia for God's plan to be accomplished in this Church Age. In reality, it has already begun.

For the last twenty years, I've read many sources that have alluded to the changes in the church, which would be forthcoming if we were going to accomplish God's plan. At first, I too was a skeptic, but during the 1990s the Holy Spirit convicted me of this radical transformation that was expedient and inevitable. Later, while reading some thoughts by Peter Wagner, he confirmed my observations when speaking specifically on the topic of church membership: "God did not stop revealing Himself and His will when the Bible was completed. He continues to be active in the world, and His works can be seen and understood. As we are told in the book of Revelation, the Holy Spirit continues to speak to the churches, and we must have an ear to hear (see Revelation 2:7). Doing theology, then, starts with understanding God's Word, but it goes on from there to understanding what God is saying and doing in the world today. . . . Whenever we find ourselves entering into a paradigm shift, terminology becomes very important. If we can learn to see the church from this perspective, we have begun to move toward a Kingdom perspective. Many of us, quite properly, have our membership in a local church. But we must keep in mind that our church membership is not our Kingdom membership. Our Kingdom membership is in the church that exists all seven days of the week wherever the people of God might be found."[236]

These thoughts about the Kingdom and church membership are not disjointed thoughts from the battle between Islam and Christianity. They both deal with the major shift going on in the Church Age that will eventually complete God's plan. If you remember from the third chapter, one of the key definitions of a peripeteia reads: "A sudden reversal of circumstances to the opposite."[237] Such events as the demise of the importance of denominations, the decreasing role of ecclesiastical headquarters, and the breakout into regional or "virtual" seminary campuses are only some of the changes affecting the church. We are also witnessing the increased secularization of Western society, the advance and volatility of a global economy, as well as the increasing power of media to persuade people toward their liberal bias. Furthermore, the isolation and open animosity that is now emerging within some political camps in the United States toward its long-time ally of Israel testifies of this dramatic reversal. Within this new archetype to the past democratic principles and biblical absolutes, it would appear that God's plan may be in jeopardy. Actually, this is far from the truth. The biblical writings prophesied regarding these bizarre developments, which would not hinder but hasten the fulfillment of God's plan as follows:

Now, brethren, *concerning the coming of our Lord Jesus Christ and our gathering together to Him*, we ask you not to be soon shaken in mind or troubled, either by spirit or by word or by letter, as if from us, as though the day of Christ had come. Let no one deceive you by any means; *for that Day will not come unless the falling away comes first*, and the man of sin is revealed, the son of perdition, who opposes and exalts himself above all that is called God or that is worshiped, so that he sits as God in the temple of God, showing himself that he is God. Do you not remember that when I was still with you I told you these things? *And now you know what is restraining, that he may be revealed in his own time. For the mystery of lawlessness is already at work; only He who now restrains will do so until He is taken out of the way.* And then the lawless one will be revealed whom the Lord will consume with the breath of His mouth and destroy with the brightness of His coming. The coming of the lawless one is according to the working of Satan, with all power, signs, and lying wonders, and with all unrighteous deception among those who perish, because they did not receive the love of the truth, that they might be saved. *And for this reason God will send them strong delusion that they should believe the lie that they all may be condemned who did not believe the truth but had pleasure in unrighteousness*" (2 Thessalonians 2:1–12, italics added for emphasis).[238]

Those who attempt to wrestle with The Book of Revelation are enthralled by the obvious implications of the Last Days. They are also concerned that believers in Christ will fully appreciate what the final peripeteia will mean both politically and spiritually. One such author explains it like this: "The main themes are abundantly clear: The church and the state are on a collision course; and initial victory will appear to belong to the state. Thus he warns the church that suffering and death lie ahead; indeed, it will get worse before it gets better (Revelation 6:8). He is greatly concerned that they do not capitulate in times of duress (14:11–12; 21:7–8). But this prophetic word is also one of encouragement—for God is in control of all things. Christ holds the keys to history, and he holds the churches in his hands. . . . It is clear from every kind of context in the Revelation that God's people will not have to endure God's awful wrath when it is poured out on their enemies, but it is equally clear that they will indeed suffer at the hands of their enemies. This distinction, it should be noted, is precisely in keeping with the rest of the New Testament."[239]

With the acceleration of cultural change in the Christian world, there are also temptations to start cloning other apparently successful ministries as the Church Age nears the end. In the whirlwind of busyness today, too many only duplicate what others are doing instead of taking the time and energy to discover what is God's unique plan for their church.

Even more, many are finding that with the rapid transformation of society that no two churches can operate alike. While personally talking with Lyle Schaller at a conference in Denver, Colorado, in 1991, he made a comment that summed up his presupposition from his earlier book: "The differences between congregations are becoming greater with the passage of time. The safe assumption today is that no two are alike. Each congregation has its own culture. . . . As they seek to understand the unique nature of their own worshipping community, as they endeavor to be attentive and responsive to God's call to this particular congregation, and as they seek to exercise foresight and wisdom in making choices, they carry a heavy burden."[240]

While the above quote may seem somewhat distant, a recent issue of *REV* magazine echoed the same basic argument today. This issue featured an article by Pastor Will Mancini about the six hazards churches and other organizations are falling into that negate their effectiveness to fulfill God's plan. He gives an exceptional delineation of what he has termed, *the thinkholes*:

1. The Ministry Treadmill—This is when a person gets so busy in the ministry that it creates a progressive and irreversible hurriedness in the leader's life. They are so caught up in the weekly grind of events and ministry demands that they do not explore the culture of their church and thereby how it relates to the community around them.
2. The Competency Trap—Because the leader has been successful in the past in another location or in another program that worked well at a specific time and place in their ministry, they keep trying to impose this program or way of working on their present church or ministry. This kind of thinking turns their leaders into talkers instead of thinkers.
3. The Needs-Based Slippery Slope—The pastor and leaders get caught into a trap of always trying to meet people's needs and expectations that they

cannot escape this slippery slope. The vision of the church is reduced to making people happy. This produces a church that is missing its unique calling and ministry to the community by attempting to be everything to all the members.

4. The Cultural Whirlpool—This is a church that is in a constant flux of change. The dangers are colossal since leaders can get to the place they never are able to settle in and find their place to produce mature fruit. In the race to always be on the "cutting edge," they drown their church in new ideas and programs that never get off the ground or develop into effective ministries in helping their community.

5. The Conference Maze—This is a pastor, leadership, or church that gets fixated and "jazzed" about every new conference that comes along. After awhile, they are always running to deliverance conferences, leadership conferences, or a myriad of other seminars to perpetually learn or get deliverances. This results in the sin of copying someone else or enjoying the conferences more than implanting the seeds to bring growth. It is a viscous cycle of going but never doing.

6. The Denominational Rut—This is a whirlpool that can drag down the local postmodern church with being driven by another distant group's vision, purpose, or anointing. Too frequently, the denominational offices simply want to continue to push their doctrinal bent or see themselves as the major motivational leaders for the future. Regretfully, they cannot centralize what each specific church needs in their particular culture, language, location, or size. The best thing these denominational leaders can do is to "come alongside" the growing churches and encourage them to seek God's plan for their local body.[241]

We have transitioned from the church universal to the local church. In both cases we can recognize the phenomenal adjustments or radical turnarounds necessary to finish God's plan. Before we move on though, I feel that the state of the Christianity in North America that has been so strong for so many years is on a fast track of deterioration. Many church leaders and politicians would deny this as they like to point out the maturity of churches to increased toleration of alternative lifestyles and the assimilation of various value systems into the church as hopeful signs of progress. In point of fact, this kind of thinking, which promotes relativism and humanism, hurls us toward a global change of negative implications. Anyone who has ever read the writings of Steve Gallagher knows how he has identified these developments as the seduction warned about in the Holy Scriptures for the Last Days. As I watched the voting returns from the last American election, Steve's admonition from 1996 seemed like it was written only yesterday:

> "The Christian nation of Germany put Adolf Hitler into power because he gave them what they wanted. Not only did they install him as their chancellor, but also they adored him! And before they knew what had happened, he was gassing Jews by the millions in the death camps of Europe. When they elected Hitler they never dreamed he would perpetrate such atrocities! The absence of total surrender to Christ and the resulting lack of discernment made them vulnerable to the powerful personality of the Fuhrer. We have so vilified the German people that it is easy to cast them all in the same mold as Hitler. We forget that most of these were simple people who, like us, just wanted to have a better life for themselves and their families. In fact, a majority of the population claimed to be Christians. Once Hitler was in power, many of them became agents of butchery because their Christianity had no hold on their consciences and the moral climate of their day overpowered them. There was nothing to stop their descent into the cruelties of hell. 'We would never do what they did,' we say. But dear reader, our culture is much more influenced by the spirit of kosmos than theirs was! We're in terrible danger of rolling out the welcome mat, not for a NAZI dictator, but for the man who will lead the world into a violent collision with God Himself. The people of America are ready for such a leader."[242]

Uncannily, as Aristotle knew so well, the nature of a peripeteia is not always a turning point to something that is good. This is a warning to everyone who leads an organization or church. There comes a pivotal moment in every peripeteia when the final act may not be played out as we envisioned or preached. In the case of God's plan, it will be accomplished in the Church, but it may not always result in a positive outcome in every person's life, church, or nation. This will certainly be determined by those who consciously and alertly move wisely and proactively at the pivotal stage of God's allotted time. I realized this the first time I watched

The Turning Point That Changed Everything

the six act play by Tennessee Williams entitled, *The Glass Menagerie*.[243] The *Glass Menagerie* was William's first successful play; he went on to become one of America's most highly regarded playwrights. *The Glass Menagerie* is looked upon by many to be an autobiographical play about William's life, the characters and story mimicking his own family more closely than any of his other works. For those who have never seen this powerful drama or read the story, let me share with you a very brief synopsis.

The play is introduced to the audience by the main character Tom as a memory play, based on his recollection. Amanda's husband (whose name is unimportant) deserted the family long ago, and she remains stuck in the past. Her son Tom works in a factory, doing his best to support them. He chafes under the ordinariness and boredom of everyday life and spends much of his spare time watching movies in cheap cinemas. Amanda is obsessed with finding a suitor for his sister Laura, who spends most of her time with her glass collection that becomes the symbol of her fragile life. Tom eventually brings a young man named Jim home for dinner at the insistence of his mother, who hopes Jim will be the long-awaited suitor for Laura. Laura realizes that Jim is the man she loved in high school and has thought of ever since. But he dashes her hopes, telling her that he is already engaged, and then leaves town abruptly to never return. Her brother Tom leaves after a short while also and never returns to see his family again. The departures of Jim and Tom leaves the audience stunned that what was hoped and expected did not happen. The powerful drama, while displaying insights into the human psyche and inciting humorous qualities typical of a Tennessee Williams' play, reveals the genre of a classical Greek tragedy.[244]

The aforementioned play is rarely matched in its ability to illustrate the gravity of a turning point in a person's life. For that matter, it excels in unfolding the lifetime consequences of decisions on both families and groups. The first time I saw this play as a teenager, it left me sitting in my high school theater stultified. Perhaps, I was not intelligent enough to understand the purpose of the story or even feeling that the last act of the play was certainly not the author's intention in the beginning. Perplexed and disappointed, I left to muse over this production for several days. As the years have gone by, I have come to appreciate the brilliance of Tennessee Williams; it comes through in many of his other plays. But The Glass Menagerie is a masterpiece that exposes life the way it really works, too frequently to be a tale. So it is with God's plan in the Church Age—not everyone is going to like or enjoy some of the events or consequences in the development of the End Times. Some of the things that occur will hurt us to undergo, other things will certainly delight our expectations; and, at the End of the Church Age, we will behold some awesome turnarounds of unparalleled proportion. This is what the writer of The Revelation saw after the greatest peripeteia of them all had taken place in mankind's history:

> Then I saw a new heaven and a new earth, for the first heaven and the first earth had passed away, and there was no longer any sea. I saw the Holy City, the New Jerusalem, coming down out of heaven from God, prepared as a bride beautifully dressed for her husband. And I heard a loud voice from the throne saying, "Now the dwelling of God is with men, and he will live with them. They will be his people, and God himself will be with them and be their God. He will wipe every tear from their eyes. There will be no more death or mourning or crying or pain, for the old order of things has passed away." He who was seated on the throne said, "I am making everything new!" Then he said, "Write this down, for these words are trustworthy and true." He said to me: "It is done. I am the Alpha and the Omega, the Beginning and the End. To him who is thirsty I will give to drink without cost from the spring of the water of life. He who overcomes will inherit all this, and I will be his God and he will be my son" (Revelation 21:1–7).[245]

With all this thrilling news for victorious Christians, there are developments that all of us need to understand. Many unbelievers today are struggling with the rapid and drastic changes in our culture. During the last year, I have asked many who would be described as the pagan crowd, about the end of the world, their future, and the way they view Christians. Almost without exception, they were confused by how Christians believe in the Coming of Jesus Christ but rarely ever take time to discuss this great imminent event with them.

My subsequent question was specific: "Do you want to hear more about what's happening on the earth and what you could do to make your life better now?" The answer was overwhelmingly, "Yes, I would." More than twelve years ago, Chuck Swindoll shared an observation he had made about so-called pagans in America. He wrote how that many unbelievers would never tell you that deep down inside they envy genuine Christians. They say this as they wonder silently: "How does she do that? How can he no longer do these things? I'm not able to stop the treadmill I'm on! What in the world has made the difference for you? Why are you so happy with so little to live on?"[246] Chuck summarized that most don't want another lecture about their lifestyle, but they would be open to a friend who would tactfully and graciously tell them how their life was changed and how they could have their life transformed

As one who has been through several "sudden turnarounds of the opposite" in my life, I am moved with compassion for such honest seekers. A peripeteia is an invitation for genuine Christians to help in guiding others beyond just being able to cope with all the maddening events, but it's an opening to assist them as these traumatic events occur like cluster lightning in this fast-paced society.

Conclusion

*In this world of change naught which comes stays,
and naught which goes is lost.*
—Madam Swetchine

If you have studied much about the narratives in Hebrew writings, you would know how important the scenes of the stories are. Jesus used this basic method in teaching parables. Rather than build a story around a single character, the most common method of storytelling in the Hebrew narrative is "scenic." The action moves along through a series of scenes that compile the whole. This has been compared to the development of television movie or theatrical drama that tells a story though a secession of scenes. Each scene has its own uniqueness, yet it becomes progressively a sequence of scenes that blend to tell a complete story that takes many surprising turns to reveal the plot of the author. Having studied this myself in Hebrew literature, perhaps this is the intent of the divine in ordering the scenes of our lives?

In this conclusion, I wanted to leave you with an appreciation for the story being played out in your life and in many organizations around you. Even a peripeteia is a call for a response by you to the events of your life. This truth has been acutely brought home by an example from Professor Gordon Fee when speaking of those same parables of Jesus: "The best clues as to what the parables are is to be found in their function. In contrast to most of the parabolic sayings, such as not reaping figs from thistles, the story parables do not serve to illustrate Jesus' prosaic teaching with word pictures. Nor are they told to serve as vehicles for revealing truth—although they end up clearly doing that. Rather, the story parables function as a means of calling forth a response on the part of the hearer. In a sense, the parable itself is the message. It is told to address and capture the hearers, to bring them to respond in some way to Jesus and his ministry. . . . The two things that capture the hearer of a joke and elicit a response of laughter are the same two things that captured the hearers of Jesus' parables, namely, their knowledge of the points of reference, which in turn caused them to recognize the unexpected turn in the story. The keys to understanding are the points of reference—those various parts of the story with which one identifies as it is being told. If one misses these in a joke, then there can be no unexpected turn because the points of reference are what create the ordinary expectations. If one misses these in a parable, then the force and the point of what Jesus said is likewise going to be missed."[247]

Is it possible that you and I may not have paid enough attention to those reference points in our life story so that we can appreciate or take the right actions when the unexpected turns have taken place? What is even more dramatic is that we may also fail to take the necessary action that calls for a response.

May I encourage you to prayerfully reflect on some of your own points of reference that will help prepare you for the next unexpected turn in your story! For in doing so, it will in most cases be the best way you can be prepared for your next unexpected twist. I never liked missing the point of a joke because I failed to pay attention to those key points in the story that make it so funny when it takes that sudden turn from the outcome I expected. Without a doubt, we need to be on high alert when the signs of a change are on the horizon.

It is my hope, one day, that this book will serve as a precursor for a class at seminaries, universities, and other practical conferences to examine the subject

The Turning Point That Changed Everything

of peripeteia. Sadly, too many leaders (believers and unbelievers) have neglected the "well of philosophy" that helps people to think soberly. I want young men and women to learn both philosophically and biblically to have a proper worldview that can guide them in a turnaround. They can only do this by revisiting history and understanding those scenes that are inevitable in their lives when changes shall come so swiftly and frequently. Indeed, to expect that such transitions are always for the good is foolish. Moreover, to ascertain that one can prevent any and all change is also childish. One must be willing to handle such transforming times with great prayer, counsel, and humility.

In the end, some things will happen that will not last; in other words, "buyers beware!" Additionally, there will be things that appear to have past or vanished, but they may reappear. I would treat both with careful examination. During the past ten chapters of this book, you have seen several scenes that aid your understanding of a turning point. Reread them at your leisure; they have taught me much:

- You have observed the intimacy of my own crisis of change.
- You have examined the concept of peripeteia.
- You have read about the unpredictable life.
- You have learned about those who resist or want to control changes.
- You have witnessed some turnarounds that are unmanageable.
- You have discovered how some people will try to profit from change.
- You have been cautioned about the improbable degree of a reversal to the opposite.
- You have been given the opportunity to understand a far more personal transformation called anagnorisis.
- You have learned that making the necessary adjustments for a complete change requires both faith and patience.
- You now must decide if you will believe and accept God's plan in this present age.

The above can be useful for developing discussion points for a class setting or a reminder to you to keep your mind open the next time there is a "sudden reversal of circumstances" in your life. God grant you courage and hope! In the end, may you be guided with this assurance: "But as for me, I trust in You, O Lord, I say, 'You are my God.' My times are in Your hand."[248]